Island Cultures and Festivals

SERIES EDITOR

Sonjah Stanley Niaah

ADVISORY BOARD

Carolyn Cooper
Julian Henriques
David Katz
Deborah Thomas
Jo-Anne Tull

Word, sound and power. This is the definition of the musical vibrations of Jamaican music. The music of Jamaica influences and has been influenced by countless other music forms throughout the Caribbean and worldwide. At the intersection of creation, production, consumption and globalization of Jamaican music, and from an interdisciplinary perspective, Sound Culture begins a long overdue focus on the history and evolution of sounds, tracing the movement from mento to ska and on to rocksteady, reggae, dub, nyabinghi, dancehall and the various styles of reggae fusion. The series covers all Caribbean music that intersects with Jamaican sounds, and artists in the region who work within the musical genres from Jamaica. It examines those who have blended their national musical forms with Jamaica's and acknowledges that, in addition to shaping culture, social relations, economics and politics, Jamaican music has influenced popular cultural production internationally. In particular, reggae has resonated with the disenfranchised and marginalized all over the world, its rhythm and melody appealing to soul rebels from Japan to South Africa, and Croatia to New Zealand. Sound Culture is intended as a record of the colossal impact that Jamaica has had on the planet through its musical vibrations.

Island Cultures and Festivals

A CREATIVE ECOSYSTEM

Edited by **EVANGELIA PAPOUTSAKI** *and*
SONJAH STANLEY NIAAH

The University of the West Indies Press
Mona • St Augustine • Cave Hill • Global • Five Islands

The University of the West Indies Press
7A Gibraltar Hall Road, Mona
Kingston 7, Jamaica
www.uwipress.com

A catalogue record of this book is available from the
National Library of Jamaica.

ISBN: 978-976-640-967-8 (paper)
978-976-640-968-5 (ePub)

Cover image courtesy of Lee Abel
Cover and book design by Robert Harris
Set in Minion Pro 11.2/15 x 24.

Printed in the United States of America

Contents

Part Two: Music, Dance and Island Identity

Preface

Island Culture Research and the Small Island Cultures Research Initiative

PHILIP HAYWARD

THE ISLAND FESTIVALS AND MUSIC TOURISM CONFERENCE HELD at the University of the West Indies in Kingston in July 2019 was the fifteenth annual event facilitated by the Small Island Cultures Research Initiative (SICRI) and the first to be held in the Caribbean. SICRI was founded in 2004 by a group of international musicologists, linguists and anthropologists interested in the maintenance and development of small island cultures. One of SICRI's core principles has been to work with activists and local communities to create opportunities for local cultures to flourish and be recognized internationally. Collaborative projects undertaken by SICRI researchers include developing local language resources, recording albums of local music, organizing local song contests and music tours, making video documentaries, organizing art exhibitions and co-authoring reports and funding applications.

The annual SICRI conferences provide valuable meeting places for local researchers, cultural activists and visiting academic researchers. The first International Small Island Cultures conference organized by SICRI was held in 2005 in Kagoshima, in southern Japan, in collaboration with Kagoshima University's Pacific Island Research Centre. The event succeeded in inspiring a disparate group of researchers to collaborate in long partnerships that have persisted to the present. A vital ingredient of the Kagoshima conference was the role of music and dance. The opening reception featured a performance by djembe drummers from the tiny volcanic island of Iojima. The audience's attention and curiosity were immediately aroused. How had a West African percussion instrument found its way to a remote Japanese island and been embraced by islanders? The answer was simple, if beguiling. Locals had invited a West African djembe drummer to visit, had fallen in love with its sounds and rhythms, had learned playing techniques and had gone on to maintain an ensemble for over twenty years that is now emblematic of Iojima. Indeed, Iojima is now home to a Djembe Academy that attracts tourists to the island to learn it.

In contrast to the modern "syncretic" music of the Iojima drummers (where elements of a foreign culture are adopted into an indigenous one), the final session of the conference at the Amami Cultural Centre in Kagoshima city featured more traditional performances. At the closing reception, delegates heard a range of *shima uta* ("island song") performances played by Amami islanders and participated in lively festival dancing that brought the conference to an animated conclusion.

Since 2004, SICRI has held conferences in a series of iconic island locations, including Norfolk Island, Guernsey, Fernando de Noronha, Newfoundland and Okinawa. All these locations share a strong sense of local identity and local culture, and all have supported festivals and encouraged tourists to visit and participate in cultural events. The idea of having a conference in Jamaica arose from a number of leading SICRI members' strong interest in and appreciation of Jamaican music and literature and their highly positive responses to Dr Sonjah Stanley Niaah's invited keynote address to the 2016 conference in Naha, Okinawa. Like the first SICRI conference in Kagoshima, the Naha conference was accompanied by a concert featuring performances by leading island musicians, and the conference itself was enriched by a presentation by noted Japanese musician Kazufumi Miyazawa. Dr Stanley Niaah's detailed discussion of how reggae operated in a relatively small national context provided pointers for understanding music cultures and industries in island locations more generally. A range of papers presented at the Naha conference were subsequently expanded and accepted for publication in a theme issue of the journal *Shima* – volume 11 number 2, *Island Music and Performance Cultures*. Available online, the theme issue is a significant resource for scholars of island music and performance traditions.

In discussions following the Naha conference, Dr Stanley Niaah and SICRI steering group members agreed that Jamaica was the ideal location for a conference dedicated to exploring two key themes – the development and operation of island festivals (of various kinds) and island tourism. The conference was also scheduled to allow delegates the opportunity to attend the major Sumfest Reggae Festival, linking the theoretical concerns of the SICRI event with the pleasures and observational opportunities offered by the festival itself. By the time of the Kingston conference, Dr Evangelia Papoutsaki (from the University of Central Asia, Kyrgyzstan) had succeeded Dr Arianne Reis (from Western Sydney University, Australia) as SICRI's international network convenor and collaborated with Dr Stanley Niaah in the organization of the conference and the editing of this volume.

The Kingston conference was an important one for SICRI as it was held in a region in which the organization had little previous engagement or profile, and the organization as a whole was refreshed by a number of delegates who had not previously been associated with it. Reading the Facebook posts and emails of various attendees, it became evident that the cultural encounters that occurred during the conference period were as significant as the formal sessions. I was reminded of the affective power of Caribbean music and dance cultures across international boundaries in a very different context shortly before writing this preface when attending a festival of Jamaican Music and Food in North Sydney (Australia) in November 2019. The headline artist, Mad Professor (aka Neil Fraser), is a London DJ of Guyanese origin, and a variety of acts had origins and professional careers that had looped them between Jamaica, the UK, Australia, New Zealand, Israel and other locations. The Jamaican-ness and island-ness of the event were thematic and culturally inclusive, rooted in an island context but equally a continuously diasporic one, reassembling itself in new locations. Watching a young Japanese couple dancing to a dancehall track on one of the side stages, I remembered conversations I had with Japanese reggae aficionados at the Kaya Hut reggae bar in Naha and the manner in which Okinawan duo Udou and Platy have incorporated elements of Okinawan festive dancing and call and response patterns into their quirky dancehall reggae sets. The "outernational" aspect of Jamaican culture continued to be evident globally and testified to the ways island musics can move beyond their shores.

This rich and engaging collection of papers illustrates the vitality of research around island music festivals and music tourism. The anthology also provides a variety of perspectives on cultural phenomena that serve essential functions for both originating communities and tourists who seek out the local roots and contexts of its production. The volume also bodes well for the future of SICRI as an organization as new voices are coming into play and new agendas are developing for the next decade of an organization founded on the reflection, festivity and camaraderie between researchers and island artists first fostered in Kagoshima in 2004.

Introduction

Island Cultures and Festivals
A Creative Ecosystem

SONJAH STANLEY NIAAH AND EVANGELIA PAPOUTSAKI

ONE FEATURE OF HUMAN EXISTENCE IS THE PARADOX of inclusivity inside exclusivity or even cohesion inside isolation as part of the character of geo-culturally specific phenomena such as islands. Islands are bounded yet, more often than not, unbounded by the movement across their multiple borders. They are also often vulnerable, with constantly considering and planning for sustainable outcomes. Among the disciplinary configurations that seek to engage these geo-cultural phenomena, it is well acknowledged that island studies has developed into an established, interdisciplinary research field (Shima Editorial Board 2007), one that has attempted to grapple with existential questions around sustainability and resilience as well as geopolitics and economics. However, specific research and comparative analysis of island cultures within a field that identifies itself as Island Studies is a more recent phenomenon. For Grydehøj (2017, 3), the former editor of the *Island Studies Journal*, it is "important that island studies not only continue deepening its internal theoretical understandings but also reach out to other fields and regions that have received limited attention within island studies".

The Caribbean is one such region. While the interdisciplinarity of island studies and the uniting of regional island studies into a wider scholarly community has been strengthened by several scholars over the past two to three decades (see Baldacchino 2004, 2006, 2008; Hayward 2016; Hay 2006; Royle 2014; Hau'ofa 1993; McCall 1994), how has the Caribbean as a distinct region with its creative ecosystem been framed in island studies? Can the Caribbean offer new ways of thinking through and theorizing in island studies? The conference around which this publication was catalysed took place in the Caribbean, which provides an interesting case study coming from the several contributions in this collection added to those of scholars such as Burke (2010), Nurse (2017), Nurse et al. (2006, 2019), Tull (2017), Stanley Niaah (2018), Stanley Niaah and Hendrickson (2018), among others.

Island studies as a distinct field is based on the notion that islands share a set of features that other territories do not (Androus and Greymorning 2016, 453). Islands for Baldacchino (2004, 278) are more than simply microcosmic research laboratories for mainlanders or worlds-unto-themselves for islanders; instead, "islandness is an intervening variable that does not determine, but contours and conditions physical and social events in distinct, and distinctly relevant, ways." Terrell (2004, 11) has similarly argued that "islands are more varied, diverse and complicated places than commonly believed" and that "isolation is not a defining characteristic of island life; to the contrary, it would be argued that islanders are generally more aware of, and in touch with, the world wide web of human intercourse than others may be". This is supported by the earlier, much-cited thesis of Hau'ofa (1993), who asserted that instead of a vast empty space in which separate islands exist, the ocean is the medium that links the Pacific Islands into a vibrant field of communication. And Ellis (1998), adding to this, argued that inter-island space is alive with relational meaning. For Hay (2006, 31), islands are special places described as "paradigmatic places, topographies of meaning in which the qualities that construct place are dramatically distilled". Baldacchino (2005, 35) demonstrated this island uniqueness in his observation, often seen in the island studies literature, that "small islands are special because their 'geographical precision' facilitates a (unique) sense of place".

Suwa's (2007) exploration of the Japanese term *shima*, denoting island, provides an additional definitional layer to the term island, which embodies a dual meaning: islands as geographical features and islands as small-scale social groups where cultural interactions are densely intermeshed.

In the context of island festivals, we can see the island/*shima* as a unique milieu within which communicative performances occur and produce communicative ecologies that fill the space with meaning. The patterns of communication exchanges develop in various interpersonal, familial, social, cultural and economic networks and accumulate as an island communicative ecology (Papoutsaki and Kuwahara 2018, 2021; Konishi and Papoutsaki 2020). An island-contextualized communicative ecology approach refers to the various forms, activities, resources, channels and flows of communication and information as well as island agents unique to an island or group of islands (ibid.). When we come to study the creative ecology of islands, these elements play a critical role in shaping unique island festivalscapes (see chapter four), reflecting aspects of the island's place, identity and "storytelling" and weaved through the island's communicative ecology. We could also argue that when festivals take place in the unique communication action context of islands, they shape, in turn, the islands' communicative ecology and sociality (ibid.), where the festival acts as a "story" about the island, created by, co-created with or imposed upon the island. The festivals, integral to the island's storytelling communicative ecology, help construct island imaginaries as a particular representation of a place that impacts how participants create communities (Baragwanath and Lewis 2010, in Baragwanath 2010, 7).

FILLING RESEARCH GAPS

The intersection between island cultures, identity, music and tourism demands greater exploration and, to fill some gaps in the literature on island cultures and their ecology, the Institute of Caribbean Studies, University of the West Indies, Mona Campus partnered with the Small Island Cultures Research Initiative and the Sydney Institute of Music and Sound Research to stage the fifteenth International Small Island Cultures Conference under the theme "Island Festivals and Music Tourism", held 9–13 July 2019. The conference, which was staged at the University of the West Indies in Kingston, Jamaica, saw presenters from various disciplines, as well as managers and practitioners with an interest in islands, festivals, and music tourism, sharing their research and experiences. This edited volume contains the selected proceedings of the 2019 conference. The focus on island music, tourism and festivals in their multiple dimensions was engaged by scholars from different disciplinary fields who shared research and experiences using case studies, policy interventions and comparative research. While island festivals and music tourism were an initial focus of the conference and are a feature of this publication, this volume also aims to promote a critical research agenda for island studies and ethnomusicology in general.

Islands have been hosts to numerous festivals that have driven music tourism and cultural development for decades. However, the intersection between festivals, music tourism, and island studies remains under-explored, particularly in the Global South. Festivals have been intertwined with islands and tourism for some time. Academic attention in the context of event and leisure studies increased in the 1990s, focusing on festival economics, event management, sponsorship and marketing, and forecasting. Within event studies, festival studies is also emerging as a distinct sub-field, in large part because festivals occupy a special place in almost all cultures and have therefore been researched and theorized by scholars in various disciplines, particularly anthropology and sociology.

While both festival studies and island studies are interdisciplinary, they have often been pursued through somewhat predictable disciplinary lenses and from particular geographical locations with binary oppositions, such as north versus south, rich versus poor, scientific versus affective, functions versus dysfunctions, sacred versus secular, high versus low culture, among others. Even as the focus on islands and islandness has been less visible in the scholarship on festivals, the festivalization of islands is an emerging sub-field, gaining needed attention.

Literature on festival tourism (Gibson and Connell 2012; Getz 2010; Cudny 2013) has centred on such dimensions as group and place identity, geopolitics, sustainable development and elements such as the cultural, community, ritualistic, ceremonial, urban versus rural as well as old and new festivals across a variety of landscapes. Festival tourism has been engaged from unique island spaces, from Australia and Hawaii to Britain and Bali. However, there is still a gap in research that renders some areas virtually invisible. Gibson and Connell (2005) took the first comprehensive look at the links between travel and music. They combined contemporary and historical analysis of the economic and social impact of music tourism, discussing the cultural politics of authenticity and identity. Music tourism evokes nostalgia and meaning and celebrates both heritage and hedonism. It is a product of commercialization that can create community, but that also often demands artistic compromise. Diverse case studies, from the United States and the United Kingdom to Australia, Jamaica and Vanuatu, illustrate the global extent of music tourism and its contradictions and pleasures.

From an examination of Christian youth music festivals to mixed arts or alternative scenes such as Burning Man, festivals have been examined through the lens of tourism and heritage (Connell and Gibson 2005), musical genres, event management, consumption patterns, promotion of tolerance, measurement of impact and perceptions, socio-economic benefits, ritual aspects and community belonging, and cosmopolitanism and transnationalism. Studies examining the de-territorialization of identities crafted in festivals include that of the European Union study (2011, 8) of arts festivals and strengthening cultural diversity, which centred the "ephemeral and non-territorial aspect of festivals that lends support to the ideas of internationalism, cosmopolitanism and trans-nationalism as alternative frameworks for understanding their cultural and socio-political significance". But have these lenses been applied to island cultures and festivals? This is one question answered by this volume.

Even when the rationales for staging festivals and their spaces of operation differ, what they share is a determination to expose audiences to novel ways of looking at and judging the world, its cultures and the arts, as well as society and politics. Magaudda et al. (2011, 57) examined the relationship between the festival and its local identity context, thereby highlighting the importance of branding at the local level and how festivals make place/space as situated events. They conceived of "collaborative identity projects" (66), when specific locations then assume a specific identity as sites of memory and recall in relation to festivals and, ultimately, communities.

Not to be missed is the way streaming, diverse online lives and the urgency of the COVID-19 pandemic, which began reorienting lives in 2020 and has now shifted the modalities of festivals both on mainlands and islands (see Mendes-Franco 2021a, 2021b). Festivals, island cultures and music tourism have all experienced profound shifts with the interruptions in travel and events, and increased fears of association. Digital lives have become more of a rule than an exception. While the economic losses have been great, innovation has led the way to even more openness for transcending the digital borders around both islands and their music and festival cultures.

EXPLORING MUSIC, FESTIVAL AND CARIBBEAN STUDIES

Most importantly, this collection bridges several gaps even as we navigate theoretical and existential boundaries related to island studies, Caribbean studies, festival studies, ethnomusicology and, at this time, epidemiology, climate change and sustainable development. Ultimately, this collection is grounded in Caribbean studies as a field of inquiry and area studies more broadly, where it has been a focus at different points, leading to the development of various programmes and departments dedicated to Caribbean studies. While Caribbean studies has impacted the academy, island studies as a more recent area has not taken full account of the Caribbean as a distinct set of islands with regional specificity. Further, the intersection between Caribbean studies and island studies through a specific focus on music, festivals and island cultures of the Caribbean helps to fill the gap in scholarship on festival studies within the academic domain of island studies.

This collection is located in the creative Caribbean. It centralizes the remarkable creative output of Caribbean islands even while many creatives remain outside the professional structures of taxation, association, access to funding and matriculation. With some forty-four million residents in the region, its creative mainstay has been embedded in various festivals, some of which have been captured in this volume. At the centre of Caribbean life are carnivals, festivals, musical genres, performances and innovation, which bind disparate islands together. The masquerade tradition is an exemplary representation of a cultural ecosystem that blends celebration, subversion, politics and citizenship with humour, chaos, transgression and liberation.

The Caribbean's creative sensibility has produced a certain vocabulary for living and livelihood imperatives that must be accounted for in the context of its sustainable development. Festivals are marketplaces inside distinct economic models, and there are efforts to include such economic components more centrally in the study of island cultures. The festival marketplace has produced local, regional and economic benefits, with some seventy Caribbean diasporic festivals spawned from Trinidad's Carnival alongside local ones (Nurse et al. 2006) as well as numerous musical genres, of which Jamaica accounts for at least eight (Stanley Niaah 2018). Outside the festivals dedicated to soca/calypso, reggae music festivals, over four hundred of which have been mapped since 1978, litter the festival landscape inside a creative economy that currently lies outside the grasp of island studies. This Caribbean cultural footprint provides a rich diet for scholarship in island studies, but it has to be considered within a context of various vulnerabilities. Since the onset of the COVID-19 pandemic, for example, there have been cancellations of numerous Caribbean festivals and events, leaving over 90 per cent of creatives and event promoters out of work. Such devastating impacts, though periodic, are enough to cripple the festival and, more broadly, the creative ecosystem that drives regions such as the Caribbean.

THE COLLECTION

The papers that comprise this collection were divided into two parts with nine chapters organized around the broad themes of "Art, Culture and Island Communities" and "Music, Dance and Island Identity". Festivals can transform island places from being everyday settings into temporary environments that contribute to the production, processing and consumption of culture, concentrated in time and place (Waterman 1998, in Derret 2008, 8). The four chapters in part one discuss how festivals can engage with island communities through art and culture, how island communities and culture can be nourished and contested and some of the challenges and opportunities for sustainable island communities involved in this process. Derret's (2008) research model for the role of festivals in community resilience identifies place, residents (in this case, islanders) and visitors as key elements whose interaction results in an overlap between a sense of community and place, image and identity, and cultural tourism. The five chapters in part two explore the music festivals' connection to island image and identity, but also a desirable cultural tourism destination.

Most of the chapters in this part focus on the Caribbean, which reflects the International Small Island Cultures 2019 conference hosted in Kingston, Jamaica. It is also worth mentioning that islands in the Caribbean region are a newly emerging music festival marketplace (Semrad and Rivera 2016). These islands are perceived as desirable festival destinations for visitors who can immerse themselves in the local island culture and live music as an experiential product.

PART ONE: ART, CULTURE AND ISLAND COMMUNITIES

Diagnosing Uneven Revitalization Outcomes among Declining Communities in a Japanese Island Art Festival by Meng Qu, Yachen He, A.D. McCormick and Carolin Funck focused on the Setouchi International Art Festival (SIAF). Also known as Setouchi Triennale, this international art festival was established to aid the revitalization of twelve remote islands and their depopulating communities through art tourism. SIAF officials and the media claim that the Setouchi Triennale is a successful model for government policies aimed at community revitalization, citing over a million visitors each year and the increase in new residents on the islands. A true understanding of the outcomes of rural revitalization-oriented art projects, however, has to be sought on the other side of art interventions: the destination community's perspective. In this chapter, the authors explore what locals think about the influence of Triennale tourism and the way art influences their community. Among the islands involved in the SIAF, Megijima and Ogijima are two important island destinations based on their population, land size and artwork number. Field research was conducted through participant observation as a visitor and art festival volunteer during SIAF 2016 and 2018, as well as through questionnaires with community stakeholders after the festival. The results of the research show that the outcomes of the art festival in the two islands are different, despite the similarities in the way the festival was carried out. In particular, Ogijima shows more positive outcomes for its growing number of small-scale creative tourism businesses created by in-migrants.

Emma Lang's chapter on *The Norseman's Home: Up-Helly-Aa and Shetland's Performance of Place* explores festivals as an opportunity to share local history. On the last Tuesday in January every year, the largest town in Shetland, Lerwick, is filled with singing, torch-bearing men in costume participating in the more than a hundred-year-old festival of Up-Helly-Aa. The men parade through the town before gathering in a park to burn a beautiful hand-crafted longboat and proceeding to community halls where they will perform dances and skits into the early morning. Through an examination of Lerwick Up-Helly-Aa's portrayal of Vikings, use of ethnic stereotypes and pop culture references, this chapter provides insight into how local festivals teach outsiders local history and how they maintain invented historical narratives about ethnic identity. These topics are all inherently connected to the role of Lerwick Up-Helly-Aa as, simultaneously, a demonstration of Shetland's historical and modern connections to the broader world – despite predominant narratives that state otherwise – and a space where the emphasis on tradition and the conflict surrounding increasing diversity in the islands are on full display.

In their case study, *Mapping Waiheke Island's Festivalscape: Community Activism and Festival Reclamation*, Papoutsaki and Stansfield explore island festivals and related forms of public culture as performance events that construct and negotiate meaning for the island community that hosts them and for visitors. Waiheke Island is the third most populated island in Aotearoa, or New Zealand. Situated in the Hauraki Gulf near the most populated city, Auckland, the island has been a food basket, a forest to plunder, a holiday and retirement community, and a bohemian retreat now catapulted through international recognition as a playground of the rich and famous. The island's vineyards and art studios, pleasant micro-climate and many beaches attract weekend visitors throughout the year. Festivals have always been an important and integral part of Waiheke's community life, island identity and economy and contribute to the tourism product of Auckland. In recent years, there has been an increase in cultural tourism events organized by Auckland Tourism Events and Economic Development, which has resulted in some events moving from a local island focus to a regional, national and global cultural festival tourism market, including the Sculptures on the Gulf annual festival and the Jazz Art and Music Festival that attract thousands of visitors annually. In this chapter, the authors map the island's festival ecology through a temporal dimension –

past, established and emergent festivals – and look at factors influencing longevity; they discuss the contribution of the island's festival culture to its identity and community organization and explore the concept of "festival reclamation" as a uniquely local celebration after a larger festival has become a tourist attraction.

The chapter by Marie-Christine Parent on *Promoting the "Creole Traditional Wedding" During the Seychelle Creole Festival as a Strategy to Sustain Cultural Traditions* explains how the Seychelles Creole traditional wedding, considered endangered, has been reintroduced into Seychellois' life through tourism and, more specifically, as being part of the most important festival of the country. Known as a honeymoon destination, Seychelles is now offering couples a "Creole traditional wedding package", which includes a traditional ceremony in Creole, local food and music, with Seychellois. These special packages are set up in collaboration with local NGOs, district administrations and the Ministry of Culture and take place during the annual Creole Festival. To better understand the context in which these weddings are organized, the author positions them in the political and social history of the country, as well as within its tourism development. The author ends with some considerations of culture, heritage and tourism in the Seychelles of the twenty-first century, showing how these are intertwined. She also expresses some concerns that she associates with the postcolonial condition.

PART TWO: MUSIC, DANCE AND ISLAND IDENTITY

In his chapter, Holger Briel explores *The Traditional Daur Music and Dance Festival Kumule on the Island Meadow by the Amur River.* The Mongolic-speaking Daur people are one of the fifty-six ethnic minorities officially recognized by the Chinese government and, according to the last census figures, number about one hundred and forty thousand people. They mainly live in Inner Mongolia and along the Amur (Heilongjiang) River near Heihe, North-Western China. Every June, they celebrate their biggest festival of the year, Kumule, which highlights their history via dance and song. Originally, the Daur community in Heilongjiang lived on the Russian side of the river, but in 1956, they were forced to flee to China due to Stalinist ethnic cleansing strategies. The Kumule Festival restages this traumatic flight. In June 2017, the author visited the Daur with his media studies students and observed the Kumule festival on an island in the huge Amur River estuary, the border between Russia and China, for almost two thousand miles. This border was only finally established in 1991 in the Sino-Soviet Border Agreement and has created much hardship for the Daur. In this chapter, the author features excerpts from the documentary film *On the Black Dragon*, shot by his students, which addresses some issues the Daur are facing. He highlights the music and theatrical presentations during this festival and stresses the insular theme, which continues in Daur culture. For centuries, the Daur have been isolated, both in Russia and in China, heavily conscripted in times of war and left to fend for themselves in times of peace. The dramatic presentation, the highlight of every Kumule Festival, reminds the Daur where they come from and teach their children their musical and cultural history.

Shauna Rigaud explores soca culture in her chapter *Soca, Pleasure and Utopia*. In the mid-1970s, soca music began its rise as a genre that would later capture the energy of the Trinidadian-style carnival. Soca's originator, Lord Shorty, wanted to create a new genre for listeners of calypso music that directly responded to the political climate of Trinidad. For him, this would be the vehicle to bring the nation of Trinidad and Tobago together. In Richard Dyer's article "Entertainment and Utopia", he discusses the pleasure that is derived through the consumption of entertainment and what he sees as utopian sensibilities. He saw the musical as a mediated vehicle that represented a way for its audience to escape: real-life scarcity and exhaustion turned into abundance and energy on the screen. In this chapter, Rigaud looks at the history of soca music and analyses its work as entertainment in the Dyer sense. Using his analysis as a framework, she discusses how soca music uses texture, tempo and storytelling to engage and draw in its audience for pleasure and the ways that utopia is conveyed in soca music.

Melville Cooke's chapter on *Rebel Salute: A Birthday Party the World Attends* analyses the impact of this festival on Jamaica's tourism. In January 1994, deejay Tony Rebel's first Rebel Salute concert celebrated his birthday in Mandeville, Manchester, Jamaica. He recalls that many people from

Jamaica's capital, Kingston, sixty miles away, attended. Overseas visitors increased with Rebel Salute's growth. Before its twenty-fifth anniversary in 2018, Minister of Culture, Gender, Entertainment and Sport Olivia Grange said Rebel Salute attracts the highest proportion of tourists among any Jamaican festival. That was 38 per cent, but Tony Rebel said it was based on a 2013 Jamaica Tourist Board survey, done in the year Rebel Salute expanded to two days and moved from Jamaica's south coast to its current north coast tourism belt location, and believes the current proportion is much higher. The festival's organizers had previously complained of low Jamaica Tourist Board support and attempted to keep track of tourist attendance in order to press for increased government sponsorship. Currently, they use online ticket sales to track the countries comprising Rebel Salute's audience. Using content analysis and interviews, this chapter tracks the Jamaica Tourist Board's sponsorship of Rebel Salute and the tourist composition of its audience, analyses a shift from intense community tourism to include the all-inclusive model, and analyses Rebel Salute's impact on Jamaica's winter tourist season.

In *A Celebration of Music, Movement and Memory: The Archival Significance of St Kitts "Sugar Mas"*, Stanley Griffin explores the historic and contemporary significance of the St Kitts and Nevis National Carnival. More popularly known as Sugar Mas, it is held at the end of the calendar year, with its festivities culminating on New Year's Day with a grand Carnival parade through the streets of Basseterre, the capital of the twin-island federation. Sugar Mas bears all the usual features of a Caribbean carnival, with its calypso and soca music, queen and teen talent shows, food fairs and displays. However, there is a strong link between the island's history of sugar production, the customs rising out of the experiences of the enslaved and the Sugar Mas celebration. It revels in the African cultural retentions as expressed in the Christmas Sport dance movements of the Masquerade and, more importantly, the memory of the socio-political and economic struggles and triumphs of a postcolonial island society. In this chapter, the author considers the significance of Sugar Mas as a "Living Archive", a space filled with materials of enduring value for reflection and reference aimed at appreciating the past and present-day St Kitts and Nevis society.

In *The Sound of Citizenship: Performance, Politics and Transgression*,

Sonjah Stanley Niaah zeroes in on island music by putting music and performance in conversation with the politics of citizenship. She uses the sound system as an instrument of the Jamaican nation, a symbol of citizenship but also in/security and transgression. What stories do island sounds tell about citizenship, the politics of belonging, suppression and identity? In this chapter, part of a larger body of work on Black Atlantic entertainment, suppression and reparatory justice, Stanley Niaah is concerned with the aesthetics of noise that have characterized sound across the Black Atlantic. The chapter is a reparatory project that privileges sound in a deliberate Afro-futuristic sense, displacing the pejorative term 'noise' to claim the drum and its sound as science, method, movement, pleasure, fantasy and transgression, its moments of silence and its high waves and tones. Located at the intersection of cultural history, cultural geography, and cultural studies more broadly, this paper is ultimately about forms of citizenry at the heart of island musics and sound revolutions across the African Diaspora at the heart of which lie questions of rights, status, participation, power and identity.

ISLAND FUTURES

We are finalizing this volume while festivals are vulnerable and face threats from internal and external shocks. Whether it is climate change, the COVID-19 pandemic or instability because of war, violence and crime, there is much to be accounted for, as island studies seeks to tackle major questions affecting small island states such as those in the Caribbean and elsewhere. For example, the impact on island communities hosting festivals and music events, where such events are the mainstay of a community's economy, needs to be accounted for in the policy and development plans for island communities.

There is a step beyond yet inside theorizing, which lies in the quotidian practices that governments and communities can effectively navigate, together with partners and stakeholders, to ensure the sustainable development of island communities. In Jamaica alone, the drop in revenue from the COVID-19 pandemic has been estimated at half a trillion Jamaican dollars since the start of measures to contain the virus (Miles 2022).

The entertainment, cultural and creative industries employ an estimated seventy-five thousand creatives, who bore the brunt of the most severe economic contraction since the start of the millennium. Not only were they the first to be hit with prohibitions on events under the disaster risk management provisions, but cultural and entertainment services provided through restaurants, cinemas, galleries, mass events and festivals (with an estimated 9.3 per cent contribution to the annual gross domestic product) took a nose dive, which later spiralled to a complete shutdown by June 2020 and continued until March 2022.

The impact of COVID-19 on the Jamaican entertainment sector is but one example of the unexpected devastation that fragile island economies can experience without warning. The climate emergency is yet another, which has caused us to question the relationship of festivals to place. When a product such as a festival, which has defined place and identity, is removed from the physical landscape because of shocks, what then of place and identity? What, then, is an island festival? Both the pandemic and climate emergencies have pushed events into spaces such as digital platforms. For example, the Caribbean saw Trinidad's Carnival, Jamaica's Sunplash and Sumfest return with digital debuts as they sought to keep audiences tuned in and eager for the return of face-to-face events. But how does one experience place within a digital festivalscape? In the Caribbean, where tourism is the mainstay of many economies and is a wholly physical experience of place, the context of vulnerability from external shocks is brought into stark focus. The vulnerability of the festival economy is directly related to the vulnerability of the tourism economy on which Caribbean islands remain dependent. There are multiple impacts for small island communities that rely on face-to-face events.

Are we to expect more upheavals in the coming years? How do we address these challenges in island studies? While the conference theme did not foreground the climate emergency or pandemics, we felt that this edited collection had to account for emerging and longstanding risks. What remains clear is that island studies and Caribbean studies scholars can no longer fragment scholarship in academic silos. Instead, we must embrace multidisciplinary approaches that calculate climate emergency projections for festival economies just as tourism projections are generated in response to the devastation caused by hurricanes. Ultimately, there is a connecting thread that weaves human existence in ways that preserve modes of celebration, identity and livelihoods and provide economic, cultural and emotional well-being.

REFERENCES

Androus, Zachary, and Neyooxet Greymorning. 2016. "Critiquing the SNIJ Hypothesis with Corsica and Hawai'i." *Island Studies Journal* 11, no. 2:447–464.

Baldacchino, Godfrey. 2004. "The Coming of Age of Island Studies." *Tijdschrift voor economische en sociale geografie*, 95 (3): 272–83. https://doi.org/10.1111/j.1467-9663.2004.00307.x.

———. 2005. "The Contribution of 'Social Capital' to Economic Growth: Lessons from Island Jurisdictions." *Round Table* 94 (1): 31–46.

———. 2006. "Islands, Island Studies, Island Studies Journal." *Island Studies Journal* 1 (1): 3–18. https://islandstudiesjournal.org/files/ISJ-1-1-2006-Baldacchino-pp3-18.pdf.

Baragwanath, Lucy. 2010. *The Waiheke Project: Overview of Tourism, Wine and Development on Waiheke Island*. School of Environment, the University of Auckland, Occassional Publication no 51.

Burke, Suzanne, 2010. *Re-imagining, Re-fashioning, Re-building: Actions for the Creative Ecosystems 2010–2012: OECS Action Plan*. Castries, Saint Lucia: OECS Secretariat.

Cudny, Waldemar. 2013. "Festival Tourism – The Concept, Key Functions and Dysfunctions in the Context of Tourism Geography Studies." *Geographical Journal* 65 (2): 105–18. https://www.researchgate.net/publication/287956579_Festival_tourism_-_The_concept_key_functions_and_dysfunctions_in_the_context_of_tourism_geography_studies.

Derrett, Ross. 2008. "Regional Festivals: Nourishing Community Resilience: The Nature and Role of Cultural Festivals in Northern Rivers NSW Communities." PhD thesis, Southern Cross University.

Ellis, J. 1998. "Literary Cartographies in Oceana." In *Message in a Bottle: The Literature of Small Islands*, edited by L. Brinklow, F. Ledwell, and J. Ledwell, 51–64. Charlottetown: PEI, Institute of Island Studies, University of Prince Edward Island.

European Union. 2011. *European Arts Festival: Strengthening Cultural Diversity*. Luxemburg: European Union.

Getz, Donald. 2010. "The Nature and Scope of Festival Studies." *International Journal of Event Management Research* 5 (1): 1–47.

Gibson, Chris, and John Connell. 2005. *Music and Tourism: On the Road Again.* Clevedon, UK: Channel View Publications.

Grydehøj, Adam. 2017. "Editorial: A Future of Island Studies." *Island Studies Journal* 12 (1): 3–16.

Hau'ofa, Epeli. 1993. "Our Sea of Islands." *Contemporary Pacific* 6 (1): 147–61.

Hay, Pete. 2006. "A Phenomenology of Islands." *Island Studies Journal* 1 (1): 19–42.

Hayward, Philip. 2016. "Introduction: Towards an Expanded Concept of Island Studies." *Shima* 10 (1): 1–7. https://doi.org/10.21463/shima.10.1.03.

Konishi, Junko, and Evangelia Papoutsaki. 2020. "From Local Media to Vending Machines: Innovative Ways of Sustaining Okinawa's Shimakutuba and Island Culture." *Shima: International Journal of Research into Island Cultures* 14 (2): 231–51. https://9408297e-0d15-410f-b5c1-f402dc747904.filesusr.com/ugd/fd99ff_e3e1111608fa43ea855c19174ac722d5.pdf.

Magaudda, Paolo, Marco Solaroli, Jasper Chalcraft and Marco Santoro. 2011. "Music Festivals and Local Identities." In *European Arts Festivals: Strengthening Cultural Diversity*, edited by Liana Giordi, Monica Sassatelli, Marco Santoro, Gerard Delanty, Jasper Chalcraft and Marco Solaroli, 57–67. Luxembourg: European Union. https://papers.ssrn.com/sol3/papers.cfm?abstract_id=1805104.

McCall, Grant. 1994. "Nissology: The Study of Islands." *Journal of the Pacific Society* 17 (2–3): 1–14.

Mendes-Franco, Janine. 2021a. "Pandemic Soca: How COVID-19 is Shaping the Sound of Trinidad and Tobago's Cancelled Festival." *Global Voices*, 28 January 2021. https://globalvoices.org/2021/01/28/pandemic-soca-how-covid-19-is-shaping-the-sound-of-trinidad-tobagos-cancelled-carnival/.

———. 2021b. "Musician Chantal Esdell on How the Pandemic is Bringing Trinidad and Tobago Carnival Back to Itself." *Global Voices*, 2 February, 2021. https://globalvoices.org/2021/02/02/musician-chantal-esdelle-on-how-the-pandemic-is-bringing-trinidad-tobago-carnival-back-to-itself/.

Miles, Kellaray, 2022. "$500-b in Losses: Entertainment, Culture and Creative Sectors Record Huge COVID Fallout." *Jamaica Observer*, 16 March 2022. https://www.jamaicaobserver.com/business-observer-daily-biz/-500-b-in-losses-entertainment-culture-and-creative-sectors-record-huge-covid-fallout_246344.

Nurse, Keith. 2017. "Regional Strategic Plan for Cultural and Entertainment Services/Cultural Industries in CARICOM and CARIFORUM States." CARICOM Secretariat, Georgetown, Guyana, July.

———, Allison Demas, Jo-anne Tull, Bruce Paddington, Winston O-Young, Michael Gray, Halcyone Hoagland and Michele Reis. 2006. "The Cultural Industries in

CARICOM: Trade and Development Challenges." https://caricom.org/documents/10191-cultural_industries_report.pdf.

Nurse, Keith, and Mira Burri. 2019. *Culture in the CARIFORUM–European Union Economic Partnership Agreement*. Paris: UNESCO.

Papoutsaki, Evangelia and Sueo Kuwahara. 2018. "Mapping Small Islands Communicative Ecologies: A Case Study from the Amami Islands." *South Pacific Studies Journal* 31 (1): 25–49.

———. 2021. "Akina: An Ecocultural Portrait of an Island Community Through the Photographic Lens of Futoshi Hamada." *OJIS: Okinawan Journal of Island Studies* 2:11–64.

Royle, Stephen A. 2014. *Islands: Nature and Culture*. London: Reaktion.

Semrad, K., and M. Rivera. 2016. "Advancing the 5E's in Festival Experience for the Gen Y Framework in the Context of eWOM." *Journal of Destination Marketing & Management* 7:58–67. http://dx.doi.org/10.1016/j.jdmm.2016.08.003.

Shima Editorial Board. 2007. "An Introduction to Island Culture Studies." *Shima: International Journal of Research into Island Cultures* 1 (1): 1–5.

Stanley Niaah, Sonjah. 2018. "Can Jamaica Put Music First?" *Caribbean Quarterly* 64 (2): 330–47.

———, and M. Hendrickson. 2018. *A Study on the Creative Industry as a Pillar of Sustained Growth and Diversification – The Film and Music Sectors in Jamaica: Lessons from Case Studies of Successful Firms and Ventures*. UNECLAC Studies and Perspectives Series 7. https://hdl.handle.net/11362/43410.

Suwa, Juni'Chiro. 2007. "The Space of Shima." *Shima: International Journal of Research into Island Cultures* 1 (1): 6–15.

Terrell, J.E. 2004. "Islands in the River of Time." Paper presented at Islands of the World VIII International Conference: Changing Islands – Changing Worlds, Kinmen Island (Quemoy), Taiwan, 1–7 November 2004.

Tull, Jo-Anne. 2017. "Caribbean Festival Arts." *Caribbean Quarterly* 63 (2–3): 291–303.

Part One

ART, CULTURE AND ISLAND COMMUNITIES

Diagnosing Uneven Revitalization Outcomes among Declining Communities in a Japanese Island Art Festival

MENG QU, YACHEN HE, A. D. MCCORMICK, CAROLIN FUNCK

INTRODUCTION

RURAL JAPANESE REGIONS, FACING SEVERE CONDITIONS OF AGEING and depopulation, have sought increasingly novel approaches to mitigate population shrinkage and preserve cultural and community vitality. A nationwide depopulation trend in Japan has seen hospitals and schools close, town centres empty out and entire villages become abandoned and consumed by encroaching wilderness. Japan's small islands, physically disconnected from mainland flows of human and financial capital, have experienced this declining crisis acutely. For many islands in the Seto Inland Sea, with communities composed primarily of elderly residents and with only a handful of children (or none at all), long-term viability is an issue of profound significance (Matanle, Rausch and Shrinking Regions Research Group 2011). Conceived largely in response to these issues, the emergence in the last decade of large-scale, contemporary art festivals in rural areas that attract domestic and international artists and visitors is understood as a new mode of rural revitalization through socially engaged rural art festival tourism (Qu 2019,

20; Qu and Funck 2021). The first, the Echigo-Tsumari Art Triennale in mountainous Niigata Prefecture, was created by Tokyo-based curator Fram Kitagawa in 2000. Based on the success of this festival, he was invited by Kagawa Prefecture to lead its island festival project, which became the Setouchi Triennale (Qu, McCormick and Funck 2020).

The Setouchi Triennale (*Setouchi Kokusai Geijutsusai*, literally Setouchi International Art Festival) is one such festival and, unlike the earlier example in Niigata, it focuses on islands specifically. Located in the Seto Inland Sea region, or Setouchi (figure 1), the festival was organized to revitalize several ageing island communities by linking them together in a triennial display of site-specific artworks. It began in 2010 across seven islands – Naoshima, Teshima, Shodoshima, Megijima, Ogijima, Inujima, Oshima – and two nearby mainland ports, Uno and Takamatsu. Starting in 2013 and continuing for the two subsequent festivals in 2016 and 2019, four other islands to the west were added for the autumn portion of the Triennale. While some of these communities had already been developed as sites for art tourism (Qu 2019), for most of the islands, this was something totally new.

Festival officials and the government of Kagawa Prefecture consider the Setouchi Triennale to be a successful model of rural community revital-

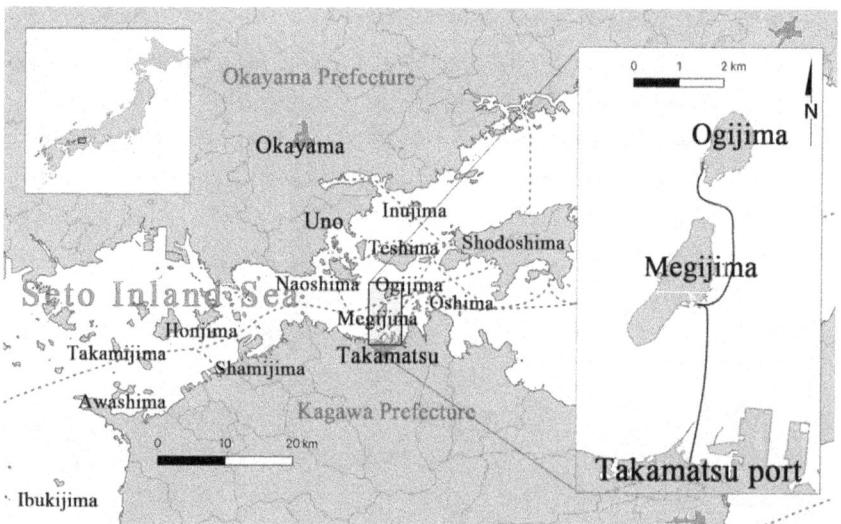

Figure 1. Map of Setouchi Triennale Islands (by the authors), source of the map: (GSI 2016), software (QGIS Development Team 2019)

ization through art tourism (Kitagawa and Setouchi Triennale Executive Committee 2016).

For this study, the authors defined revitalization as creating the conditions necessary to return a community to long-term viability – not simply adding vitality to a community. This study sought to uncover whether, how and to what extent this revitalization had manifested by comparing different islands. To minimize extraneous variables, the authors chose Megijima and Ogijima for fieldwork. These two neighbouring festival islands were of similar size, population, number of artworks and distance to the central port city of Takamatsu, which administered both islands. As shown in table 1 and figure 1, both islands have similar population sizes: at the time of the Setouchi Triennale's debut in 2010, they each had approximately two hundred inhabitants.

Table 1. Secondary data of Ogijima and Megijima islands (by the authors) (NPO Ogijima Life Research Institute 2018; Setouchi Triennale Executive Committee 2017)

	Ogijima	Megijima
Size	1.38 square kilometres	3 square kilometres
Population (October 2019)	170	154
Distance from Takamatsu city port	40 minutes by ferry	20 minutes by ferry
Number of festival artworks (2016)	16	13
Number of visitors (2016)	54,232	49,276
Number of in-migrants (2018)	more than 50 people	around 4 to 5 people
Main industry	agriculture, fishing, tourism, information technology	agriculture, fishing, tourism
Infrastructures (2017)	more than 3 vacant houses, kindergarten, elementary and junior high school	limited vacant houses, share kindergarten with Ogijima, share school with Takamatsu city
	similar internet connectives, food stores, water, electricity and gas providers, bank, simple post office, ATM, and garbage collection services	

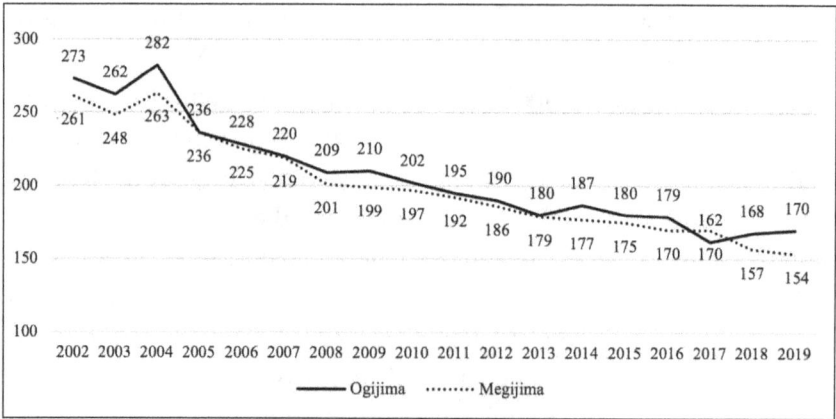

Figure 2. Demographic changes in Ogijima and Megijima (by the authors) (Takamatsu City Official Website 2019)

According to secondary data on both islands obtained from a non-profit organization on Ogijima (NPO Ogijima Life Research Institute 2018), from 2014 to 2018, Ogijima attracted more than fifty in-migrants, compared with less than five in-migrants on Megijima in the same period. While Megijima's population stayed the same or fell every year since the start of the festival, Ogijima's population saw a small but significant rebound after 2017 (figure 2). Nakashima (2014, 101) attributed Ogijima's success at drawing new in-migrants to a quality of "cultural openness". However, during fieldwork, the authors quickly dismissed "cultural openness" as a trait unique to Ogijima and sought deeper insights to explain the in-migrant gap.

This study followed a mixed methods research design (Creswell 2017), expecting employing both quantitative and qualitative approaches would yield the most complete possible understanding of the disparate outcomes between islands. Quantitative methods provided a broad view of bottom-up, small-scale business responses to the festival on Megijima and Ogijima. At the same time, qualitative data uncovered more nuanced explanations of the situation on each island. The qualitative results became the core of the study, with interviews and participant observation providing the main support for the conclusions. Much of the fieldwork was conducted during off (non-festival) periods for two reasons: First, islanders were much more willing to complete surveys than they would have been during the busy festival period. Second, working then allowed the authors to observe how many local tourism businesses were closed during the long off-festival periods versus the comparatively short art festival periods.

Data were collected via 1) a questionnaire distributed to local tourism micro-firms (Ogijima, n=14 of 17 total tourism micro-firms, or 82.3 per cent; Megijima, n=15, representing all local micro-firms) in which business owners were asked about their motivations for establishing businesses on the islands; 2) analysis of secondary data (table 1) from national government statistics, festival reports, local publications and scientific literature; and 3) twenty semi- and unstructured interviews (table 2) with different festival stakeholders. For this study, tourism micro-firms (or businesses) are defined as businesses serving tourists with ten or fewer employees, which were predominantly food service or accommodation businesses. The study used snowball sampling to interview festival officials. For community festival stakeholders, the study employed purposive sampling to target different groups on both islands: long-term island residents, new urban-rural in-migrants, former in-migrants and seasonal commuters, and business owners. The interview questions covered topics related to art, the festival, businesses and in-migrants. Interviews lasted an average of forty minutes and were recorded with the interviewees' permission. The authors transcribed and translated them from Japanese to English before processing them for this study. Supplementing the three methods described above, participant observation was conducted during and between art festival periods in the 2016 and 2019 Triennale years, as well as during non-art festival years (2017–18) on both islands.

The quantitative and qualitative findings revealed disparate outcomes were tied to a uniform strategy of revitalization-through-tourism applied identically by festival organizers to islands with highly varied local circumstances and dynamics. This, in turn, demonstrated that while multi-community art festivals have the potential to facilitate community revitalization, unique challenges on the ground are difficult or impossible for outside organizers to solve and require the involvement of the communities themselves. Both local infrastructure and local leadership are necessary to reach revitalization goals. This study also found that, in the right circumstances, islands can successfully attract significant numbers of in-migrants despite the challenges of rural island life. This highlights both the development

Table 2. Interview survey with Setouchi Triennale officials and on both islands (by the authors)

	Type of Interview	Interviewee title	Gender	Quotes within text
Festival officials	Semi-structured	Setouchi Triennale Executive Committee spokesperson	Male	
		NPO Koebi Network general manager	Female	Interviewee 1
		NPO Koebi Network core-management group (5 people)	Group	
	Unstructured	Setouchi Triennale general director	Male	
		NPO Koebi Network Ogijima manager	Male	
		NPO Koebi Network Megijima manager	Female	
		NPO Koebi Network public relations	Female	
Ogijima	Semi-structured	Independent IT worker (in-migrant)	Male	Interviewee 2
		Business owner (local long-term resident)	Male	
		Business owner (local long-term resident)	Male	
		Business owner (local long-term resident)	Female	Interviewee 3
		Residents' association leader (in-migrant)	Male	Interviewee 4
		Business owner (in-migrant)	Male	Interviewee 5
		Business owner (former in-migrant)	Male	
	Unstructured	Business owner (former in-migrant)	Female	
		Self-employed (1 household, 2 person)	Couple	Interviewee 6
Megijima	Semi-structured	Business manager (local long-term resident)	Male	Interviewee 7
		Business owner (seasonal commuter, birth from island)	Male	Interviewee 8
		Business manager (seasonal commuter)	Female	Interviewee 9
		Business owner (local long-term resident)	Male	

potential of festival-based revitalization strategies as well as the need for further study regarding the changes and challenges brought by such social restructuring (see Gosnell and Abrams 2011) in precarious communities.

There were some limitations to this study, including the fact that some fieldwork was conducted only during the non-art festival period. While this was planned in order to reach business owners when they had more time to speak to researchers, it may have influenced the data in unexpected ways. Additionally, over-research on Ogijima, as well as at least one negative experience islanders had with a previous researcher whose carelessness with private information led to divisions within the community, caused unforeseen difficulties in communicating with some potential respondents.

SOCIALLY ENGAGED RURAL ART FESTIVAL TOURISM AND ISLAND REVITALIZATION

Art festivals have the power to shape destinations into creative places by promoting cultural tourism (Prentice and Andersen 2003) and packaging creative experiences as attractions to draw festivalgoers to rural areas (Richards and Wilson 2006). Recent research has shown that a significant number of art festivals in both urban and rural settings result from bottom-up or grassroots initiatives, conceived at a small scale by local, deeply dedicated creative placemakers (Quinn 2010). In this regard, the Setouchi Triennale, organized at the prefectural level and directed by a Tokyo-based curator, is notably distinct.

Festivals provide not only leisure and recreation for tourists but also improve destination infrastructure for local residents, improve social development and foster exchanges of ideas and information (Cudny 2013). Art festivals thus present a relational or participatory model of rural development, contributing to the tourism economy while also foregrounding and even strengthening community relations (Crawshaw and Gkartzios 2016; Prince, Qu and Zollet 2021). The Setouchi Triennale typifies this model, offering cultural exchanges (Nakashima 2012; Qu 2020; Qu and Funck 2021) between locals and non-locals through creative, relational and interactive experiences.

The number of art festivals worldwide has surged in recent years, dominating in developed countries (Cudny 2013). Pointing to the sharp increase in art festivals in urban locales, Quinn (2010) argued that this rise has not resulted in a corresponding increase in local prosperity. Such issues have followed festivals as they move to rural locales. In rural Japan, which is almost universally ageing and depopulated, the unifying characteristic has been an emphasis on the potential of art festival tourism to spur community revitalization (Yamashima 2014; Qu and Funck 2021). Such festivals have the potential to offer a point of departure from (or even outright resistance to) the commercial, hyperglobal art market by re-situating contemporary art on unconventional, rural soil, commissioning artists to create site-specific artworks within host communities (Qu 2019; Qu, McCormick and Funck 2020). Alongside the potential and actual benefits of these festivals, observers have pointed to negative impacts on host communities and sites, including damage to natural environments, disruptions to daily life and local infrastructure, and conflicts between locals and tourists (Cudny 2013). A study of two other islands in the Setouchi Triennale revealed disconnects, with some locals ascribing a "theme park" atmosphere on the islands to the festival (Qu 2019, 19).

Can Japan's rural art festivals really trigger community revitalization? The recent introduction of the term "festivalization" has carried both positive and negative connotations. On the one hand, it suggests superficial, commercialized and privatized events; on the other hand, it implies the stimulation of cultural economies, creative experiences and social capital (Richards and Colombo 2017). Until now, efforts to identify social outcomes in Setouchi have been lacking. While valuable contributions to the literature on the Setouchi Triennale have been made in the fields of art history and criticism (see, for example, Favell 2016), evaluation of the Setouchi Triennale's community revitalization outcomes requires a social science approach.

As researchers have observed, in the emerging rural art festivals in Japan, it is not simply art tourism but contemporary art itself, which presents a possible medium for regional revitalization (Klien 2010; Qu and Funck 2021). Within Seto Inland Sea island communities, locals respond better to examples of particular festival artworks that link to island landscapes, local histories and collective memories (Qu 2019, 2020), suggesting that the characteristics of individual artworks are important to communities. On the other hand, Setouchi Triennale organizers prioritize *interactions*, not artworks themselves, as the vehicle for revitalization. They describe how visitors celebrate with locals rather than just coming to the islands to "see art" (Qu 2020). Some authors writing about rural Japanese art festivals have attempted to reinforce such ambiguous links between urban-rural interactions (whether tourist interactions or participatory artist-resident activities) and community revitalization, particularly as an aspect of place-making initiatives (Nakashima 2014; Koizumi 2016).

However, efforts to measure cultural exchange have yielded incomplete and misleading data that do little to either prove or disprove revitalization claims. For example, a report on the island of Teshima carried out during the 2013 Setouchi Triennale revealed that only 8.3 per cent of festival tourists said they were interested in interacting with locals (Yamamoto, Kawahara and Hara 2014). Yet this report failed to establish what interactions occurred or how long and how deep such local-visitor interactions were. Even if this data were present, such an evaluation would leave unanswered the critical questions of whether and how those interactions translated to specific revitalization outcomes.

To better establish conditions for long-term community viability, the authors turned to more tangible benchmarks. Duxbury and Campbell (2011, 14) suggested evaluating the success of art-and-culture-related development by a "creative class"-as-"residents-with-businesses" pattern. Whether communities in the art festival attract newcomers who start small businesses, thus creating a bottom-up response to the top-down festival structure, would be a significant and lasting outcome. Therefore, the authors sought such creative-newcomer entrepreneurship on Ogijima and Megijima.

FINDINGS ON UNEVEN REVITALIZATION OUTCOMES

In interviews, officials representing the three entities managing the festival all emphasized that the Setouchi Triennale is a revitalization initiative employing art festival tourism, not simply a tourism development programme. When the first author asked what the most significant challenges were for sustaining the art festival, answers mainly highlighted threats – such as ageing and depopulation – that were out of their control, originating from within the communities themselves. No officials reflected on real or potential failures in their own management or other internal weaknesses.

Officials generally agreed that the continued viability of the island communities was essential to the continued existence of the art festival. The general director of the Setouchi Triennale explained that revitalization is not simply a matter of increasing the number of island inhabitants, but seeing new in-migrants establish services and facilities to serve the island communities. After analysing multiple official interviews, the authors developed figure 3 to explain the stated mechanism of Setouchi Triennale, according to its organizers. The three-stage process is weighted heavily toward the second stage, where islands shift from hosting tourists to attracting a certain number of in-migrants. These in-migrants thus become a major reference point for examining the community development process within the art festival's revitalization agenda.

> So, after ten years, Ogijima now has more in-migrants. They have about fifty in-migrants, which means that 30 per cent of the population is in-migrants. Well, that's great. Yeah, it's a rare story. (Interviewee 1)

Exemplified by this quote, most festival officials mentioned Ogijima among the twelve festival islands as being a noteworthy example of revitalization at work. The number of in-migrants was frequently indicated as a cause for celebration.

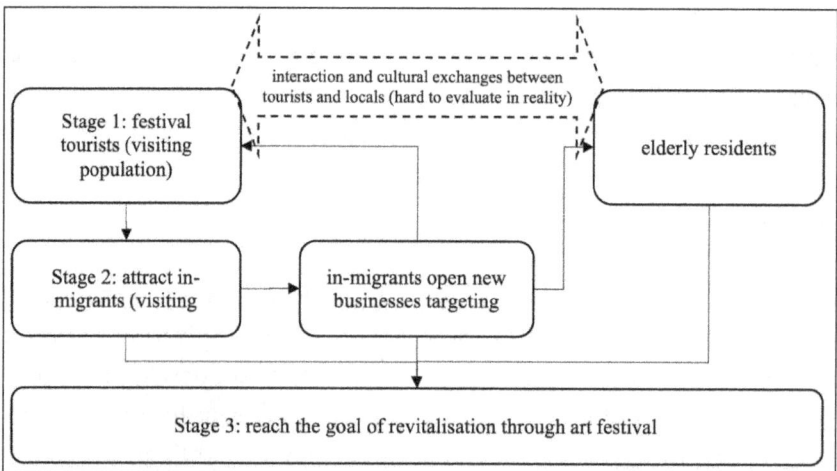

Figure 3. The model of the revitalization mechanism by Setouchi Triennale (by the authors)

The questionnaire distributed to tourism businesses gleaned insights from twenty-nine business owners on both islands. In fieldwork, during which the questionnaire was circulated, the authors observed that only about 60 per cent of island businesses remained open for the non-art festival periods. As shown in table 3, the ages and resident status of business owners, along with their target customers and business types, varied substantially between the two islands. More than half of the local businesses on Ogijima were mixed businesses (for example, a combined cafe and guest house), while on Megijima, most businesses were cafes, restaurants and guest houses or other

Table 3. Characteristics of respondents from questionnaire survey with local tourism businesses (by the authors)

		Ogijima			Megijima	
		Frequency (n=14)	Percentage		Frequency (n=15)	Percentage
Age groups	20–49	8	57.1		3	20.0
	50–79	6	42.9		12	80.0
	Non-response	0	00.0		0	0.0
Type of resident	Local long-term resident	6	42.9		5	33.3
	In-migrant	6	42.9		2	13.3
	Return migrants	1	7.1		0	0.0
	Commuter	1	7.1		8	53.4
	Non-response	0	0.0		0	0.0
Type of businesses	Mixed business	8	57.1		2	13.2
	Souvenir shop	0	0.0		1	6.7
	Tourist facility	0	0.0		1	6.7
	Grocery store	1	7.2		1	6.7
	Restaurant/café	4	28.5		6	40.0
	Accommodation	1	7.2		4	26.7
	Non-response	0	0.0		0	0.0
Target customers	Tourist	4	28.6		9	60.0
	Local	1	7.1		4	26.6
	Both	9	64.3		1	6.7
	Seasonal	0	0.0		1	6.7
	Non-response	0	0.0		0	0.0

accommodations. More than half of the Ogijima businesses had relatively young proprietors (20–49 years old), while 80 per cent of the businesses on Megijima were run by older people (50–79 years old). The respondents on Ogijima mainly comprised local long-term residents and in-migrants. However, on Megijima, they were mainly commuters who lived in the nearby city, Takamatsu, and worked on the island. Additionally, Ogijima businesses aimed their trades at both locals and tourists; Megijima's businesses were likely to target tourists expressly.

The authors also identified the reasons respondents established their businesses. As shown in figure 4, the results indicated that liking their island and the desire to make a living were the dominant reasons for both islands. While the Setouchi Triennale ranked fourth among the eight choices for Ogijima respondents with 21.4 per cent of the total, only 6.7 per cent of Megijima respondents cited the festival as a primary reason for starting their businesses.

Respondents on Ogijima indicated positive outcomes from the festival, particularly the new opportunities presented by the island's nascent tourism industry. This resulted in the island becoming more well known, which led to an increase in lifestyle in-migrants from Japanese cities, some of whom opened new tourism businesses. According to one respondent, "I can see that [the Triennale is] shining a spotlight on the region and introducing a lot of economic opportunities for local people other than the traditional

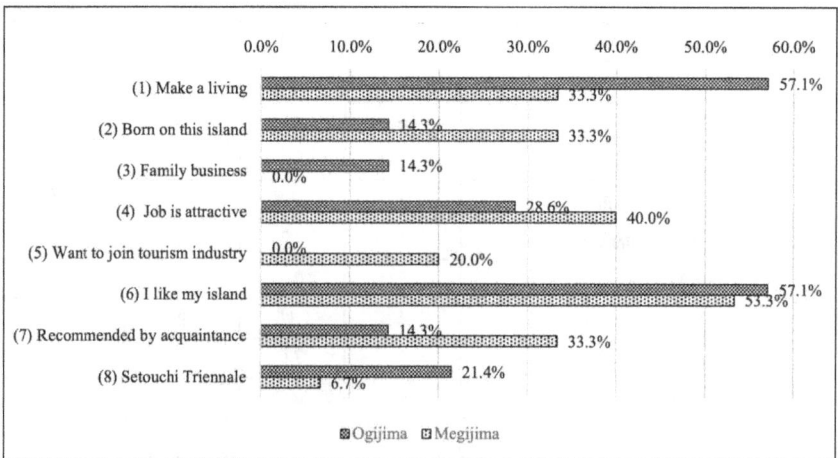

Figure 4. Reasons why business owners opened their businesses (by the authors)

industries like fishing and agriculture . . . A lot of [new in-migrants] are working either remotely or with businesses they've created on the island" (Interviewee 2).

Newly created businesses, such as the privately operated Ogijima Library (figure 5), were likely to attract both tourists and local customers. The library's small adjacent kitchen served curry, drinks and desserts, which visitors could eat on repurposed school desks inside the main building. Books in the library's collection, accumulated entirely through donations, were available for visitors to peruse and for islanders to borrow.

Another development widely promoted by festival organizers was the reopening of Ogijima's school, which was also viewed locally as highly attractive to in-migrants. Shuttered in 2011, the combined elementary and junior high school reopened in 2014 when three families relocated to the island (Takamatsu City Ogi Elementary and Junior High School 2014).

> The Triennale led to the school reopening . . . After the school reopened, the number of students gradually increased. There are more babies on the island now . . . Because of the Triennale, the population is growing. This is because the younger generation is willing to have children. That is [what we] expected. (Interviewee 3)

Figure 5. At the Ogijima Library, visitors could buy lunch, read books and interact with locals. Additionally, island residents could borrow books and participate in occasional educational events at the library (Photo by A. D. McCormick)

> I moved to this island on March 31, 2014. I put my children into school last year . . . Ogijima lost its future once due to the closure of primary and secondary schools. (Interviewee 4)

Ogijima respondents stressed that the school played a critical role in retaining the island's younger generation when they had children of their own, as well as attracting newcomers. While there were conflicting accounts regarding the precise causes of the school's reopening, there was a general sense that the Triennale had played at least a contributing role in this significant symbolic and practical victory for the island.

However, as the school's reopening was linked to the island's influx of in-migrants, this influx deserves more careful consideration, particularly as neighbouring Megijima did not share in Ogijima's success. Interviews on the island pointed to the efforts of a key figure in the community as central to the island's in-migrant boom. The leader of the residents' association, who was born on Ogijima but had left, returned to the island with his family in 2014 and quickly assumed an active role in helping outsiders who were interested in moving to Ogijima. With no government office on the island offering relocation services, he connected outsiders with other in-migrants. He provided information on matters related to island life, including local culture, available housing, transportation, education and job opportunities. Speaking on the diversity of in-migrants' backgrounds and vocations, he said:

> Engineers, designers, editors . . . some of them are really separate [from the tourism industry], but the most important reason people come to Ogi is in order to do what they want to do. (Interviewee 4)

In-migrants on Ogijima pointed to a range of benefits to life on the island, from the lifestyle benefits of living amid natural beauty and within a close-knit community to practical considerations such as the availability of high-speed internet and other services. However, without the active involvement of the residents' association leader, matters as basic as finding a house could have easily become overwhelming for prospective newcomers.

Opportunities connected to festival tourism were motivating to in-migrants interested in starting new tourism-focused businesses on Ogijima. This situation drew mixed comments from respondents.

The most obvious thing is the sudden influx of people wandering around, and the number of shops and stalls open. I see a lot of people return to Ogijima from Takamatsu and beyond seemingly lured in by the economic opportunities. When the crowds are not here, shops will only be open a couple of days a week, but during the festival a lot of shops didn't take a single day off during the spring period. (Interviewee 5)

Several respondents pointed to the inconsistent flow of tourists between the Setouchi Triennale's on- and off-seasons as creating a condition where there were alternately either too many or too few tourists on the island.

I felt that [the number of Triennale tourists] was really crazy. There were 1,700 visitors in May of this year [2019], and it started to feel like a war. Originally, the library was designed for [local] people who came here to read books and maybe have some snacks at the same time. [Now it's mostly tourists coming for lunch.]. (Interviewee 4)

During the festival period, the increase of foreigners on the island was also a challenge for long-term residents operating businesses who struggled to communicate with them.

During non-festival times, most of the faces you encounter on the streets are familiar and will always greet you warmly. During Setouchi Triennale, it can be difficult because I assume people are Japanese, but they don't respond to my greetings, and then I hear them speaking another language (to my untrained ears, it regularly sounds like Mandarin). (Interviewee 6)

The authors also uncovered challenges brought on by the rapid increase in in-migrants, which had caused a noticeable cultural shift toward openness to outside ideas on the island. Some respondents mentioned that as newcomers and new ideas gain weight against traditional values and systems, it can be difficult for long-term residents to adapt. Additionally, there was no guarantee that recent in-migrants would remain on the island indefinitely. The authors observed more than fifteen cases where in-migrants to Ogijima had already left the island or did not permanently reside there.

One negative impact on locals is over-research. Ogijima's success attracted many researchers, some of whom published their findings without protecting local respondents' privacy. The exposure of candid views given by islanders under the assumption of anonymity triggered rifts among locals. Now, Ogijima's community council website includes this language for researchers:

> In recent years, we have received a lot of reports regarding these research interviews, and we are struggling with too much ... Please consider the privacy of the islanders. Exposure to the media and publication of papers have sometimes hindered the private matters of the islanders and the relationships between them. Be sure to obtain the approval before publication from the interviewees and the organizers of the interviews. (Ogi District Community Council 2013)

Megijima received far fewer in-migrants (five or fewer) but many more commuters who operated tourism businesses on the island while living on the mainland. Respondents generally remarked upon a lack of positive changes since the debut of the Setouchi Triennale. All of this was in stark contrast to Ogijima.

> It's true that [the Setouchi Triennale] is not a bad thing for Megijima, but [revitalization] is not the current reality yet ... In our case, it was behind Ogijima. (Interviewee 7)

> Basically zero [changes]! That's why we accepted [the Triennale], but we helped to finish it. There is nothing left now. (Interviewee 7)

> I can't live without having a job. The art festival can't bring jobs to Megijima. Every three years, tourists come, and there are short-term economic benefits during that period. But after that, there will be a lot of less people, so it won't be a stable thing. (Interviewee 8)

> I don't recommend [the Setouchi Triennale to people]. Locals [on Megijima] don't have much interest in the festival, so I can't justify spending time on it. But the younger people on Ogijima are interested. (Interviewee 7)

> Japan is full of such mistakes from the past. In order to revitalize [areas], the government threw a lot of money into them, and after the projects failed and no one came, they left ruined tourist facilities and empty golf courses everywhere. By the way, the Japanese government is a tourist business. They can only create a period of [visitor number] bloom rather than a new culture ... [These ideas are] like Disneyland. (Interviewee 8)

Megijima respondents were far less likely to express faith in either the art festival or economic opportunities related to it. For some, the Setouchi Triennale felt like an echo of failed government projects from the nation's late twentieth-century bubble economy. One tourism-related business announced its closure at the start of 2019, claiming a poor economic outlook, even though the 2019 Triennale was a few months away. Instead, seasonal, commuter-run businesses had become common, such as a pop-up coffee shop (shown in figure 6) run out of a vehicle by the port, reflecting a lack of interest in in-migration and a lack of confidence in regular customers from within the community.

Respondents on Megijima also frequently expressed a sense that the art on their island was inferior and getting worse with successive festival iterations.

> If it's unique, it's a work [of art], but I don't feel that kind of artistry [on Megijima]. From my point of view, I think it's a state art festival where fake and real things are mixed. (Interviewee 8)

Figure 6. Rather than new resident-operated businesses, Megijima saw an increase in commuter-run businesses like this pop-up coffee truck, which appeared during the spring session of the 2019 Setouchi Triennale (Photo by Meng Qu)

Somehow, I think [Setouchi Triennale] has gotten worse and worse, and especially artistically, and this is a threat for long-term sustainability. There have been a lot of ugly artworks. As the festival has repeated twice and three times now, the [quality of the] artwork become [equivalent to what's found in] a university art or cultural festival. (Interviewee 9)

These sentiments represented a strong disconnect between the community and the festival. While respondents on Ogijima reported problems associated with the Setouchi Triennale, their overall impression of recent developments on the island was one of enthusiasm and pride. On Megijima, respondents saw little benefit from the festival, which felt neither rooted in local concerns nor supported by local constituents.

BETWEEN SUCCESS AND STAGNATION

Setouchi Triennale officials claim credit for Ogijima having received more in-migrants and new businesses over the last nine years. However, respondents on both islands did not consider the existence of the Setouchi Triennale as being, on its own, more significant than financial or lifestyle benefits. Most mentioned liking their island, making a living, or the attractiveness of the job as being far more critical. The "cultural openness" of Ogijima (Nakashima 2014, 101) appeared far less significant in drawing in-migrants to the island than concrete factors like the reopening of the school and, more importantly, the efforts of a key individual, the residents' association leader, to support those interested in settling on the island. While the festival was not directly tied to these factors, it played a contributing role in establishing conditions necessary to return Ogijima to long-term viability, particularly by thrusting it into the spotlight and thus advertising it to prospective in-migrants. This was not without its challenges, as the changes and new ideas brought by a large class of newcomers were not always well received by long-term residents, causing divisions within the Ogijima community. This tension seemingly complicates Crawshaw and Gkartzios's suggestion that art festivals can *reveal* community relations (2016). A negative side effect of Ogijima's high-profile successes, the excessive and careless research conducted on the island, may have exacerbated these divisions.

With Megijima, the island's failure to attract sufficient in-migrants resulted when seasonal commuters from the mainland operated more small businesses. These types of businesses mainly focused on tourists, as the business owners did not have significant community ties and were, therefore, more profit-minded. This appears to have had something of a cyclical effect, with observed examples of local businesses closing because of a lack of customers in the off-season, further tilting the small business environment toward commutership and pop-up food vehicles amid a hollowing out of the residential business community. Complaints about the festival were rampant on Megijima. They covered everything from the failure of the revitalization effort to the quality of the artwork itself, which was seen as inferior to that of other islands in the festival and declining with successive festival iterations. Echoing locals on a neighbouring island who described the festival as a "theme park" (Qu 2019), a respondent on Megijima dismissed the Triennale, referring to it as "Disneyland".

By processing these findings using the revitalization model in figure 3, which was developed out of interviews with festival officials, the results were summarized in table 4. The Setouchi Triennale had a noticeable impact on both islands, transforming them into well-known and highly visited tourist destinations by positioning artwork in a festival format as a creative spectacle (Richards and Wilson 2006). However, both over-tourism and under-tourism, caused by the intermittent festival structure, led to problems

Table 4. Applying research findings into the model of the revitalization mechanism by Setouchi Triennale (by the authors)

Stages of revitalization by Setouchi Triennale	Ogijima	Megijima
Stage 1: festival tourists	Island becomes tourist destination for revitalization. Over-tourism during festival; under-tourism in off season	
Stage 2: attract in-migrants	Obtains substantial number of in-migrants. Tourism businesses target both tourists and locals	Commuters heavily outweigh in-migrants. Their businesses target tourists exclusively
Stage 3: reach the goal of revitalization through art festival	Conditions for revitalization achieved with help of major local efforts (population, tourism development, other new industry growth)	No clear sign of revitalization

on both islands. Both islands had a similar number of tourism businesses, and respondents emphasized a sense of over-tourism during the Triennale period, while they were more likely to dwell on under-tourism during the non-festival period when income was insufficient to maintain their businesses. Ogijima actively worked to mitigate this issue by expanding beyond in-migrants seeking to capitalize on the tourism economy and reaping the rewards for their efforts, reaching Stage 3 in the revitalization model. Ogijima offers an example of an island where more in-migrants led to increased small business development by island residents. These small businesses catered to both locals and tourists. While festival organizers pointed to this revitalization outcome as a success that aligned with their hopes for communities within the Triennale, hailing the improvements to the quality of life for locals (Cudny 2013), this outcome directly resulted from local efforts. The failure of Megijima to reach a similar outcome suggests that, without significant local leadership, the Setouchi Triennale cannot effect true revitalization in participating communities.

CONCLUSION

This chapter evaluated the potential of Japan's socially engaged rural art festival to bring about conditions necessary to create long-term viability in participating island communities. In particular, it focused on the idea of festivals attracting new types of in-migrants who engage in the "residents-with-businesses" pattern linked to revitalization by Duxbury and Campbell (2011, 114) by studying two islands in the Setouchi Triennale with similar demographics and scale. The findings revealed that the same top-down revitalization strategy could lead to drastically varied results depending on local conditions, particularly if no effort is made to customize the strategy to those conditions. Ogijima offered an example of a relatively successful revitalization outcome, having attracted sufficient urban-rural in-migrants (Stage 2) to achieve the stated goal of revitalization through small business development (Stage 3). On the contrary, Megijima failed to attract in-migrants and, as a result, remained at Stage 1 after nine years of festival development.

The "cultural openness" of locals (Nakashima 2014, 101) and the art festival both established favourable conditions for in-migration to Ogijima but were not the main reasons Ogijima was successful. Nor was the role of "medium" played by the festival's tourism and artwork (Klien 2010, 519) alone sufficient to achieve revitalization. Instead, the strategic and supportive efforts of a community leader, along with the symbolic and practical reopening of the school in 2014, took advantage of the festival's favourable conditions to intentionally create a pathway to long-term community vitality. Put, socially engaged rural art festivals have triggered socially responsive changes toward rural revitalization.

New in-migrants gradually bring changes in the social structure of the community. As in-migrants and their ideas gain weight against traditional values and systems, it can be difficult for long-term residents to adapt. Islands that can attract more in-migrants benefit by having more small businesses operated by residents. Small businesses run by locals who cater to other locals as well as tourists are much stronger markers of revitalization. This study shows that, since the festival is held once every three years, tourist flows alternate between short periods of high tourist traffic and longer periods of significantly reduced tourist visitation. This, in turn, has forced small businesses to operate intermittently, which challenges both socio-economic and population stability. The long-term sustainability of the Setouchi Triennale and the marginal communities hosting it requires festival organizers to prioritize achieving a balance between over-tourism during the festival and under-tourism during non-festival periods. For future research, an in-depth study of how "revitalization" is perceived among various stakeholder groups within a large-scale socially engaged rural festival like Setouchi Triennale is required, as this moving target has caused much uncertainty. Moreover, focusing on additional cases of community revitalization within Setouchi Triennale is needed.

ACKNOWLEDGEMENTS

The authors gratefully acknowledges the financial support from the Japan Society for the Promotion of Science Grant-in-Aid for Scientific Research Projects 22K13251. Special thanks to Yaqian Liu, Art Island Center on Naoshima, as well as community members on both islands, whose assistance with data collection in the field was tremendously beneficial to this research.

REFERENCES

Crawshaw, Julie, and Menelaos Gkartzios. 2016. "Getting to Know the Island: Artistic Experiments in Rural Community Development." *Journal of Rural Studies* 43:134–44.https://doi.org/10.1016/j.jrurstud.2015.12.007.

Creswell, John W. 2017. *Research Design: Qualitative, Quantitative, and Mixed Methods Approaches*. Los Angeles: Sage Publications.

Cudny, Waldemar. 2013. "Festival Tourism – The Concept, Key Functions and Dysfunctions in the Context of Tourism Geography Studies." *Geographical Journal* 65 (2): 105–18.

Duxbury, Nancy, and Heather Campbell. 2011. "Developing and Revitalizing Rural Communities through Arts and Culture." *Small Cities Imprint* 3 (1): 111–22.

Favell, Adrian. 2016. "Islands for Life: Artistic Responses to Remote Social Polarization and Population Decline in Japan." In *Sustainability in Contemporary Rural Japan: Challenges and Opportunities*, edited by Stephanie Assmann, 109–24. London and New York: Routledge.

Geospatial Information Authority of Japan (GSI). 2016. "Global Map Japan." https://www.gsi.go.jp/kankyochiri/gm_japan_e.html.

Gosnell, Hannah, and Jesse Abrams. 2011. "Amenity Migration: Diverse Conceptualizations of Drivers, Socioeconomic Dimensions, and Emerging Challenges." *GeoJournal* 76 (4): 303–22. doi:10.1007/s10708-009-9295-4.

Kitagawa, Fram, and Setouchi Triennale Executive Committee. 2016. *Setouchi Triennale 2016 Official Guidebook*. English Ed. Tokyo: Gendaikikakushitsu.

Klien, Susanne. 2010. "Contemporary Art and Regional Revitalisation: Selected Artworks in the Echigo-Tsumari Art Triennial 2000-6." *Japan Forum* 22 (3–4): 513–43. doi:10.1080/09555803.2010.533641.

Koizumi, Motohiro. 2016. "Creativity in a Shrinking Society: A Case Study of the Water and Land Niigata Art Festival." *Cities* 56:141–47. doi:10.1016/j.cities.2015.10.002.

Matanle, Peter, Anthony. S Rausch, and Shrinking Regions Research Group. 2011. *Japan's Shrinking Regions in the 21st Century: Contemporary Responses to Depopulation and Socioeconomic Decline.* New York: Cambria Press.

Nakashima, Masahiro. 2012. "Community Involvement and Quality of Life with Setouchi International Art Festival." *Hiroshima Journal of International Studies* 18:71–89.

———. 2014. "Community Regeneration of Aging Society and an Art Festival on a Remote Island." *Hiroshima Journal of International Studies* 20:93–104.

NPO Ogijima Life Research Institute. 2018. "Island Living Guide Book." http://shimagurashi.info.

Ogi District Community Council. 2013. "For the Media and Students Who Want to Interview Ogijima." *Ogijima Info.* http://ogijima.info/contact/.

Prentice, Richard, and Vivien Andersen. 2003. "Festival as Creative Destination." *Annals of Tourism Research* 30 (1): 7–30. doi:10.1016/S0160-7383(02)00034-8.

Prince, Solène, Meng Qu, and Simona Zollet. 2021. "The Making of Art Islands: A Comparative Analysis of Translocal Assemblages of Contemporary Art and Tourism." *Island Studies Journal*, 1–20. doi:https://doi.org/10.24043/isj.175.

QGIS Development Team. 2019. "QGIS Geographic Information System." *Open Source Geospatial Foundation Project.* http://qgis.osgeo.org.

Qu, Meng. 2019. "Art Interventions on Japanese Islands: The Promise and Pitfalls of Artistic Interpretations of Community." *The International Journal of Social, Political and Community Agendas in the Arts* 14 (3): 19–38. doi:https://doi.org/10.18848/2326-9960/CGP/v14i03/19-38.

———. 2020. "Teshima – From Island Art to the Art Island." *Shima: The International Journal of Research into Island Cultures* 14 (2): 250–65. doi:10.21463/shima.14.2.16.

———, and Carolin Funck. 2021. "Rural Art Festival Revitalizing a Japanese Declining Tourism Island." In *Cultural Sustainability, Tourism and Development (Re) Articulations in Tourism Contexts*, 51–68. London and New York: Routledge. doi:10.4324/9780367201777-6.

Qu, Meng, A.D. McCormick, and Carolin Funck. 2020. "Community Resourcefulness and Partnerships in Rural Tourism." *Journal of Sustainable Tourism.* Routledge, 1–20. doi:10.1080/09669582.2020.1849233.

Quinn, Bernadette. 2010. "Arts Festivals, Urban Tourism and Cultural Policy." *Journal of Policy Research in Tourism, Leisure and Events* 2 (3): 264–79. doi:10.1080/19407963.2010.512207.

Richards, Greg, and Alba Colombo. 2017. "Rethinking the Eventful City." *Event Management Special Issue* 21:527–31.

Richards, Greg, and Julie Wilson. 2006. "Developing Creativity in Tourist

Experiences: A Solution to the Serial Reproduction of Culture?" *Tourism Management* 27 (6): 1209–23. doi:10.1016/j.tourman.2005.06.002.

Setouchi Triennale Executive Committee. 2017. "Setouchikokusaigeijutsusai 2016 Sōkatsu Hōkoku 瀬戸内国際芸術祭2016総括報告 [Setouchi Triennale 2016 General Report]." https://setouchi-artfest.jp/seto_system/fileclass/img.php?-fid=press_release_mst.20170217195217a6457f2b91cb302fa36db1fae1083e73.

Takamatsu City Official Website. 2019. "[Tōkei] Tōroku Jinkō (Jūmin Kihon Daichō Jinkō) 統計】登録人口 (住民基本台帳人口) [Statistics] Registered Population (Basic Resident Registration)." http://www.city.takamatsu.kagawa.jp/kurashi/shinotorikumi/tokei/jinko/toroku/index.html.

Takamatsu City Ogi Elementary and Junior High School. 2014. "Takamatsu City Ogi Elementary and Junior High School." http://www.edu-tens.net/syoHP/ogisyouHP/index.html.

Yamamoto, Akemi, Susumu Kawahara, and Naoyuki Hara. 2014. "Role and Influence of Art and Culture Activities in Regional Development 2013 Setouchi International Art Festival Visitors' Survey Report." *"Kanko Kagaku Kenkyu"* 観光科学研究 *[Tourism Science Research]* 7:59–64.

Yamashima, Tetsuo. 2014. "Naosima – The Island of ART in Setonaikai." *Utsunomiya Kyowa University Annual Report on Urban Economics* 14:90–96.

Chapter Two

The Norseman's Home
Up-Helly-Aa and Shetland's Performance of Place

EMMA LANG

ON THE LAST TUESDAY OF JANUARY, LERWICK SHETLAND is filled with men and boys in costumes of all kinds, hundreds of torches ready to be set alight, and a beautiful hand-crafted wooden boat built for being burned. All business is put on hold for the annual festival of Up-Helly-Aa, an event more than a hundred and thirty years old, where the performance of what it means to be a Shetlander and Shetland's place in the world, historically and today, takes centre stage. Up-Helly-Aa has come to represent Shetland culture to the world, and many Shetlanders see it as an integral part of their culture. Up-Helly-Aa sits at the core of Shetlanders' negotiating cultural understanding.

This chapter will examine how Lerwick Up-Helly-Aa – the largest of the Up-Helly-Aa festivals that occur in communities across Shetland from January to March – can be interpreted as a demonstration of how the archipelago is, and has always been, globally connected. Up-Helly-Aa is

---

Authors Note: In the six years since this article was written, public debate around cultural representations and the exclusion of women from Lerwick Up-Helly-Aa has increased, due in large part to a steady increase in visitors to Shetland prior to the COVID-19 pandemic. In 2023, women were allowed to participate for the first time, but the long-term impact of those discussions and changes on Lerwick Up-Helly-Aa has yet to be determined.

uniquely Shetlandic in its form, yet similar to many other traditions across the world, from masked performances put on in conjunction with religious holidays to many bonfire nights and parades. Lerwick Up-Helly-Aa, although only lasting one day, is a deeply complex festival that incorporates music, dance, acting, material culture as costumes, foodways, the galley (a wooden longship), language and tales. It is a festival that has been well documented for most of its history, in large part because of its age – the first Up-Helly-Aa is thought to have been held in 1881. This has meant that letters, newspaper articles and, most of all, photographs exist chronicling the festival's evolution. Photography in particular has played a major role in documenting the festival. Beginning in the early twentieth century, every single group or squad participating in the festival has been photographed, class-photo-like, both in full costume and unmasked, and an extensive number of photographs, both official and unofficial, have been taken during the festival itself (Brown 2002, 22–23; Shetland Amenity Trust n.d.a, n.d.b, n.d.c, n.d.d, n.d.e, n.d.f, n.d.g; Up-Helly-Aa Committee n.d.a, n.d.b, n.d.c).

CONTEXT

In focusing on how Lerwick Up-Helly-Aa serves as a performance of global connectedness, I have been forced to narrow in on some parts of the festival while leaving others out. Most notably absent is any analysis of the group performances that make up the latter part of the festival and the different Norse legends chosen each year to be embodied by that year's Guizer Jarl, or festival leader. This chapter builds on the work of the three books written about Up-Helly-Aa C.E. Mitchell's *Up-Helly-Aa Tar Barrels and Guizing: Looking Back* (1948), James W. Irvine's *Up-Helly-Aa: A Century of Festival* (1982) and Callum G. Brown's *Up-Helly-Aa: Custom, Culture and Community in Shetland* (1998) as well as the history of the festival written by Brian Smith (n.d.) and published on the official Up-Helly-Aa website, www.uphellyaa. org, and literature about the negotiation of Shetland island identity as it relates to Scandinavia, works explicitly by Adam Grydehøj (2010, 2013a, 2013b), Silke Reeploeg (2017) and Angela Watt (2012). In addition, I examined Viking and Up-Helly-Aa-related ephemera produced by Shetland institutions and available for tourists, which I collected during the summer of 2016 on a research trip to Shetland, and reviewed online references to Up-Helly-Aa aimed at tourists, both those produced as advertising and those created by travel writers. Lastly, I have asked friends in Shetland to share their thoughts on the festival with me. However, in undertaking an analysis of such a complex festival on which a limited number of secondary sources exist, I would like to emphasize that the research I conducted on Up-Helly-Aa should be viewed as only scratching the surface of the material that could be examined.

Up-Helly-Aa's creation and current form are directly connected to Shetland's place on the globe. The geographic location of Shetland has led to its cultural connection to a multitude of nations and its active participation in the global economy for centuries. Lerwick, the main town in Shetland, is approximately the same distance from Bergen, Norway, as it is from Aberdeen in Scotland and is closer to both Oslo and Amsterdam than it is to London. Norse presence in Shetland is understood to have begun in the late eighth century and the archipelago, along with Orkney to the south, were under Norwegian rule until 1469, when they were given to Scotland by the Danish rulers of Norway as part of a dowry. Shetland was ruled by the Scots until the 1707 Act of Union brought it, and the rest of Scotland, under the control of London (Schei 2006, 11–16). While it is far from what is generally considered prime colonial real estate, Shetland's location at the confluence of the North Sea and the Gulf Stream in the Atlantic Ocean gave Shetlanders easy access to rich fishing grounds, making it desirable to nations with growing economies across Europe (Grydehøj 2013a, 41–42; Shetland Museum and Archive n.d.d.; Shetland Museum and Archive n.d.e). The fish caught and salted by Shetlanders provided a vital source of cheap, easily transportable protein needed by the growing European population of the early modern period (Pope 2004, 11). Much of this fish was sold to the Henseatic League, which dominated Northern European trade at this time, and later, as the Henseatic League lost dominance, to other traders on the continent. This economic relationship put Shetlanders in contact not only with Norwegian and Scottish sailors and traders but also with seafarers from across Northern and Western Europe and beyond (Grydehøj 2013a, 41–42; Nicolson 1978, 22–23). These interactions with companies and people from far away continued as Shetland's export economy evolved to include wool products, most notably Fair Isle sweaters (named after Shetland's most southerly island), the wearing of which has been a recurring fashion trend for over one hundred years (McHattie, Champion and Broadley 2018; Shetland Museum and Archive n.d.b.) and expanded even further with the discovery of North Sea oil in 1971 and the building of the Sullom Voe oil terminal. The latter resulted in Shetland becoming host to thousands of outsiders who moved to Shetland to build the terminal and work in the oil industry (Wills 1991). More recently, the number of tourists visiting Shetland has exploded, as affordable flights and regular cruise ship visits to Lerwick have made the islands more accessible to global travellers. This history shows how, despite appearing in a box on a map of the United Kingdom, Shetland has always been a site of cross-cultural interactions and a player on the global economic stage, a position not unlike many other island groups (Stratford 2013; Gillis 2001; Grydehøj 2010, 2013; Immerwahr 2019).

ORIGINS OF UP-HELLY-AA

Up-Helly-Aa began as a formalization of the nineteenth-century Christmas season tradition of what could broadly be called "fire-play" combined with a tradition of guizing, the act of a group going around in a costume with a particular goal (Brown 1999, 41–43). At the core of these traditions was the practice of tar-barrelling, found across Great Britain in this period. Tar-barrelling consisted of working-class men and boys, often in costume or disguise, rolling or carrying a flaming barrel of tar or pulling a wooden sled with flaming tubs of tar on top of it, through the streets of the town until the fire had burned out (Mitchell 1948, 18–20). This act was frequently accompanied by a combination of homemade explosives and destruction, targeting property owners who were viewed to have slighted the participants (Brown 1999, 91–95). Not surprisingly, Shetland community leaders were interested in putting a stop to the practice of tar-barrelling and began working to end the practice by the late 1860s (Mitchell 1948, 38–49; Brown 1999, 96–98).

The men who participated in tar-barrelling activities in Lerwick were residents of the town and employed in a range of skilled and unskilled occupations. In the literature, they are collectively referred to as "working men" to differentiate them from business owners or professionals (Brown 1999; Irvine 1982; Mitchell 1948; Smith n.d.). Brown, citing Brian Smith, stated that Up-Helly-Aa was an organic creation of the community of working-class men and boys who had previously participated in tar-barrelling (Brown 1999, 44–45). This is borne out by Mitchell's research, for which he spoke to early participants of the festival. Mitchell stated that Up-Helly-Aa evolved from tar-barrelling to an interim period beginning in 1876 when torchlit parades were allowed by the authorities, to a torchlit parade that included some of the guizing aspects of tar-barrelling and shifted again to an event where only those in costumes and members of registered groups or "squads" may participate in the parade (Mitchell 1948, 90–98). The final significant evolution of the festival took place in the early twentieth century when the festival gained its "Viking" flair with the addition of a Norse-style longship (referred to as the Galley) being brought through the streets and burned. The adoption of the term "Guizer Jarl" to refer to the rotating leader of the event (Irvine 1982, 32, 133–35).

We can only hypothesize why the authorities were so willing to allow the first shift to a torchlight parade. But it seems likely that it was allowed as a compromise, facilitating the positive aspects of tar-barrelling. This long-held tradition served as a fun winter distraction while removing those aspects that were viewed as negative, primarily the moving of a flaming barrel of tar through the narrow streets of the town while drinking and destroying property. The torchlit parade could be interpreted as an elite-created, watered-down version of tar-barrelling, developed to reduce the autonomy of working-class men. However, the development of the Lerwick Up-Helly-Aa committee, which in its early years did not include members of the Lerwick elite and at times ran in direct opposition to the town elites, combined with Smith's argument that the festival developed organically, counters that interpretation (Brown 1999, 162–68). From this history, we can understand that despite how it is currently framed in promotions to tourists, and despite Mitchell's assertion that the festival is rooted in Viking or Scandinavian traditions, Up-Helly-Aa is decidedly British and Shetlandic in origin and is far from an ancient Norse rite of winter (Leslie 2011; Mitchell 1948, 2–3).

UP-HELLY-AA TODAY

Preparations for Up-Helly-Aa begin soon after the last of the previous festival's costumes have been packed away. The Lerwick Festival's organizing is done by the Up-Helly-Aa committee, who have the final say in all festival-related decisions. Currently, the event includes forty-seven squads who, over the year, must prepare a costume and a related skit or dance for the event. No theme for costume or performance is allowed to be repeated either from a past year or by multiple squads in a year. One squad is chosen to be the Jarl Squad. This squad will dress as Vikings and lead the event. The leader of that squad is known as the Guizer Jarl. The role of the Jarl Squad rotates among the squads based on the seniority of the leader on the Up-Helly-Aa committee. To be the Guizer Jarl or even on a Jarl Squad is considered an honour and a sign of commitment to both the festival and the community. Aside from the preparations of each squad, the Galley must be built, torches constructed, funds raised, and as the festival draws nearer, the eleven halls across Lerwick where the squads perform their skits and dances must be decorated, food must be prepared and bars must be stocked (Brown 1999; Irvine 1982; Mitchell 1948; Smith n.d.).

Lerwick Up-Helly-Aa begins early on the morning of the last Tuesday of January with the posting of Da Bill. This large hand-painted announcement declares the charitable goals of Jarl Squad and its commitments to the community. It also includes jokes written by a jokes committee that poke fun at current events, local people and often Lerwick Up-Helly-Aa itself. Over the course of the day, the contents of Da Bill will be analysed and debated by Shetlanders around the world, including the quality of the jokes and who or what was (or was not) included. Throughout the morning, the Jarl Squad parades through Lerwick in full costume before going to visit schools, nursing homes, the hospital and local museums, giving small gifts and singing the "Up Helly Aa Song". The squad also stops by the Lerwick town hall for an official ceremony that includes drinking from the Måløy Cup, a silver cup donated by the Norwegian town of Måløy to thank Shetland for its support of the Norwegian resistance movement during World War II. This act reiterates the connection between Shetland and Scandinavia. By early afternoon, the other guizers have left work to get into costume and join their squads. By evening, all the squads are assembled and march in a torchlit procession through the Victorian neighbourhoods of Lerwick. As they parade, they sing the "Up Helly Aa Song". The Jarl Squad and the Galley lead the procession, and the route is selected for maximum dramatic effect. The procession ends at the "burning site", an empty area in a local park. At this point, the guizers sing the "Galley Song" and throw their torches into the Galley. As the Galley burns, the song "Norsemen's Home" is sung. Following the burning of the Galley, the squads board buses and travel between the eleven halls, each squad visiting every hall. It is in the halls that the skits and dances associated with the costumes are performed. Following each performance, the squad will dance with those in the halls and eat and drink for a short while before moving on to the next hall, where the process will be repeated. The squads do not complete their visits to all the halls until Wednesday morning. The day after Up-Helly-Aa is a holiday, and after the clean-up from the festivities is completed, participants begin to think about the next year's festival (Brown 1999; Irvine 1982; Mitchell 1948; Smith n.d.).

CULTURAL NEGOTIATIONS

Dominating the performance of cultural identity that is Lerwick Up-Helly-Aa are demonstrations of Shetland's historic and modern connections to the rest of the world, which also counter any argument that Shetland is isolated and that Shetlanders are behind the times. That Up-Helly-Aa would become associated with Vikings, and Shetland's Viking history is not serendipitous. In the nineteenth century, Victorian Britons were fascinated with all things Viking, as Andrew Wawn discusses in his 2000 book, *The Vikings and the Victorians: Inventing the Old North in Nineteenth-Century Britain*. Wawn explores the place of Viking and Norse references in popular literature and academic work produced during the period (Wawn 2000). The language of the songs sung as part of Up-Helly-Aa mirror the romantic portrayals of Vikings during the Victorian era. This is clearly seen in the chorus and one verse of the "Up-Helly-Aa Song", written by J.J. Haldane Burgess:

Grand old Vikings ruled upon the ocean vast
Their brave battle-songs still thunder on the blast
Their wild war-cry comes a-ringing from the past
We answer it "A-oi"!
Roll their glory down the ages
Sons of warriors and sages
When the fight for Freedom rages
Be bold and strong as they!

Of yore, our firey fathers sped upon the Viking Path
Of yore, their dreaded dragons braved the ocean in its wrath
And we, their sons, are reaping now their glory's aftermath
The waves are rolling on.
(Up Helly Aa Committee n.d.c)

In addition to writing this song, Burgess, who was educated in Edinburgh and was an active member of the Socialist community in Lerwick, is viewed as a major force behind the "Norsification" of Up-Helly-Aa, including conceiving of added the Galley to the festivities (Brown 1998, 139–44). Burgess is one of many writers of the late nineteenth and early twentieth centuries who encountered the popular fascination with Vikings and all things Norse and made it their own by seeking out and writing about connections between Shetland and Norse traditions (Grydehøj 2013a; Reeploeg 2017).

The use of Viking imagery and history, both real and imagined, can be understood as a way for Shetlanders to define their islands as both a part of Great Britain, as seen in their participation in a national obsession with all things Norse, but also as separate from the rest of the country though their more recent and thus authentic connection to Scandinavia. Further analysis of this can be seen in Silke Reeploeg's 2017 article, "Peripheral Visions: Engaging Nordic Literary Traditions on Orkney and Shetland", where she argued that Burgess's writings, including his Up-Helly-Aa-related material, along with other writers in both Shetland and Orkney in this period, could exploit the wider British interest in and desire to connect British history and culture to Norse roots by highlighting the more recent connections between the islands and Norway. This moved the islands away from the periphery of both British cultural identity and global cultural understanding into a more central position and, thus, one of greater interest and value to the broader world. The accomplishment of this movement was assisted by a broader phenomenon around how islands are viewed, which John R. Gillis puts forth in his 2001 article, "Places Remote and Islanded", whereby the "appeal of islands seems directly proportional to their perceived remoteness" (Gillis 2001, 41). By exploiting this phenomenon, Shetlanders were able to promote the islands' importance as the homeland of what could be called "authentic Anglo-Scandinavian identity", an identity around which interest was increasing when Up-Helly-Aa first emerged (Grydehøj 2010; Grydehøj 2013b; Watt 2012).

How this negotiation of Shetland's cultural location between modern Great Britain and ancient Scandinavia took place is visible in the text of a pamphlet from 1877 believed to include the first published use of the phrase "Up-Helly-Aa" in relation to a winter festival. Callum Brown describes the pamphlet as making fun of the churches in Lerwick and demanded the "restoration of the ancient Norse faith of Shetland". Those wishing to participate in this restoration are then called to join in a "festival of uphellya" [sic] (Brown 1999, 32–33). Though produced as satire, the pamphlet's placing of the "ancient" and, it is implied, true faith of Shetlanders against the "outsider" and modern churches from Scotland and England would have been understood by readers as Shetland having a claim to Viking heritage in a way that others in Great Britain did not (ibid.). The fascination among Shetlanders with their Norse ancestors was bolstered by an increasing local and outside interest in Shetland history, particularly its archaeology and historic ties to Scandinavia. This interest brought increasing numbers of travellers and researchers to the islands in the late nineteenth and early twentieth centuries. This is evidence itself of the movement Reeploeg describes where Shetland positioned itself as no longer at the periphery of the British imagination, as well as of Gillis's argument that islands that are perceived as remote, but not so remote as to be completely inaccessible, attract increased interest (Brown 1999; Reeploeg 2017; Gillis 2001, 41).

In understanding the modern context of Shetlanders' perception of their location at the intersection of Great Britain and Scandinavia, it is useful to look to research presented in Angela Watt's 2012 unpublished doctoral thesis, "The Implications of Cultural Interchange in Scalloway, Shetland with

Reference to a Perceived Nordic-based Heritage". Watt's research explored the impact of focusing on the connections between modern Shetlanders and Norse heritage using a cultural anthropology framework. She explored the concept of "Norsemen's bias" to describe the long-term implications that defining Shetland as Norse or Viking has had (Watt 2012). In viewing the impact of an emphasis on Shetland's Norse connections, we can understand the Norsemen's bias as allowing Shetland and Shetlanders to locate themselves as part of two normally separate regions, Scandinavia and the British Isles, on a personal level. Through Watt's framework we can understand Shetland's movement away from the periphery into a liminal space between the two, both culturally and historically. This liminality is directly tied to the interest in Vikings being, if not explicitly a fad, certainly a component of ongoing popular culture. That Shetland's Norsemen's bias is based, in part, on an aspect of popular culture that has become integral to the culture of the place and is dominant in how it performs its relationship to the globalized world, demonstrates Up-Helly-Aa's power as a conduit of popular culture across time and space.

Lerwick Up-Helly-Aa's continued use of global popular culture has taken many forms, but the most visible one is in the theme chosen by various squads. Over the years this has included themes such as Charlie Chaplin (1920), Popeye (1930), Snow White (1939) – for which the squad obtained permission from the Walt Disney Company – Donald Duck (1953) and astronauts (1970). More recent themes have been Men in Black (2009), Angry Birds (2012), the vampire craze (2014), emojis (2016), and tributes to Michael Jackson (2017) and Roald Dahl (2017). (Shetland Museum and Archives n.d.e; Up Helly Aa Committee n.d.a) Proceedings are, of course, always led by the Vikings of the Jarl Squad, who continue to be romanticized and included in popular culture around the world (Coutts et al. 2009; Irvine 1982; Shetland Amenity Trust n.d.a, n.d.b,, n.d.f, n.d.g; Up Helly Aa Committee n.d.a, n.d.b 2009–19). The use of an integral component of Up-Helly-Aa to present interpretations to global popular culture, through demonstrated knowledge of that culture as well as, in more recent years, mass produced costumes, serves to counter the assumption that Shetland is isolated or even backwards and old fashioned.

While Up-Helly-Aa reinforces to Shetlanders their global connectedness and, one could argue, cosmopolitanism, it is used to do the opposite in the materials created for tourists and potential tourists to the islands. In this context, the terms "Up-Helly-Aa" and "Viking" are used to define Shetlanders as "the folk": rural, bound by tradition and not necessarily connected to the broader world (McKay 1994, 10–13). The understanding of Shetlanders as "folk" and, by implication, as "primitive" dates back at least as far as the late eighteenth and early nineteenth centuries, as seen in the analysis of Shetland travelogues by Watt, but is perpetuated today through the continued presence of Viking culture (Watt 2012, 82–87). A more concrete example of the romanticization of Shetlanders as "the folk" is the frequent appearance of the Jarl Squad in full Viking costume in tourism marketing. The costumes, in particular, are presented as an example of authentic Shetland culture, but they are based on a modern interpretation of how Vikings dressed. Despite Lerwick Up-Helly-Aa occurring in late January when the temperatures hover around zero degrees Celsius and when there is often a brisk cold wind off the sea, the Jarl Squad is almost always dressed in knee-length skirts and boots, with a large amount of bare skin visible. While not historically based, these costumes fit in with the concept of "the folk" being hardy and not always smart, in this case not smart enough to make sure all skin was covered against the elements (Promote Shetland n.d.b; Shetland Amenity Trust n.d.a, n.d.b, n.d.c, n.d.f, n.d.g). However, as previously noted, the Vikings who provide credibility to Shetlanders as "the folk" are a mix of the Victorian construct of Vikings, as portrayed in all Up-Helly-Aas, and the actual historic Vikings who visited and lived in Shetland, a topic discussed in much greater depth in Adam Grydehøj's 2010 article, "Uninherited Heritage: Tradition and Heritage Production in Shetland, Åland and Svalbard". This conflation of the historic Viking and Norse presence in Shetland and the locally born tradition of Up-Helly-Aa is seen in all its permutations in the brochure about Vikings produced for tourists by the Shetland Amenity Trust, the governmental heritage agency. This flier includes information about historic sites related to the Viking presence in Shetland. Still, the photograph on the cover and more than half of the images within are from Up-Helly-Aa, not of sites where the Vikings were present or of Norse artefacts found in Shetland. In addition, the images in the brochure, both of the Lerwick Up-Helly-Aa exhibit at the galley shed and of the town hall's nineteenth-century art portraying Vikings, fail to note that these portrayals of Vikings are less than historically accurate (Shetland Amenity Trust n.d.g.).

The effectiveness of the tourism marketing, which includes the portrayal of Shetland as a place where the authentic "folk" can be found, is seen in recent online travel writing describing Shetland as a "rugged outpost in the North Atlantic" and a "sleepy quiet place" (Everfest Inc. n.d.; Wherever Family 2017). The 2006 edition of the only printed guidebook exclusively for Orkney and Shetland describes Shetlanders using animal parallels: "There is plenty to inform and entrance in this scattering of rugged islands, whose people are probably best epitomized by that truly native inhabitant, the sturdy little Shetland pony – hardy, self-reliant, enduring and friendly" (Penrith and Penrith 2006, 155). From an emic perspective, it is obvious that Shetland and Shetlanders are aware of and active participants in the world beyond their shores, both economically and culturally. Yet the participation in the performance of global culture as part of Lerwick Up-Helly-Aa, either directly as a member of a squad or as an audience member who understands the references made by squad costumes, can nonetheless produce a much-needed counterbalance to assumptions around isolation with which Shetlanders are bombarded during the tourist season and when they travel. Shetlanders often have to use a map to explain where they live and frequently get questions regarding access to basic technologies (toilets, the internet, aeroplanes). They are often asked why they choose to stay there (Christie 2017; Huda 2017).

Up-Helly-Aa's location in Shetland culture as a space where issues related to globalization and local identity are negotiated has also been tied to the festival's ongoing debate about who should and should not be allowed to participate in the festival's squads. The question of a residency requirement for squad participation first came up after oil was discovered in the 1970s and Shetland experienced a massive influx of outsiders (Brown 1999, 170–71; Wills 1991, 59–65). These newcomers excitedly joined in on the fun of Lerwick Up-Helly-Aa and were keen to become more actively involved. However, the organizers of Lerwick Up-Helly-Aa were less excited about the influx of new participants. As Brown stated, and as I heard anecdotally multiple times during my time in Shetland, the "oilies" were thought to have brought crime and disorder to the islands and were felt by many to be an invading force (Brown 1999, 173–74; Christie 2017; Johnson 2017; McMillan 2007). In response, the Lerwick Up-Helly-Aa committee passed a rule that stated that a five-year residency in Shetland was required for participation in an Up-Helly-Aa squad. The residency requirement stayed in place until the 1990s (Brown 1999, 174).

It is important to note that, despite the regulations put in place, the definition of an outsider has more to do with ethnic and cultural heritage than residency. This can be seen in the fact that every year, Shetlanders who live overseas and those descended from Shetlanders who moved overseas are welcomed to come back and participate in Lerwick Up-Helly-Aa (Brown 1999, 28). That Up-Helly-Aa serves to demonstrate Shetland's links to the broader world through the use of global popular culture and the inclusion of expatriate Shetlanders and their descendants in Lerwick Up-Helly-Aa while simultaneously excluding some current residents – including all women – makes clear the ambivalence of some Shetlanders – most notably those on the Lerwick Up-Helly-Aa committee – around Shetland's current existence as a heterogeneous and globally connected community.

The exclusion of outsiders who moved to Shetland during the oil boom from a festival that celebrates a historic tie to Vikings who were themselves outsiders who moved to Shetland is ironic. However, the Viking history of Shetland is understood to facilitate a positive romantic understanding of Shetland as a globally connected place that welcomes the cultural shifts and global economic connections that come with the arrival of outsiders. Unfortunately, modern industrial workers do not suggest the same bucolic picture as Vikings seem to. The same dichotomy that simultaneously holds these two different perspectives of outsiders is at play when looking at the inclusion of ethnic stereotypes in Up-Helly-Aa squads' costumes and performances. The ethnic caricatures depicted by squads bring outsiders into Up-Helly-Aa in a way that is acceptable and controlled, unlike the actual participation in the festival of non-ethnic Shetlanders. Using caricatures (including painting skin to represent a given group) has been a part of Up-Helly-Aa for its entire history. Without viewing the skits or dances associated with these costumes, it is difficult to ascertain the degree to which these caricatures are racist or culturally appropriative. However, it is clear from the photographs of the squads in costume, the names of the squads and the long history of certain cultural stereotypes that some of these caricatures are deeply problematic.

Some ethnicities that have had squads based on stereotypes of them are nationally identified either in their depiction or the squad name, including Americans (particularly those from the American South), Chinese, Dutch, German, Indian, Irish, Japanese, Mexican (one of the most frequently stereotyped groups), Russian, Spanish, Swedish. Others are more broadly identified, as with squads depicting indigenous peoples of North America, people from the Middle East (another of the most frequently stereotyped groups) and various depictions of people from the continent of Africa or its diaspora, which can be divided into three loose categories: general carica-tures of blackness, Africans and people from the islands of the Caribbean (Shetland Museum and Archive n.d.e; Up Helly Aa Committee n.d.a). Some squads that portray stereotypes, such as the 2009 squad "A Sheik Up at Sullom", include members in costumes that stereotype an ethnic or regional group (in this case, some members of the squad are dressed in kaftans and keffiyehs to represent people from the Middle East) and mem-bers in Western dress (in this case, members dressed as sailors, oil workers and one dressed as a clown) (Up Helly Aa Committee n.d.a). Squads often perform skits that directly address the relationship between Shetlanders and outsiders or relate to local news items (Coutts et al. 2009, 12). As this example also shows, an in-depth analysis of the use of ethnic caricatures in Up-Helly-Aa would need to include a survey of how they are, or are not, contextually linked through their performances in the halls to other stereotypes. This deeper investigation would allow for the place of ethnic caricatures within the festival to be understood in more depth. Suffice it to say that despite the lack of discussion of the presence of ethnic caricatures in the extant literature, their frequent appearance across the years and clear use in negotiating the relationship between global and local make them a key element of Up-Helly-Aa.

Since its creation, Up-Helly-Aa has provided a space for Shetlanders to perform their negotiations for their place in the world. In taking an informal tradition, tar-barrelling, and turning it into a regularized festival that is now broadcast around the world and has even been used in a reality television show challenge (*Skin Wars* 2016, Season 3,), it has helped shape the global perception of Shetland, which in turn has shaped Shetlander's perceptions of themselves. This chapter has only touched on the many ways that Up-Helly-Aa is a site where Shetlanders negotiate cultural understanding. Far more research needs to be done into the use of ethnic caricatures as a continuing part of Up-Helly-Aa and how insiders and outsiders are defined in relation to the festival. But without a doubt, the performance of Lerwick Up-Helly-Aa provides insight into Shetland's complex relationship with globalization over the last 130 years. As global interconnectedness continues to accelerate and, Up-Helly-Aa becomes known to a more diverse audience. As the demographics of Shetland residents and tourists shift, Lerwick Up-Helly-Aa will probably evolve as well. What those evolutions will entail will no doubt tell us a great deal about how the archipelago locates itself in the world.

REFERENCES

Brown, Callum G. 1999. *Up-Helly-Aa: Custom, Culture and Community in Shetland.* New York: Mandolin.

Christie, Steven. 2017. Interview by Emma Lang. 11 November.

Coutts, John, Ivan Hawick, Craig Sim, and Malcolm Younger. 2009. *Up-Helly-Aa 2009 Annual.* Lerwick: Millgaet Media.

Everfest Inc. n.d. "Up Helly Aa 2018." Accessed December 2017. https://www.everfest.com/e/up-helly-aa-lerwick-scotland.

Gillis, John R. 2001. "Places Remote and Islanded." *Michigan Quarterly Review* 40 (1): 39–58.

Grydehøj, Adam. 2010. "Uninherited Heritage: Tradition and Heritage Production in Shetland, Åland and Svalbard." *International Journal of Heritage Studies* 16 (1–2): 77–89.

———. 2013a. "Ethnicity and the Origins of Local Identity in Shetland, UK – Part I: Picts, Vikings, Fairies, Finns, and Aryans." *Journal of Marine and Island Cultures* 2 (1): 39–48.

———. 2013b. "Ethnicity and the Origins of Local Identity in Shetland, UK – Part II: Picts, Vikings, Fairies, Finns, and Aryans." *Journal of Marine and Island Cultures* 2 (2): 107–14.

Huda, Ayesha. 2017. Interview by Emma Lang. 12 December.

Immerwahr, Daniel. 2019. *How to Hide an Empire: A Short History of the Greater United States*. London: The Bodley Head.

Irvine, James W. 1982. *Up-Helly-Aa: A Century of Festival*. Lerwick: Shetland Publishing Company.

Johnson, Angus. 2017. Interview by Emma Lang. 4 December.

Leslie, Brydon. 2011. "Up Helly Aa: An Ancient Viking Festival." *The New Shetlander*, no. 258:7–9.

Levitt, Michael, and Jill Goularte, executive producers. 2016. *Skintastic Celebration*. Season 3, Episode 1. "Skin Wars." Michael Levitt Productions.

McHattie, Lynn-Sayers, Katherine Champion, and Cara Broadley. "Craft, Textiles and Cultural Assets in the Northern Isles: Innovation from Tradition in the Shetland Islands." *Island Studies Journal* 13 (2): 39–54.

McKay, Ian. 1994. *The Quest of the Folk: Antimodernism and Cultural Selection in Twentieth-Century Nova Scotia*. Montreal: McGill-Queen's University Press.

McMillian, Alexander. 2007. Multiple conversations with Emma Lang, June–August.

Mitchell, C.E. 1948. *Up-Helly-Aa: Tar Barrels and Guizing, Looking Back*. Lerwick, Shetland: T & J Manson "Shetland News" Office.

Nicolson, James R. 1978. *Traditional Life in Shetland*. London: Robert Hale.

Penrith, Deborah, and James Penrith. 2006. *Scottish Islands: Orkney and Shetland*. Guilford, CT: Globe Pequot Press.

Pope, Peter. 2004. *Fish into Wine: The Newfoundland Plantation in the Seventeenth Century*. Chapel Hill: University of North Carolina Press.

Promote Shetland. n.d.a. Accessed December 2017. http://www.shetland.org/.

———. n.d.b. "Up Helly Aa." Shetland. Accessed December 2017. http://www.shetland.org/things/events/culture-heritage/up-helly-aa/.

Reeploeg, Silke. 2017. "Peripheral Visions: Engaging Nordic Literary Traditions in Orkney and Shetland." *Scandinavica* 56 (1): 34–58.

Schei, Liv Kjørsvik. 2006. *The Shetland Isles*. Grantown-on-Spey, Scotland: Colin Baxter Photography.

Shetland Amenity Trust. n.d. "Archaeology: Discover Yesterday Tomorrow."

———. n.d.b. "Lerwick: Britain's Most Northerly Town."

———. n.d.c. "Museums and Heritage Centres: Island Treasures."

———. n.d.d. "Place Names: Signposts to the Past."

———. n.d.e. *Shetland Museum and Archives*. Accessed December 2017, May 2019, September 2019. https://www.shetlandmuseumandarchives.org.uk/.

———. n.d.f. "Shetland Museum and Archives Photo Library." *Shetland Museum and Archives*. Accessed December 2017. http://www.shetlandamenity.org/.

———. n.d.g. "Vikings! Explore Our Exciting Viking Past Today."

Shetland Museum and Archives. n.d.a Accessed December 2017, May 2019, September 2019. https://www.shetlandmuseumandarchives.org.uk/.

———. n.d.b. Wall Text, Fickle Trends.

———. n.d.c. Wall Text, Harvest from the Sea.

———. n.d.d. Wall Text, Meeting Currents.

———. n.d.e. "Shetland Museum and Archives Photo Archive." Accessed December 2017.https://www.shetlandmuseumandarchives.org.uk/collections/museum/photos.

———. Shetland Museum and Archive Smith, Brian. n.d. "The History of the Up Helly Aa." *Up Helly Aa.* Accessed December 2017. http://www.uphellyaa.org/about-up-helly-aa/history.

Stratford, Elaine. "The Idea of the Archipelago: Contemplating Island Relations." *Island Studies Journal* 8 (1): 3–8.

Up Helly Aa Committee. n.d.a. "Songs." *Up Helly Aa.* Accessed December 2017. http://www.uphellyaa.org/about-up-helly-aa/up-helly-aa-songs.

———. n.d.b. "Up Helly Aa Procession." *Up Helly Aa.* Accessed December 2017. http://www.uphellyaa.org/about-up-helly-aa/procession.

Watt, Angela. 2012. "The Implications of Cultural Interchange in Scalloway, Shetland, With Reference to a Perceived Nordic-based Heritage." PhD diss., University of Aberdeen.

Wawn, Andrew. 2000. *The Vikings and the Victorians: Inventing the Old North in Nineteenth-century Britain.* Rochester: D.S. Brewer.

Wherever Family. 2017. "Winter Festivals with the Family." https://whereverfamily.com/winter-festivals-with-the-family/.

Wills, Jonathan. 1991. *A Place in the Sun: Shetland and Oil Myths and Realities.* St. John's, Newfoundland and Labrador: Institute of Social and Economic Research, Memorial University of Newfoundland.

Chapter Three

Mapping Waiheke Island's Festivalscape
Community Activism and Festival Reclamation

EVANGELIA PAPOUTSAKI AND JOHN STANSFIELD

WAIHEKE ISLAND IS THE THIRD MOST POPULATED ISLAND in Aotearoa, New Zealand. Situated in the Hauraki Gulf and its Marine Park and close to the most populated city, Auckland, the island has played many roles. Before colonization, it was a food basket for the region. After colonization, it has been a forest to plunder, a holiday and retirement community and a bohemian retreat that is increasingly attractive to the moneyed class, which has contributed to a higher cost of living. The island's vineyards and art studios, pleasant microclimate and many beaches attract weekend visitors and increasingly unsustainable numbers of cruise-ship day trippers throughout the year. Along with its expanding tourism, wine industry and rural gentrification, the island is also known for its growing significance as a maritime suburb and a "political hotbed" with an activist culture (Baragwanath 2010, 15).

Waiheke was chosen as the focus for this study because festivals have always been an important and integral part of this island's community life and are often linked to the island's rich activist culture, which has used festivals as a way of community-building and protesting on social issues. Waiheke's island identity and economy also contribute significantly to the tourism product of Auckland City. In recent years, there has been an increase in cultural tourism events organized by the Auckland Tourism Events & Economic Development, which has resulted in some events taken over from their local island focus to a regional, national and even global cultural festival tourism market, including the *Sculptures on the Gulf* biennial festival and the *Jazz Art and Music Festival* that attracts thousands of visitors annually.

In this chapter, we explore island festivals and related forms of public culture as performance events that construct and negotiate meaning for the hosting island community and the visitors that come to the island to participate (Magliocco 2001). Through the mapping of Waiheke Island's *festivalscape*, we explore related concepts like *festivalization* and *festival reclamation*, and we discuss the contribution of the island's festival culture to its identity and community organization. We conclude by linking these to the interconnected concepts of *strange island* and *island imaginaries*. Data for this research was collected through in-depth interviews with island inhabitants who have been involved in organizing and volunteering for festivals and ethnographic observations, partly participatory, by one author, John Stansfield, who has been a Waiheke Island community member and activist for over three decades.

AN ISLANDS AND FESTIVAL CONCEPTUAL FRAMEWORK

> When you are on an island you are in quite a unique position where everyone is kind of together by the fact that we are surrounded by a body of water, so ... although sometimes it feels like quite a great battle to get stuff up and going, once you do people will want to come on board. (Waiheke Island inhabitant)

Conkling's (2007) well-known definition of islandness seems to reflect partly what the Waiheke Islander quoted above tries to convey in their description of island life. For Conkling, islandness is a "metaphysical sensation that derives from the heightened experience that accompanies physical isolation" that is "reinforced by boundaries of often frightening and occasionally impassable bodies of water that amplify a sense of a place that is closer to the natural world because you are in closer proximity to your neighbours" (201). He continues by providing another important feature of islandness. This "sense is absorbed by islanders through the obstinate and tenacious hold of island communities" that visitors to the island can also experience "as an instantaneous recognition" (201). It is this unique sense of islandness that, according to Conkling, helps to sustain these island communities despite often challenging conditions.

> The strong sense of community is among Putz's key features of islandness. One notices not only essentially practical attributes, like earthy common sense, independence, vigilant cooperation, and polydextrose and multifaced competence, but also a tolerance of eccentricity and a complex oral tradition (1984, 26–27)

He went on to argue that,

> Island institutions are deep and traditionally effective, for they seldom operate solely for the advantage of their members. What is gained in them is a celebration of identity and fellowship. They are a blend of romanticism, of oral literature, of forum, of unity in rites, of security, sharing of wit, art, and commiseration – all the truly important things in life. (Putz 1984, 27)

One of the Waiheke Island festival organizers aptly described how these island features translate into reality and how island life shapes festivals:

> Because we live on an island and we don't have reticulated water and sewerage, for example, we live a bit more close to the environment and that has become part of our identity. Certainly, I felt like Junk to Funk [Festival] was another expression of that artistic, clever, can do, supportive community that makes living here so nice. (Festival organizer)

When we come to study such cultural events as festivals on islands, all these features play an important role in shaping them into unique island events, reflecting aspects of the island's identity and weaving through the island's communicative ecology. This ecology refers to the various activities, forms, resources, channels and flows of communication and information unique to an island context and identity, as well as the topics of communication and how things are communicated (see Papoutsaki and Kuawaha 2018; Hearn and Foth 2007). It also refers, perhaps most importantly in this context, to a milieu of island agents and island storytelling networks that island events like festivals are part of. These island networks are created through a storytelling process in which island inhabitants, organizations and local media work with each other to construct a reality for their island communities as places where they belong and in which they create events that express this islandness (Papoutsaki and Kuwahara 2018, adapted from Wilkin et al. 2007).

In an island like Waiheke, which has a rich activist culture and high community engagement, these storytelling networks become vehicles for island storytelling agents to not only articulate in unique ways how festivals form part of the island's life but also to raise their voices about their impact. Waihekians are well aware of the unusually high number of festivals on their island. When, for instance, *Sister Shout*, Waiheke's all-woman choir, performed their show aptly titled WAIMAD in 2019, they intended to provide a satire on the "astounding array of festivals that seem to continuously arise on Waiheke's shores, valleys and hilltops" (Caitcheon and Johnson 2019, 24). Attendees were issued festival wristband "tickets", asked to scrub their shoes upon entering – in imitation of the island's ecosystem protection efforts for kauri tree disease that is often applied in festival venues – and were entertained by several festival-themed songs and skits, one of which featured a lost *Walking Festival* tramper who turned up at every other festival, poking fun at how *festivalization* has permeated island life. And in a typical Waiheke fashion, the performances raised funds for a worthy cause, Living Without Violence. This pertinent satirical performance stands as an example of the island's rich storytelling culture expressed in a milieu of island agents, in this case, the women's choir performers, who seek to take ownership of and, indeed, reclaim their island's *festivalscape*.

Having explored some features of islandness and how they shape island identity and activities, we now turn to how festivals have been defined in the literature and some features that make them distinctive events. Wilson et al. (2016) defined festivals as public, short, themed celebrations that are held regularly, while Uysal and Gitelson (1994, 3) saw them as traditional events staged to increase the tourism appeal to potential visitors. Getz, Anderson and Carlsen (2010, 30) considered them a celebration of community values, ideologies, identity and continuity ("When we celebrate our values together we build collective identity. We are saying, 'this is us; this is what we believe; this is who we are; this is what sets us apart'", Waiheke Island Junk to Funk festival volunteer). Julien (2007, 246) argued that they create a sense of belonging and pride among local residents, thus fostering the sharing of local resources and local purchases. For Turino (2008, quoted in Johnson 2015, 18), festivals, like other "public expressive cultural practices are a primary way that people articulate the collective identities that are fundamental to forming and sustaining social groups, which are, in turn, basic to survival". More specific to the islands, Magliocco (2001) saw festivals as performance events that construct and negotiate meaning for the island community and the visitors, a type of cultural celebration that comes under events tourism. Island festivals, according to Magliocco, can be seen as "arenas where the combination of ideologies, coordinates of power and performances of identity that characterize cultural contact and conflict on the island are played out". This definition adds a level of complexity to festivals that Magliocco saw as more representative of the context of small islands.

The benefits festivals bring to their hosting communities are well documented. Tull's (2012, 2014) festival model has identified both benefits and constraints for the hosting community. Festivals, according to Tull (2014), construct and showcase social and cultural experiences through ritual and traditions, cultural and artistic objects, aesthetics, performance and engagement to create unique, public celebrations. In this case, we could say that the island culture is a driver of development led by the growth of the creative economy. Festivals are often seen as tools that enhance their communities' economies and landscapes. However, their success often depends on whether volunteers can be encouraged to dedicate their time to these events (Getz and Frisby 1988; Gursoy, Kim and Uysal 2004). The strong cooperation characteristic of island communities often translates to a strong volunteering culture, which has been a key feature of Waiheke Island's festival scene, both community- and commercial-focused:

> One of the great things with Waiheke is, especially with Junk to Funk, once it got up and running and it had been on a couple of times, it was very easy to rope in volunteers. It was something that was focused primarily at young people and Waiheke has a great culture for supporting its young people and for wanting to make that happen, so lots and lots of people – mums, dads, uncles, aunties – all put their hands up and helped. (Waiheke Island festival volunteer)

But this is where the constraints become visible. Festivals often fall within the domain of the creative economy. In islands, festivals can become an instrumental tool in tourism and economic development, as well as in place marketing and the selling of attractions and venues. When linked to such an instrumentalist approach, art festivals can generate tensions for the island hosting communities, as one Waihekean shared: "You know, I love Waiheke, but the problem is it has become known as the island of wine and dance parties. I wish it was something else" (Waiheke Island inhabitant).

The island context, with its unique characteristics, and the specific events and nature of festivals all contribute to shaping an island's *festivalscape*. Referring to Getz, Anderson and Carlsen's study of *festivalscapes* as contact zones that reinforce group identity, Johnson (2015) further added that they bring together aspects of culture that celebrate and display under one banner an idea of solidarity or distinctiveness. Lee et al. (2008, 56) saw this "scape" as an amalgam of the tangible factors and the intangible "atmosphere" associated with a festival which informed how people relate to it. Lee et al. (2011) identified a set of dimensions for this scape that could include, in the context of island festivals, the island's ambience, aesthetics, functionality and socio-cultural factors. Gursoy, Kim and Uysal (2004) mentioned that festivals depend highly on the driving forces of key individuals acting within festival networks, who support their emergence and occurrence regularly. Attachments to a certain cultural community can have a significant impact on intentions to revisit festivals. Festivals also provide a context for social relationships and shared experiences that represent one's values. When asked about the social benefit of participating as a zero-waste volunteer at the Jazz festival on Waiheke, one volunteer said, "As a zero-waste volunteer, I met new people ... I also got to meet up with other volunteers that I had met at previous zero-waste events I had helped with. I was then able to meet up with friends after my shift." Felsenstein and Fleischer (2003, 385) referred to the "perceived destination image" as a crucial factor in encouraged repeat visits to festivals. As one Waiheke festival volunteer said, "If you go to a [Waiheke Island] festival, and it's not zero waste, go find the event organizer and ask them why!", alluding to the island's sustainable eco-friendly image that added significantly to the perceived destination image Felsenstein and Fleischer spoke about.

WAIHEKE ISLAND: THE "JEWEL IN THE CROWN" OF THE HAURAKI GULF

> I have an identity as an islander because I know that we won't take shit. I know that we will stand our ground and fight on anything that is fair. I know that we have strong environmental values but also, it is the artiest place I have ever lived. (Waiheke Island inhabitant)

Popularly referred to by locals as the jewel in the crown of the Hauraki Gulf, Waiheke Island is just seventeen kilometres away from central Auckland, to which a forty-minute ferry ride connects it. However, its status as a contemporary tourist hotspot (Campbell, McNair, Mackay and Perkins 2019) belies a much more interesting and vibrant past. Waiheke Island was traditionally called *Te Motu Aria Roa* in Māori ("the long sheltering island"). Seen by many as a residential maritime suburb of Auckland, it is the most populated of New Zealand's smaller islands (aside from North Island and South Island). It has been occupied since the earliest phase of Māori presence in Aotearoa, and there is archaeological evidence of headland *Pa* (fortresses) predominantly occupied by the *Hauraki* and *Te Arawa* tribes but periodically contested from both North Island and South Island.

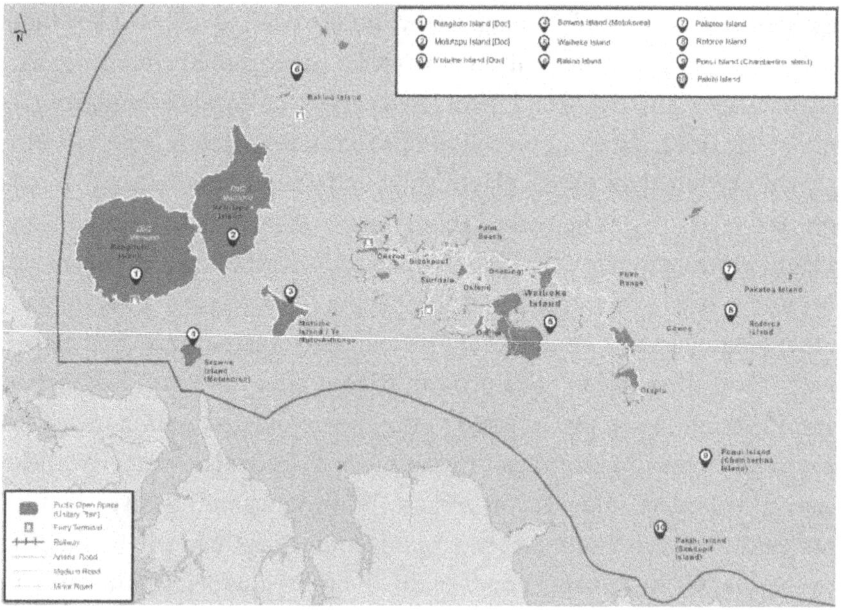

Figure 1: Waiheke local board boundary map (Auckland City Council n.d.)

Indigenous history and early European writers identify Waiheke as rich in natural resources, sitting at the centre of North Island's busiest waterways in pre-European and early colonial times (Monin 2012). The abundant fish in the area's protected waters were an important food source for the region. As one early photograph shows, three thousand sharks were dried over six weeks to prepare for a major feast (Peart 2016). Much *Mana* or prestige was accrued in traditional societies by being able to lavishly feed visitors to such events, which celebrated and preserved identity (Crespi-Vallbona and Richards 2007).

The first recorded festivals on Waiheke were coastal sale days where farmers would gather to sell their stock. Scours and barges served the sale yards on the southern foreshore of Man-of-War Bay. They were a great occasion for gatherings where auctioneers, visitors and locals could lunch upon cold meats, vegetables and desserts prepared by local women (Day 1989). With the advent of a regular ferry service, homesteading declined, and its importance to the island community was reduced as regular food supplies became available from offshore. Since the 1970s, there has been an influx of those seeking a quieter lifestyle outside of the city (Baragwanath and Lewis 2014). While pastoral farming continued, residents became alarmed at the loss of forest and habitat, and agricultural enterprises diversified. Kim and Jeanette Goldwater established the first vineyard. She thus began the thriving Waiheke Island wine industry, which produces some of the most sought-after and expensive wines in the country. With the development of the wine industry came the first of the wine festivals, which served not just to celebrate the vintage but to establish the island as a significant wine-growing area (Hall and Sharples 2008).

The 2012 census and its subsequent interpretation by the local government provide us with a snapshot of what was once a loose collection of small villages. While in the 1970s, the island population was under three thousand, by 2013, it had grown to 8,340, 28 per cent of which had been born overseas, with another three thousand non-residents who kept holiday homes on the island (Statistics NZ 2013). This number increases dramatically in summer, with estimates up to thirty thousand to forty thousand people (Waiheke Island Community Board 2009). Households are predominantly single-family households, and there is a higher proportion of single-person households than in Auckland. The median age of residents, at 45.3 versus 35.1 for Auckland, reflects the substantial retired population, with 19 per cent of the population being over sixty-five versus 12 per cent in Auckland (Statistics NZ 2013). Some would argue that this has implications for festivals, as the dominant generation is used to making its own entertainment rather than having this provided by the market.

The island has three schools and, according to the 2012 census, over twelve hundred businesses employing 2,250 people. Tourism (accommodation and food services) is the largest employer of both resident and non-resident islanders. Because of its reputation as a place for moneyed people to go, the island had a modest median household income of NZ$51,100 versus NZ$76,500 for greater Auckland (Statistics NZ 2013). Contemporary Waiheke is enjoying a boom both in settlement and tourism, and it has developed somewhat of an international reputation, with the Lonely Planet Guide listing it as the fifth-best island in the world (*NZ Herald* 2018). Some of its contemporary festivals are clearly aimed at the tourist market, while others are less clear as they have evolved towards this. However, there remains a very strong tradition of festivals by the island for the island.

MAPPING WAIHEKE ISLAND'S *FESTIVALSCAPE*

Festival sites, according to Johnson (2015), are "contact zones that reveal not only the content of the performances on display but also meaning that is embedded in the purpose of the events in the first place" (18). One way of mapping festivals is through their hosting community. As Mackley-Crump (2012, quoted in Johnson 2015) suggested, studying festivalscapes "can be used to help understand the cultural geographies of particular localities" (107), like small islands, in this case, and their distinctive communities. Another way of mapping is through the type of festival event. Mapping them according to their perceived benefits to and impact on island life and identity can also provide a nuanced analysis.

Mapping Waiheke's festivals through their primary focus (that is, the type of event) resulted in the following descriptive categories: food and wine, music, film and dance, art, heritage, sports, seasonal, community, gardening and nature, and sustainability. The table below attempts to group

Table 1: Waiheke Island Festivalscape

Food/Wine
• W Vintage Festival – W Olive and Artisan Food Festival
• Oyster Festival – Island Styles Events
Music/Film/Dance
• W Jazz, Arts, Music Festival – Dance Party – Latin Film Festival
• W Playwright Festival – Waiheke Radio Dance Party
Art
• W Sculpture on the Gulf – Storytelling Festival – Sculpt Oneroa
• Poetry Jam on National Poetry Day – W Winter Arts Festival
Heritage
• Auckland Heritage Festival on Waiheke
Sports
• W Beach Races – Rocky Bay Regatta – Fullers Festival of Football – Beach Sports Day
Seasonal
• Fossil Bay Spring Festival – Harvest Kai Festival – Guy Fawkes Fireworks – Mid-Winter Ball – Santa Parade/Fossil Fuel Free Fiesta – Matariki – Carols by Candlelight – Easter Book Fair – Harvest Fair
Community
• W Primary School Fair – Santa Parade – Waitangi Day – Teddy Bears Picnic – Carols by Candlelight – Blackpool Fair – Easter Book Fair – SKP Impromptu Festival for Fundraisers – WICOSS Annual Celebrate Volunteering Day
Nature/Gardening
• W Garden Festival – W Walking Festival
Sustainability
• Junk to Funk – Fossil Fuel Free Fiesta

them thematically, with some, like the *Fossil Fuel Free Fiesta*, fitting under more than one theme as it is both seasonal and community-focused and has a strong sustainability character. While some of these festivals are no longer held, like the *Junk to Funk*, and while some are coming back to life with a different focus, like the *Santa Parade*, most of these festivals still take place, demonstrating a distinctive island festival culture. Waihekeans seem to thrive around community events that are used not only to celebrate the island's arts, culture and nature but also as fundraising for community causes, like the *Fossil Bay Spring Festival*, and protecting and celebrating their island's natural habitat, like the *Junk to Funk* festival, a unique expression of Waiheke Island's eco-friendly values, which was revived in 2023.

Waiheke's rich and highly diverse *festivalscape* is mainly focused around six villages – Oneroa, Blackpool, Surfdale, Ostend, Rocky Bay and Onetangi – that are home to most of the island's population. Each of these villages has its own community gathering point, usually a community hall, and its own distinct entertainments for village-, island- and visitor-focused events and festivals. Onetangi village, for instance, has a much-loved Community Hall with a kitchen and outdoor facilities where community music theatre and celebrations are held regularly. It is also home to the *Onetangi Beach Races*, an annual celebration of island culture and a fundraising event hosted by the Rotary Club. The seaside spectacle is a smoke-free and zero-waste event which attracts more than five thousand attendees, mostly locals. The other sports festival held on Waiheke is the *Rocky Bay Regatta*, a popular annual community sailing event that has been a fixture since 1948. It is organized by the Waiheke Boating Club and staffed entirely by volunteers. The strong focus on community has fostered a unique volunteering culture that sits at the core of all festivals on the island, both commercial and not-for-profit.

Surfdale also has a popular Community Hall and Youth Centre, whose grounds are used for community picnics beside the sea. The shallow waters of Shelley Beach host a regular regatta for young sailors and small craft, and the Shelley Beach community holds a regular beachside neighbours' day. Ostend is home to the regular weekly Waiheke-wide market, and its sheltered harbour is home to the Waiheke Boat Club immediately adjacent to the Waiheke Sports Club, which is a busy focal point for events such as the annual fundraiser, *Show and Shine*, and numerous well-attended sports tournaments. Blackpool Village boasts its own monthly pop-up pub, The Dog and Pony, and a regular car boot sale, as well as events associated with its old school reserve. The *Blackpool Fair*, an annual fundraising and volunteer-run event, is held by the Blackpool Residents Association targeting the local suburb.

Oneroa, the main village closest to the ferry terminal at Matiatia Bay, hosts several events, including the *Waiheke Easter Book Fair*, the *Sculpture on the Gulf Festival*, the *Sculpt Oneroa Festival*, the *Waiheke Santa Parade* (in its various manifestations) and the *Gulf News Trolley Derby*, as well as events focused around a Sustainability Centre, the Community Hall and the galleries, cinema and theatre. The *Sculpture on the Gulf*, held every two years, was originally a small fundraiser for the Waiheke Art Gallery in Oneroa, but has now grown to an international art event supported by locals, both as volunteers and as participants. Offshore and international artists increasingly dominate it and attract enormous crowds from the city. The *Sculpt Oneroa* festival, a free not-for-profit event, is run by local sculptors and began in response to the commercialization of the *Sculpture on the Gulf*. Primarily aimed at locals as a way of sharing local artists in a space easily accessible to all, it is hugely popular, particularly with local businesses along Ocean View Road, where most cafes and restaurants are, which benefit from the festival because this is where it is held. It also attracts a following from the arts community in the city. The seasonal *Waiheke Santa Parade*, funded by the local board, has been one of the most popular annual festivals on the island. It is predominantly a local event, with local community groups and clubs spending weeks preparing their floats. Following the island's long tradition of environmental activism, the event has become a *Fossil Fuel Free Fiesta* that challenged local groups and businesses to consider the environment as part of their entries: "Bikes, horses, skateboards, rollerblades, scooters, prams, wind, solar and electric vehicles, are all okay, and people-powered entries are especially welcome" (OurAuckland 2018).

Aside from the villages that host festivals closely linked to their communities, the island also hosts several other festivals that embrace the island's solidarity spirit, like the annual *Garden Festival* that began in 2001. It is supported by the Jassy Dean Trust, which was formed in 1993 when the Dean family needed support for the costly medical care of their teenage daughter. It attracts visitors from the island as well as many from offshore, with participants spending months preparing gardens as exhibits and festivalgoers visiting various island gardens over the weekend of the festival. This community spirit also manifests in several other fundraising-focused festivals like the *Fossil Bay Harvest Festival*, hosted at the popular communal farm in Fossil Bay, which attracts locals along with some visitors to the island. It has been held annually for twenty-five years. It is an important part of the funding of the Fossil Bay Kindergarten, although many island-ers who are not associated with kindergarten donate their time because they are sympathetic to environmental and sustainability issues. Similarly, the *Fossil Bay Spring Fayre*, primarily a local event and running with the backing of the highly successful harvest festival, is another fundraising venture by the Waiheke Steiner Kindy group.

Along with community-focused festivals, the island also has many com-mercially oriented events that focus on the island's branding as a tourist destination, particularly for day-trip visitors. These events, like the *Waiheke Olive Festival* and *Wine and Food Festival*, generate income for island busi-nesses. The latter, previously known as *the Vintage Festival,* was a creation of the Waiheke Winegrowers Association, mainly catering to visitors and was always commercial. Islanders, however, have been unhappy with the level of drunkenness at the festival in recent years, which was held in the hot sun without free water and with expensive food.

Part of Waiheke's image is linked to its vibrant art community, which has played an important role in shaping several festivals around the arts, culture and music, including the island-grown *Waiheke Playwright*, the *Storytelling Festivals* and *Sculpt Oneroa*, but also festivals that mirror bigger local events like the *Waiheke Poetry and Song Love Jam*, formally *Waiheke Poetry Festival*, or *Poet Jam*, held on National Poetry Day each year, hosted by the library in Oneroa village and organized by an informal group of poetry volunteers. The *Auckland Heritage Festival on Waiheke* is the local branch of an Auckland regional festival hosted by the Waiheke Library and its staff. It is attended primarily by locals, features local historians and historic artefacts and includes a heritage feast. The *Waiheke Latin and Spanish Film Festival*, a free not-for-profit event sponsored by the Spanish and some Latin American embassies in Wellington, is very popular among the locals, partly reflecting the multicultural population of the island, as Waiheke has a large population of Latin American, particularly Argentin-ian, young people on working holidays.

Many Waiheke festivals reflect the involvement and representation of different island generations. Young people often find island life restrictive, with one report identifying that "preliminary results [Youth2020] show that youth who feel 'trapped' on the island due to their financial and family circumstances are more vulnerable to issues relating to drugs, petty crime and others" (Boladeras 2020):

> One of the problems that we have here on Waiheke is that in the wintertime, the beaches are not a whole lot of fun so that takes away the young people's main source of fun during the winter and means that a lot of them turn to other sorts of mischievous fun such as alcohol and parties. So, we wanted to show that Waiheke could have an event for young people that was drug and alcohol-free, that was still a whole heap of fun and where people could get together and just hang out. (Waiheke Island youth)

While festivals like *Junk to Funk* had a particular focus on the younger population of the island to educate them about waste management and substantiality in a fun way, other events like *Super Awesome Mega Epic Day/Night* (*Same Day/Same Night* for short) are organized by the youth themselves. Part of the Waiheke Youth Voice and supported by the Home Grown Youth Change Makers programme, this event acted as a ground for youth self-organization:

> It was run by young people and it was set up by young people and it was participated by young people – for youth by youth – and if you want to have festivals on your island later on and more adult events, you need to invest in these young people festivals as well because if they learn the skills how to organize, then they can continue those on later in life and hopefully, the biggest thing is that they will feel valued in their community and they will want to stay there and they will want to continue to partake and to organize these festivals later on in life as well. (Waiheke Island youth member of organizing committee)

The above quote not only indicates the multiple benefits of festivals for young people – serving as a space to build community learning skills ("amazing opportunity to learn about funding applications and to really grow and develop these skills in organizing and delegating") – but also reflects the particular nature of island life that requires strong community participation. This leads us to the following section, which discusses the benefits festivals bring and the impact they have on islands.

PERCEIVED BENEFITS AND IMPACT: *FESTIVALIZATION* AND *ISLAND RECLAMATION*

Following Tull's (2014) festival benefits typology, we could link several Waiheke festivals to the perceived benefits they bring to the community, but also the adverse impact they might have on island life. Festivals like the *Waiheke Jazz, Arts and Music Festival* act as image makers and destination branding with an urban, regional outlook. At the same time, the *Waiheke Walk Festival* contributes to diversifying the island's tourism product and economic development by focusing on the island's natural assets. Whereas festivals like the outdoor *Sculpture in the Gulf* have transformed the island's physical landscape and *Sculpt Oneroa* have contributed towards retaining the island's artistic expression and heritage, others like the *Garden Festival, Junk to Funk* and the *Santa Parade* have significantly contributed to community-building and act as a model for a sustainable environment. The latter, being community-grounded, showcases island ingenuity, community spirit, social cohesion and sustainability.

While the largest number of festivals on Waiheke are island-grown and focused, with local community volunteering and attending, there are also festivals that, while island-grown, now cater primarily to visitors from the Auckland region, like the *Waiheke Jazz, Arts and Music Festival*. There are also festivals that, although locally initiated, have now become major global events that are attracting international visitors, like *Sculpture in the Gulf*. There is another emerging category that falls under island festival reclamation, like *Sculpt Oneroa*, referring to events the community felt the need to reclaim or recreate with an island focus.

The *Waiheke Jazz, Arts and Music Festival* was originally launched as the *Montana Waiheke Island of Jazz Festival* by Jazz musician David Paquette in 1996. It stopped in 2006 and was restarted by another musician, John Quigley, as *Waiheke International Jazz Festival*. This three-day event was renamed a third time to the *Waiheke Jazz, Arts and Music Festival*. It took on a different format: "while retaining many inspirational jazz performances, a new focus is on contemporary music, demonstrations of abstract and figurative painting and collaborative performance art involving painters, musicians and the audience" (Worthy 2018). Staged across the island in different venues, including a vineyard, a winery and a wine bar, it is evident that this new format is aimed at maximizing the island's revenue from the event and cleverly building a destination brand that pairs art and music with an island lifestyle that is associated with its wine-making image. It attracts large visitor numbers with many locals volunteering:

> This is a long-running iconic Waiheke festival, and it is great to see that it is still going today. It creates events at multiple venues on Waiheke, showcasing our wonderful vineyards, restaurants and bars. The festival definitely contributes to Waiheke's culture of lounging around with a glass of wine in hand and a bit of a boogie. (Waiheke Island festival volunteer)

Figure 2. waiJAM Festival 2020 poster (*Source:* authors)

Festivals of this scale are often commercialized and contribute significantly to the regional tourist product. As one of the managing directors of the regional iTicket event booking company indicated, "the festival will add interest, colour and excitement to the Auckland regional events scene" (Worthy 2018). Despite its commercialization, the festival still reflects some of the island's values about sustainability. Some venues have had zero-waste stalls and volunteers:

> I helped make sure there was enough zero-waste volunteers onsite to support the event- I helped to speak with participants about reusing their cups instead of single using them. I supported participants to sort their own waste at the waste station and spoke to them about the on-island composting facility that processes all of the food scraps and PLA cups from the event. (Waiheke Island festival volunteer)

What we see with this type of festival is an ambivalence about what image of the island is projected to outsiders. Here, we have juxtaposed images of "island coolness" ("lounging around with a glass of wine in hand, and a bit of a boogie") and eco-friendly values with herding large numbers of visitors to venues that have a commercial character.

This brings us to festivals as sites of *(re)presentation* and the *politics of (re)presentation*, a combination of presentation of self and representation by and for others (Odermatt 1996, 85, in Magliocco 2001). The festivals that are most strongly associated with the politics of (re)presentation are *Sculpture on the Gulf* and its counter-response *Sculpt Oneroa*, which emerged because of the *festivalization* of the island's festival culture. Getz, Anderson and Carlsen (2010) defined *festivalization* as an over-commodification of festivals exploited by tourism and place marketers. The biennial *Sculpture on the Gulf* was originally a small fundraiser for the Waiheke Art Gallery but has now grown to an enormous international event supported by locals both as volunteers and participants, but increasingly dominated by offshore and international artists and attracting huge crowds from the city.

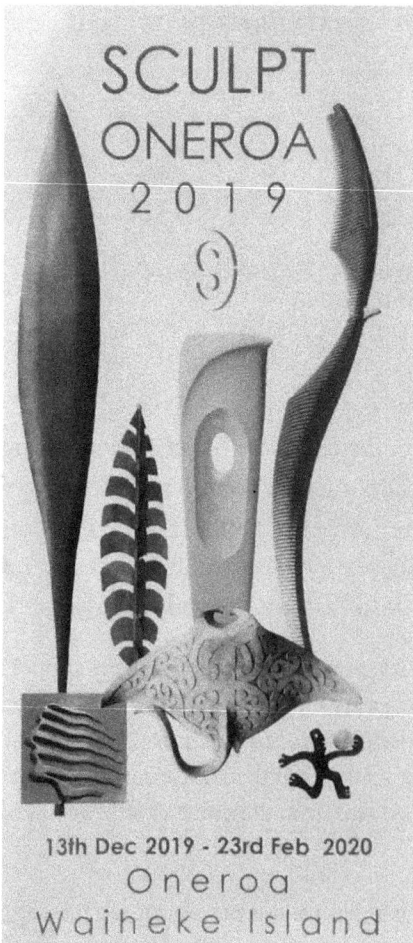

Figure 2. Scupt Oneroa Festival 2020 poster (*Source:* authors)

> It used to be something that the locals had a lot more access to and now it has become a major art event which is fine but its connection to the community is more removed and the ones who benefit from it are basically tourism operators rather than the wider community. (Waiheke Island inhabitant)

Waiheke is known for its distinctive community that values its unique culture and is prepared to protect it from inappropriate change (Baragwanath and Lewis 2010). *Sculpt Oneroa's* key message on bringing Waiheke art to Oneroa village over the summer is a political statement and an act of self-presentation. When asked by the authors what they hoped to achieve with *Sculpt Oneroa*, Paora toi Te Rangiuaia, one of the festival's driving forces, pointed to a strong need to self-represent through self-recognition:

> I guess self-recognition, Tino Rangatiratanga, [is] the idea that you have it within yourself and within your network to stand forward and be assured that you can do that with that support around you. In a Maori sense of Tuakana Teina – to be there to assist others . . . Even if they don't sell, it is still that recognition of being part of something that is intrinsically our village, our island – it is us, we are doing it. (Paora Toi Te Rangiuaia)

Island inhabitants recognize its value to their community but also express an awareness of how this festival is an act of self-representation and a reflection of the island's identity, a form of self-identification:

> You know, the exhibition here is by far better than the larger exhibition. It has so much heart; it is very honest and we love seeing people within the Waiheke Community, their artistry, their expertise and the engagement. The engagement not only of our own community but of people coming in, the tourists. (response from the community)

In a similar tone, the organizer of the *Junk to Funk Festival* expressed the importance of self-identification when asked about the uniqueness of this event in relation to the island:

> One of the things that was really cool was it was definitely one of those uniquely Waiheke things. Out in the big wider world you have a world of wearable arts and trash to fashion, but none of that matters because here on Waiheke, in our own little microculture, we had *Junk to Funk*, which was bigger and better in our eyes. Our big goal was creating a platform of, 'Oh yeah, on Waiheke Island they did that. It is achievable and look at the benefits.'

The question of who is producing what for whom is key, according to Friedman (1990, 323, in Magliocco 2001), to understanding different reactions to tourism, especially on a small island. When the islanders are in charge of their own (re)presentations, the development of a tourist-driven

festival economy does not have to undermine the continuation of a distinct island identity. Instead, Friedman argues, "when tourism exploits,
displaces and instrumentalizes its object, resistance to tourism and the
creation of a contrasting selfhood is the likely result" (Friedman 1990, 324,
in Maglioccio 2001).

While identity politics plays an important role, there is another more
pragmatic aspect of festival reclamation. The local artists perceived the
internationalization of their festival and gradual exclusion of their work
from it as "an act of war", one that had direct implications for the financial
survival of the island's artist community and also the community itself.
The *Sculpture on the Gulf* festival directs visitors arriving at the ferry terminal over to the coastal Maitiatia headland sculpture trail. Though an
additional shuttle bus route runs to other locations, most visitors stay on
the sculpture trail, purchasing food and drinks from authorized stalls and
returning to the ferry terminal without visiting the rest of the island or
Oneroa village. As the festival takes place in the summer and Headland
is exposed to the heat of the sun, visitors are rather tired by the trail and
often return to the ferry for departure. *Sculpt Oneroa* was thus a response
to the need to bring income to the island and keep it there:

> What were we going to do? It was going to kill the economy of the island. We
> have been up here and working 360-odd days a year for the last fourteen or
> fifteen years, and they were going to rob us of that economy.

In our question about who has benefitted economically from reclaiming
the sculpture festival, Paora's response was clear: "I would suggest it is
the community because most of us who have sold through that spend our
money back here on the island."

Festival reclamation, in this case, is seen as an exclusively local celebration after a larger festival has become a tourist attraction. Following
the line of Friedman and Appadurai, Magliocco (2001) argued that in the
twin processes of globalization and localization, festivals serve as sites for
the construction of identity and authenticity. The two Waiheke sculpture
festivals fit within Appadurai's argument that "for polities of smaller scale,
there is always a fear of cultural absorption by polities of a larger scale,
especially those that are nearby" (Appadurai 1990 295, in Magliocco 2001).

And to paraphrase Maglioccio (2001), when an island festival no longer performs an identity narrative to which islanders can subscribe, like *Sculptures on the Gulf*, the island community may choose to transform the festival through new activities or to designate a new, separate festival, like with *Sculpt Oneroa*, to perform the identity with which the community identifies.

A "STRANGE ISLAND"

Despite the festivalization of Waiheke's festivalscape, many of these events, past and present, reflect its distinct "strange island" identity. The concept has been used by Baragwanath and Lewis (2010) to describe Waiheke. It is borrowed from Sarah Neal, a British academic whose expression of *"strange towns"* – meaning different from the norm – was used to explore why some small, rural towns in Britain have become associated with progressive politics and radical or countercultures. Baragwanath and Lewis (2010, in Baragwanth 2010, 8) viewed Waiheke as a "strange island" in terms of its high levels of activism and ways in which different groups mobilize in order to preserve its distinctiveness, including its strong values of sustainability embedded in the island way of life. As the organizer of one festival expressed:

> Waiheke in general has always had this very staunch, well for my lifetime at least, sustainability-focused culture and *Junk to Funk* was just an amazing opportunity to show that off and to really celebrate our uniqueness and our artsiness and our creativeness, our eco-warriorness which we all have here on the island too. (Junk to Funk organizer)

This resourcefulness around sustaining the eco-friendly values that living on a small island demands is manifesting in different aspects of the island's festivalscape, including the strong festival volunteering tradition. When one local was asked why they volunteer for the zero-waste stall in one festival, the reply was indicative of the island's strong sustainability ethos:

> I struggle when I go to events that are not organized using a zero-waste *kaupapa*, so attending events where waste [is] minimized and sorted makes me happy. It is better for the venue and event organizers as they are thinking beyond the walls of their events and thinking about the footprint they are having on their environment. The wider community benefits by having access to compost that

> is created from food scraps and compostable and jobs are created through this process. It also spreads the message about minimising waste to vendors and an audience of participants that may not be familiar to this way of being. (Waiheke Island festival volunteer)

Part of Waiheke's strong island identity has to do with its earlier low-income, single-parent households and its artist and activist population, but also with the fact that until 1989, it was governed by the Waiheke County Council. To the islanders' disappointment and strong protest, it was then amalgamated into Auckland City Council, and one of the first effects of this change was the loss of their fledgling recycling scheme. The highly successful *Junk to Funk Festival*, run by the Waiheke Resources Trust (then Waiheke Waste Resources Trust), had as its principal sponsor the community-owned company Clean Stream, which ran the local rubbish enterprise until it was stripped of its contract by the Auckland City.

> Exporting waste out of Waiheke is quite an expensive thing, so being able to minimize the waste that is leaving the island has economic value in itself. On top of that, importing stuff to Waiheke is expensive because of the ferry costs, so being able to go out into the waste stream and recover what you need and being able to be resourceful and find that stuff for yourself is of huge value in terms of the economy. Furthermore, the actual event itself was catered and had food trucks there from local stores and was a great way for sustainable businesses to show off. (Junk to Funk organizer)

Waihekeans, like many island communities, are sensitive to loss of sovereignty (Prescott 2003) and have developed a culture of demanding more control over where they live. This desire for self-determination is a persistent theme in the island's history, and its challenging relationships with government bodies can be linked to this value, making a fertile ground for community development.

> I think a festival like this [Junk to Funk] brings different community groups together and creates further relationships between people helping one another, understanding organizations and what they stand for. (festival volunteer)

Developed by the WRT Education team, the much-loved festival showcased the island's creative talent by producing wearable art from the waste stream. It involved twelve hundred people (out of a population of just four thousand). It used strategies where existing events, such as the local market and music festivals, provided opportunities for community engagement. These events were the forerunners of the *Sustainability Festival* – spanning ten days and hosting over fifty events involving many other clubs and environmental organizations.

> I think it really did contribute to the identity and culture of the island, and that was a deliberate ploy on our part. We were out to create social norms around reducing and reusing, particularly before you recycle … So, the culture we were fostering was one of togetherness; we are all in this together looking after the planet; we are here to look after each other as well; we are here to not squander the precious resources of the earth, and I think that is an integral part of the identity of Waiheke Islanders. (Junk to Funk Festival organizer)

When Clean Stream lost its licence, the transfer station, a favourite scavenging point, was declared off-limits to the public, and ever-increasing volumes of reusable material were consigned to landfill. Without the financial backing of the company, the *Junk to Funk* festival stopped running in 2010, although islanders still have great hopes that they will regain the contract and the festival can be brought back to life. But it did leave a lasting legacy, especially in the younger generation that was actively involved and trained in community activism:

> I think it had lasting social value to the community at large about bringing us all together and giving us a chance to show off the wonderful works of our young people. And I think, extending a bit further from that, it taught a whole generation and a half really of young people on the island how to be resourceful for themselves and how to think of art in a very unique way and how to get involved and be engaged in waste in a very Waiheke way. (Festival organizer)

Another festival that reflects similar values is the *Fossil Fuel Free Fiesta*, which focuses on creating a seasonal Christmas festival with a strong sustainability focus:

> The festival brought up a lot of conversation around how many electric cars there are on Waiheke; it is pretty tremendous and how we, again, want to become this example to New Zealand and how we can define that through the festival and maybe remind people of what we want to be in the community. Where we are heading towards what we are aiming for. (Festival volunteer)

This festival, despite its strong sustainability focus and the engagement of different groups, particularly young people and children, was not viewed positively by some islanders. The festival replaced the long-running and very popular *Santa Parade*, which the islanders ran as a big seasonal party that expressed Waiheke Island's strong community and creative spirit. But this was not the only reason *Fossil Fuel Free Fiesta* was not embraced. Some islanders saw it as an imposition from above, commissioned by the local board and thus not a grassroots event. Some argued that the island did not need yet another trendy festival and that, by necessity, islanders were already well-versed in sustainable ways of living. The island's changing demographics, though, might mean that newcomers need to find ways to take part in the island's storytelling practices, and festivals such as this one help to create inclusiveness and build identity.

IN LIEU OF CONCLUSIONS: FESTIVALS AND ISLAND IMAGINARIES

It is evident from the above that Waiheke has a unique *festivalscape* that reflects its island identity. *Festivalization* is firmly established and, despite the increasing number of commercial festivals that aim at branding the island as a tourist and cultural events destination, there is still a persisting culture of and desire for local festivals for the islanders and by the islanders (*community engagement*). As one of the festival volunteers expressed:

> I hope that these festivals and community occasions continue to happen because I think that there is something truly magic around the arts, around festivals that the media and that television and movies just don't have. It is a different type of magic, and it is very unique, and it takes a little bit more energy, but it is a whole lot more satisfying. (Waiheke Island festival volunteer)

Local festivals are often associated with the concept of sustainable islands, and Waiheke has proven that to be the case. One of the emerging themes from this research was a "just do it" Waiheke culture that many locals believe is part of their island identity. This island seems to be rich in human capital, which is in line with the literature on island character (see above for Conkling 2007 and Putz 1984). High levels of volunteerism, necessary for sustaining such a rich festivalscape, are part of this. Waiheke's openness to experiment, part of its "strange island" nature, manifests as a "voyage of discovery" for the community when they embark on something new, as so many of its festivals have demonstrated.

However, as the island's population is changing due to increasing unaffordability, its entrenched association with alternative lifestyles, counter-cultural developments and activism is also affected (Baragwanath 2010, 18). Although one can still identify elements of this distinctive character in many island activities, including the festivals, they might be interpreted differently by different groups.

> I think with Waiheke becoming a growing destination with all sorts of different types of people coming here, there has been a fear that we are losing our sense of identity and a lot of people are moving off the island. So, I think a festival like this really brings people together and makes them think about what is important to them. They have to create something together. It is around what our values are as a community, what we want to protect. What we want our children, the future generation, to be investing energy into and really coming up with ideas which sort of celebrate Waiheke and what it means to be. (Fossil Fuel Free Fiesta volunteer)

The concept of geographical imaginaries (Baragwanath 2010) is useful in referring to the different visions of what Waiheke is and should or could be, with the consequence that the ways in which people imagine Waiheke, in turn, affect how they behave. An imaginary, Baragwanath and Lewis (2010, in Baragwanath 2010, 7) argued, is more specific than abstract imagination, as the latter implies an opening up of new possibilities and even utopian notions, while a geographical imaginary is a particular representation of a place that has effects on how participants create communities. It implies a cultural and political project in which the imagination is connected to identity and political economy, becoming, in effect, a discourse of place.

The festivals, integral to the island's storytelling communicative ecology, help to construct island imaginaries but also act as a barometer in this changing island- and festivalscape. And on Waiheke, we have a paradox on display, one that sees the island's imaginaries mobilized by different actors in different ways and for different reasons, creating tensions between the island community's perceived notion of their identity and that of outsiders.

REFERENCES

Auckland City Council. n.d. "Waiheke Local Board Boundary Map." https://www. aucklandcouncil.govt.nz/about-auckland-council/how-auckland-council-works/ local-boards/all-local-boards/waiheke-local-board/Documents/waiheke-local-board-boundary-map.pdf.

Baragwanath, Lucy. 2010. "The Waiheke Project: Overview of Tourism, Wine and Development on Waiheke Island." School of Environment. University of Auckland. https://static1.squarespace.com/static/5b1dd83a372b9624b25936a3/t/5bce1673f4e1f-c7d5d0e9e22/1540232838204/Waiheke+Report+Dr+Lucy+Baragwanath.pdf.

——, and Nicolas Lewis. 2014. "Waiheke Island." In *Social, Cultural and Economic Impacts of Wine in New Zealand*, edited by Peter J. Howland, 211–26. London: Routledge.

Boladeras, Sophie. 2020. Students' New Petition Boosts Drive Towards Free and Fair Ferry Fares. *Gulf News*, 12 March 2020.

Caitcheon, Baz, and Erin Johnson. 2019. "WAIMAD Show Pokes Fun at Festivals." *Gulf News*, 9 May 2019.

Campbell, Malcolm, Hamish McNair, Michael Mackay, and C. Harvey Perkins. 2019. "Disrupting the Regional Housing Market: Airbnb in New Zealand." *Regional Studies, Regional Science* 6 (1): 139–42. https://doi.org/10.1080/21681 376.2019.1588156.

Conkling, Philip. 2007. "On Islanders and Islands." *Geographical Review* 97 (2): 191–201.

Crespi-Vallbona, Monserrat, and Greg Richards. 2007. "The Meaning of Cultural Festivals." *International Journal of Cultural Policy* 13 (1): 103–22. https://doi. org/10.1080/10286630701201830.

Day, Dixie. 1989. *Waiheke Pioneers*. Ostend, Waiheke: Waiheke Historical Society.

Felsenstein, D., and Fleischer, A. 2003. "Local Festivals and Tourism Promotion: The Role of Public Assistance and Visitor Expenditure." *Journal of Travel Research* 41(4), 385–92. https://doi.org/10.1177/0047287503041004007

Getz, Donald, Tommy Anderson, and J. Carlsen. 2010. "Festival Management Studies. Developing a Framework and Priorities for Comparative and Cross-Cultural Research." *International Journal of Event and Festival Management* 1 (1): 29–59.

Getz, Donald, and Wendy Frisby. 1988. "Evaluating Management Effectiveness in Community-run Festivals." *Journal of Travel Research* 27 (1): 22–27.

Gursoy, Dogan, K. Kim, and Muzaffar Uysal. 2004. "Perceived Impacts of Festivals and Special Events by Organizers: An Extension and Validation." *Tourism Management* 25 (2): 171–82.

Hall, C. Michael, and Liz Sharples. 2008. *Food and Wine Festivals and Events Around the World*. London: Routledge. https://doi.org/10.4324/9780080887951.

Hearn, Gregory, and Marcus Foth. 2007. "Communicative Ecologies: Editorial Preface." *Electronic Journal of Communication* 17:1–2.

Johnson, Henry. 2015. "Asian Festivalscapes: The Festivalization of Asia in the Making of Aotearoa/New Zealand." *New Zealand Journal of Asian Studies* 17 (2): 17–39.

Julien, Pierre-Andre. 2007. *A Theory of Local Entrepreneurship in the Knowledge Economy*. Cheltenham: Edward Elgar.

Lee, J.-S., C.-K Lee, and Y. Choi. 2011. "Examining the Role of Emotional and Functional Values in Festival Evaluation." *Journal of Travel Research* 50 (6): 685–96.

Lee, Y.-K., C-K Lee, S.-K. Lee, and B.J. Babin. 2008. "Festivalscapes and Patrons' Emotions, Satisfaction, and Loyalty." *Journal of Business Research* 61 (1): 56–64.

Magliocco, Sabina. 2001. Coordinates of Power and Performance: Festivals as Sites of (Re)presentation and Reclamation in Sardinia. *Ethnologies* 23 (1): 167–88.

Monin, Paul. 2012. *Matiatia: Gateway to Waiheke*. Wellington: Bridget Williams Books.

NZ Herald. 2018. "Waiheke Named Among Best Islands in the World – Again." *NZ Herald*, 11 July 2018. https://www.nzherald.co.nz/travel/news/article.cfm?c_id=7&objectid=12087115.

OurAuckland. 2018. "Parade Goes Fossil Fuel Free." *OurAuckland*, 30 November 2018. https://ourauckland.aucklandcouncil.govt.nz/articles/news/2018/9/waiheke-parade/.

Papoutsaki, Evangelia and Sueo Kuwahara. 2018. "Mapping Small Islands Communicative Ecologies: A Case Study from Amami Islands." *South Pacific Studies Journal* 31 (1): 25–49.

Peart, Raewyn. 2016. *The Story of the Hauraki Gulf*. Albany, Auckland: David Bateman.

Prescott, Victor. 2003. A Geography of Islands: Small Island Insularity. *The Professional Geographer* 55 (2): 294–95.

Putz, George. 1984. "On Islanders." *Island Journal* 1:26–29.

Statistics NZ. 2013. "2013 Census Usually Resident Population Counts." Statistics New Zealand. https://www.stats.govt.nz/information-releases/2013-census-usually-resident-population-counts/.

Tull, Jo-Anne. 2012. "Gathering Festival Statistics: Theoretical Platforms and their Relevance to Building a Global Rubric." *Journal of East Caribbean Studies* 37 (3/4): 40–70.

———. 2014. "Festival Economic Impacts on Small Developing Economies: A

Case Study of Grenada's Spice Mas." Paper presented at *SALISES 15th Annual Conference*, Port of Spain, Trinidad & Tobago, 23–25 April 2014.

Uysal, Muzaffer, and Richard Gitelson. 1994. "Assessment of Economic Impacts: Festivals and Special Events." *Journal of Festival Management and Event Tourism* 2 (1): 3–10.

Wilkin, Holley, J. Sandra Ball-Rokeach, Matthew Matsaganis, and Pauline Hope Cheong. 2007. "Comparing the Communication Ecologies of Geo-ethnic Communities: How People Stay on Top of their Community." *Electronic Journal of Communication* 17:1–2. http://www.cios.org/EJCPUBLIC/017/1/01711.HTML.

Wilson, Juliette, Arshed Norin, Shaw Eleanor, and Pret Tobias. 2016. "Expanding the Domain of Festival Research: A Review and Research Agenda." *International Journal of Management Reviews* 19 (2): 195–213. https://doi.org/10.1111/ijmr.12093.

Worthy, Diana. 2018. "Jazz to Meet Art at Waiheke Island Easter Festival." *Stuff*, 22 January 2018. https://www.stuff.co.nz/entertainment/music/100714027/jazz-to-meet-art-at-waiheke-island-easter-festival.

Chapter Four

Promoting the "Creole Traditional Wedding" during the Seychelles Creole Festival as a Strategy to Sustain Cultural Traditions

MARIE-CHRISTINE PARENT

LOCATED IN THE INDIAN OCEAN, NORTHEAST OF THE island of Madagascar and about a thousand miles from the East African coast, the Seychelles archipelago was uninhabited until its colonization in 1770 by French settlers and then by the British from 1811. During the very first years of colonization, a plantation system was set up. Enslaved people were brought from La Réunion and Mauritius islands (then named Bourbon and Île de France, also colonized by the French), Mozambique and Madagascar to work not only on the main islands of Mahé, Praslin and La Digue but also on the outer islands. The British administration prohibited slavery in 1835, but African and some Asian workers (mostly Chinese, Indian and Malay) continued to immigrate to the Seychelles. The current population considers itself Creole, which, in Seychelles, means native to their country of ancestry (Chaudenson 1992). Creole traditional culture developed in the Seychelles territory from the meeting of diverse populations and strengthened as a national culture from the independence of the country. For many Seychellois, it is a landmark and contributes to their sense of identity.

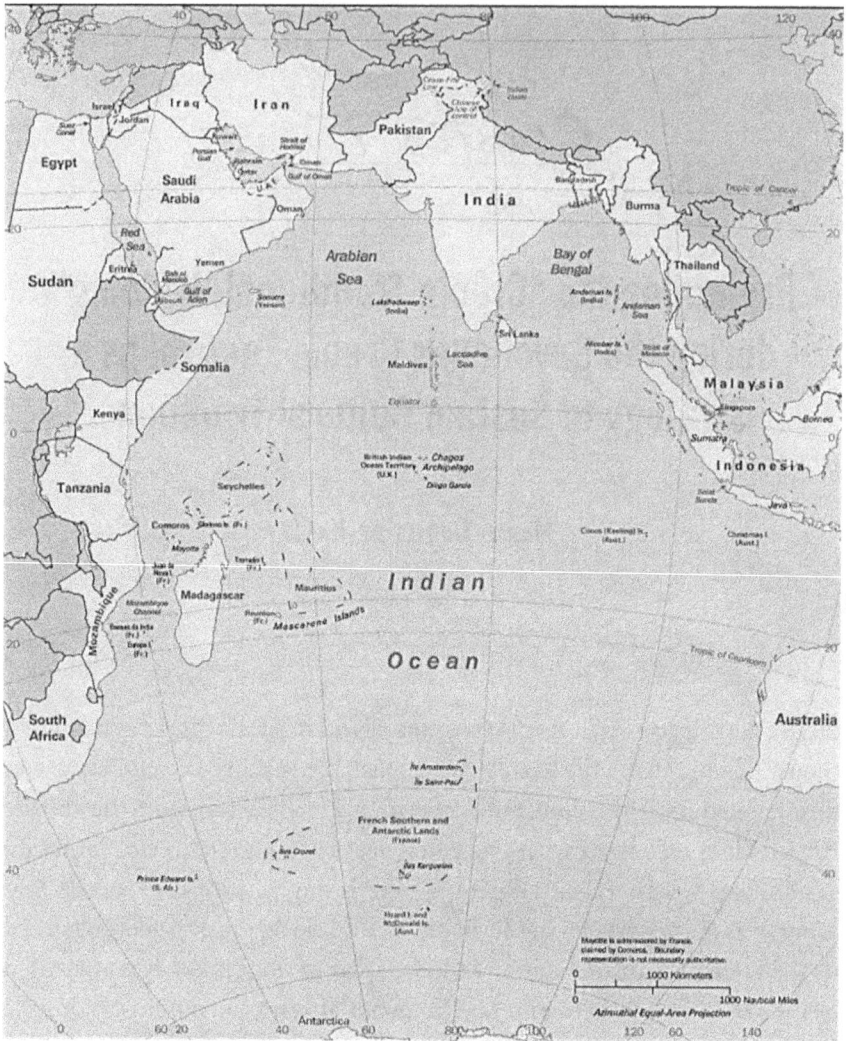

Figure 1. Map of the Seychelles in the Indian Ocean. (University of Texas Library n.d.a)

The Seychelles islands, with their stunning landscapes and beaches, are a well-known holiday destination. Since the end of the colonial period, tourism has been the main driving force in the country's economy. Tourism and culture in Seychelles are intertwined and affect each other, a phenomenon described as touristic culture (Picard 1992; Picard and Wood 1997). As in other islands, the tourism industry is shaped along the paths of colonial and postcolonial power (Rommen 2014, 1). Although culture is

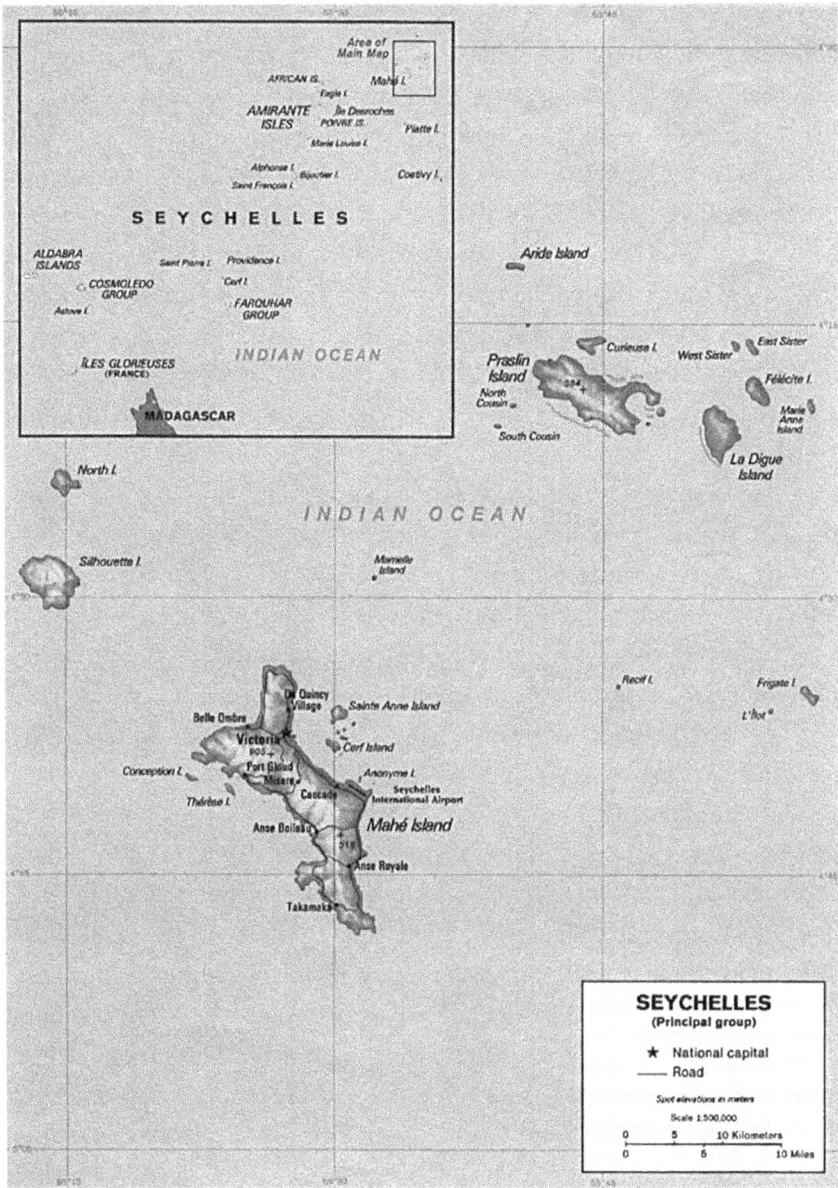

Figure 2. Seychelles archipelago (University of Texas Library n.d.b)

an important component in the global tourism industry, the connection between authorities in the fields of tourism and culture in Seychelles has never been integral. Culture was integrated into the Ministry of Tourism between 2012 and 2016, but no complimentary proficiencies have been demonstrated or exploited as was hoped by several Seychellois artists (Amesbury 2018; Parent 2017). However, tourism and festivals in Seychelles may be considered as incentives to give local cultural expressions – including traditional music – a second life, particularly when they no longer occur within communities (see Parent 2012; 2016b; 2017). The case studied here is an example demonstrating an attempt at collaboration between the cultural and tourism authorities at the time of their merger with the Ministry of Tourism and Culture.

The information and data for this article were mostly collected in Seychelles between 2011 and 2014, when the author was conducting her doctoral research in ethnomusicology. The methodology included ethnography and interviews with musicians, tradition bearers and government officials. It was completed by a review of local newspapers and scientific literature, including an ethnography of traditional Creole weddings in the Seychelles just before independence, which brings historical depth and serves as a starting point in the discussions with Seychellois and in the analysis.

This chapter aims to explain how the Seychelles Creole traditional wedding has been reintroduced into Seychellois' life through tourism. Seychelles offers future married couples a variety of honeymoon options, most including cultural entertainment ranging from private musical performances to a celebration of a traditional Creole wedding. This chapter is particularly interested in the latter, which involves the participation of the local population. Future couples can celebrate their union by buying a traditional Creole wedding package, which includes a traditional ceremony in Creole and local food and music, surrounded by Seychellois who dress for the occasion and participate in the activities. This complete formula is offered on rare occasions. It is scheduled during the Creole Festival, one of the most important cultural manifestations in Seychelles, coordinated and managed by the Department of Culture since 1986. To better understand the context in which these weddings are organized, we will position them in the political and social history of the country as well as within its tourism development.

THE DEVELOPMENT OF TOURISM AND THE MAKING OF A
TOURISTIC CULTURE IN SEYCHELLES

The Seychelles tourism industry represents the most important non-government sector of the country's economy, although its development is quite recent. It was not until 1972 that Mahé International Airport launched its first international flights. The 1970s saw very strong growth in the number of tourists, but the craze diminished during the following two decades. The reasons behind this development are based, as Jean-Christophe Gay (2004) explained, on cyclical factors: rising oil prices, rising airfares, internal political events in the early 1980s and the Gulf War in 1991–92.

In 1964, power from the colonial authorities was transferred to Seychellois officials and local political parties were created. As early as 1970, preparations were made for the establishment of an internal autonomy statute, and the foundations for a draft constitution were drawn up. This desire for sovereignty over the entire territory was part of the movement for the independence of African states. In Seychelles, two political parties were at the centre of debates about the country's future. The Seychelles Democratic Party, led by lawyer James R. Mancham, advocated for maintaining close ties with the United Kingdom. They also promoted tourism as a means of social and economic development. On the other hand, the Seychelles People's United Party, led by another lawyer, France Albert René, pushed for the country's independence. René criticized the tourism quota, arguing that it caused inflation, allowed foreign capital to dominate and risked the collapse of Seychellois society (Campling, Confiance and Purvis 2011; Gay 2004). Mancham won the 1970 elections and became the prime minister. In 1976, when the country's independence was declared, he became head of the coalition government. In 1977, his prime minister, France Albert René – a *Grand Blanc* – seized power with his party, *Seychelles People's United* Party, and created a one-party socialist system, prescribing a social-Marxist orientation.

Tourism was then seen as a threat to local culture, and the authorities introduced tourism restrictions and control policies, which lacked a vision of cultural development. This changed a few years later with the new country's need to construct a national identity based on the multicultural heritage of its inhabitants. The new government promoted the diversity of cultural and musical heritage – including cultural practices stemming from the colonial inheritance, but also from the former enslaved – trying to combine them at the same level and increase awareness among the population. This movement of developing and re-appropriating all local culture led by the cultural authorities is known as the Cultural Revolution (see Parent 2017; 2020). Workshops and classes were organized in each district, and the participants who stood out became the first cohort of the National Troupe, created in 1981. Soon, most local music and dance had been adapted for the stage. All this resulted in the institutionalization of music and dance practices, with a selection of new musical and stage settings and a certain control by official institutions. For some music that used to be played at weddings, like *kanmtole* and *contredanses*, dance postures, positions and steps have been through a process of "standardization", to use the expression of Seychellois, meaning that codes and rules have been elaborated to designate aesthetic canons. This was especially needed, according to authorities related to culture, for the assessment of *kanmtole* dances, for which there were contests. In the enthusiasm of the revolution, the first cultural festival took place in 1978, intending to promote all Seychellois' cultural practices. It would only be a few years later that a major cultural event combining the desire to make the local culture better appreciated by the Seychellois and, eventually, tourists was created. Created in 1986, the Creole Festival has always been managed and organized by a committee inside the Department of Culture. Held annually in October, it is an important cultural event that aims to promote and bring together Creole cultures from around the world, including local Seychellois culture.

The Cultural Revolution movement initially did not have a touristic ambition, but a political and social goal. However, this resulted in a propensity for these music and dance practices to be staged in the context of tourism. The folklorization of a national Creole culture and the political climate of the 1980s had the effect of confining several musical practices to the touristic environment.

During the 1980s and 1990s, it was common for tourists to be greeted at Mahé Airport by a trio of musicians. Even today, musical performances in hotels and restaurants remain the main source of income for Seychellois musicians (see Amesbury 2018; Parent 2012 and 2017). Since the 1970s, tourism has always been part of Seychellois' everyday life and has had a strong influence on their way of life and employment. When comparing the population of Seychelles in the 1970s and the number of visitor arrivals during the same years (Republic of Seychelles 1980, 6–7), one notices that the latter exceeded the former in 1978. The number of tourists in 2017 was three hundred and fifty thousand for a population of fewer than ninety-six thousand inhabitants. The tourism industry provides direct or indirect jobs – which did not exist before the 1970s – to a big part of the population, including musicians and artists.

At the beginning of the 1980s, major changes in everyday life – because of the development of tourism, new audio and visual technologies arriving in the country, and the political situation and revolution (the years following independence and the coup) – impacted the social life and musical practices of Seychellois. Most Seychellois working on the outer islands came to Mahé, Praslin and La Digue, seeking the new opportunities offered by the tourism industry following the closure of the plantations. Also, with the advent of radio and television, Seychellois changed their way of life and their hobbies drastically. Many Seychellois believe that so many changes in their social, cultural and political life in such a short time are probably responsible for a loss of traditional social values, like mutual help for the benefit of individualism and a strong urge for technologies.

All this can explain why, during my research, when discussing traditional local music and dances, Seychellois always referred to the past and called it "folklore" or "music for tourists". Most venues hosting live music in Seychelles are hotels and restaurants, which are often frequented primarily or even exclusively by tourists. Even before going to Seychelles for my research, my first contacts with Seychellois authorities were concerned about the "disappearance" of local music and culture. Knowing the history of the country, born in slavery and colonization, most of the local heritage is intangible, and the idea of preserving it leads to several questions and challenges. As we can see, most cultural practices were documented during the Cultural Revolution at the beginning of the 1980s. Still, archives are limited and, most of the time, not accessible to Seychellois (see Parent 2016a). As observed during my research and pointed out by a research collaborator, since traditional music and dances are no longer part of the daily life of Seychellois, young people must attend tourist establishments and events to see and hear their cultural heritage (Jean-Marc Volcy, interview with the author, 15 March 2013; Parent 2015, 57–58; 2017). The Creole traditional wedding was not identified as national folklore at the time of the Cultural Revolution, but most of the music repertoire associated with it was. Some of this music repertoire is still played in touristic contexts. Some others tend to be forgotten.

THE CREOLE TRADITIONAL WEDDING DURING THE COLONIAL ERA

Seychelles's musical heritage can, in a simplified way and as it is usually advanced in official documents from the Department of Culture, be described as music and dances of mixed African and European origin, categorizations inherited from the colonial era. In the past, Seychellois referred to the African origins of their musical heritage as "dancing in the dust". On the other side, there was ballroom dancing, practised in the houses of the *Grands Blancs*, the first French pioneer families of the early settlements. This is where music and dance, known today as *kamtole, contredanses* and even sometimes *romances*, were practised and developed with a local touch, experiencing a process of creolization. Indeed, it was not rare for former enslaved or domestic workers to watch and even participate in the dances. They also learned to play musical instruments by imitation and would replace musicians when they were tired. *Kamtole* and *contredanses* were traditionally played on one or two violins, accompanied by a banjo or guitar, a bass drum and a triangle. A *komander*, a person calling the choreography, is also part of the *contredanses*. The wedding celebrations, which used to be reserved for the *Grands Blancs*, included these music and dances. The small disparate communities of *Grands Blancs* on the territory would meet for wedding ceremonies, either involving a day of walking or a sea voyage. The latter represented a certain investment, evidenced by the extent of the ritual and the complexity of the musical expressions associated with it (Kœchlin 1981, 22). In a report written in 1981, the French researcher Bernard Kœchlin, recounting facts from the end of colonial times, explained the wedding ceremony as a ritual that lasted at least a week and was accompanied by complex musical expressions. We can imagine these sumptuous receptions between *Grands Blancs* at the end of the eighteenth century, with the enslaved acting as spectators, waiters and, sometimes, musicians. Soon thereafter, this prestigious model was adopted, imitated and modified by the entire population, who sometimes added other local instruments, like the *bomn* or the *zez*.

According to Kœchlin's report, the Creole traditional wedding was composed of different moments (1981, 22). The stages leading up to the wedding ceremony could span up to two years (Moka 2016). The first step is the marriage proposal, which is to say the procedure between families when asking for a woman's hand in marriage is officialized. Second comes the scene of the acquiescence of the spouses, during which the future wife must catch the *ponm damour* (a variety of tomato) thrown by her future husband to demonstrate her agreement to the marriage. The date of the wedding is then fixed. The third moment, the '*solicitation des augures*', occurs before the wedding. The future bride's mother consults various fortune tellers, from *bonnonm dibwa* – a soothsayer with traditional knowledge – to card drawing sessions to make sure her daughter will be in good hands. The Catholic God is also solicited. The wedding can finally be celebrated, first at the church and then at the guest house reception where we find *lasal vert* (the green room – a traditional leaf arbour), where the banquet of traditional Creole food is served.

Kœchlin (1981) described the wedding celebration as follows. The first musical moment of the ritual is the nuptial procession from the church to *lasal vert*. This is a long walk, lasting about an hour, with an orchestra composed of a bass drum, one or two violins and a triangle playing what is called *laserenad*. Traditionally, the procession would stop in each house in the community for a *pti lasante*, to have a drink to the health of the newly-weds. Once in *lasal vert*, a bridesmaid gives a speech and sings a *romance*. The bride's mother and the bridesmaids continue with other *romances*. Only the bride and groom do not sing. Specific traditional appetizers are served, and *romances* and *serenades* continue until the end of the meal. At the end of the feast, the bride and groom and the guests move to the dance room and start the repertoire of *kamtole*, including *contredanses*, music associated with couple dances. Around midnight, when the couple leaves for the nuptial room, the music goes back to *romances* and *serenades* for a while and then returns to *kamtole* and *contredanse*. Another *serenade* accompanies the parents and step-parents for the "achievement" at around six o'clock in the morning, confirming that the bride was a virgin by displaying the soiled linen, followed by more *romances*. The celebration continues into the next day and concludes with a ritual called *l'arrache bouquet*, when a guest walks between the dancers holding high a bouquet, and someone grabs a flower, signifying that he will take charge of (by organizing or financing) the *retour de noces*, another celebration that happens at least a week after the wedding. This type of wedding celebration does not exist anymore in Seychelles. This ritual, described by Kœchlin and for which there is documentation at the National Archives of Seychelles, started to change (and many parts of it to disappear) towards the end of the 1970s. However, even before that, not all Seychellois getting married could afford these sumptuous celebrations.

FROM DECLINE TO A TOURISTIC REVIVAL

Since the revolution and the advent of tourism, the cost of living has gradually increased for Seychellois, while wages remain relatively low. The 2008 economic crisis only worsened this situation. Political, social and economic development have seriously affected local values, choices and ways of life. Young people identify more with American and pan-African values than those of the early settlers or previous Seychellois generations. A wedding is now optional. Even though the traditional wedding is Creole, borrowing values and traditions from different groups, it is still considered a Roman Catholic tradition. It turns out that only 76 per cent of Seychellois are Catholic today – others are part of other Christian groups, Hindus or Muslims – and, at the time I was in Seychelles (between January 2011 and February 2014), I saw many Catholics changing religion or exploring other beliefs. During my research stays, the only wedding ceremonies I witnessed or was told about were not Catholic but Muslim or Evangelistic. Weddings with live music still exist but are increasingly rare. Most Seychellois would say it is because it is too expensive to pay for musicians; they may favour other expenses. Charles Davidson Lesperans, a musician who has been playing in weddings since the early 1960s, offers an example and explanation when he says that people now prefer to rent a big car with air conditioning to go to *lasal vert* rather than walking under the hot sun, something that would remind Seychellois of the misery within their difficult past (interview with the author, 4 April 2013).

In speaking with musicians, some of them told me how rich the traditional wedding music repertoire was and how live music was essential to celebrations until the 1970s. Musicians needed to be in good shape to play non-stop for at least an hour, walking in direct sun from the church to *lasal vert*, and they had to know enough repertoire not to repeat the same song during a whole ceremony. According to Charles Davidson Lesperans, one of the few violinists in the country, young Seychellois are not interested in learning how to play the violin. He said:

> Learning the violin is something serious and you need to work . . . But today's youth want everything now, without many hours working. We do not give enough value to the musicians' work and competences in our country. (interview with the author, 4 April 2013)

Charles Davidson Lesperans started to play the violin when he was a young teenager observing other musicians. Young Charles would play his father's violin in secret. His first gig was in the early 1960s at a distant cousin's wedding. His remuneration, at that time, was the equivalent of fifty cents for a ballroom dancing night and CA$1.50 to play *laserenad*. Ton Charles, as everybody in Seychelles knows him, said, "We played music for the love of music because this was not a lot of money" (interview with the author, 4 April 2013). Today, he does not play *laserenad* for less than CA$50–60 when he plays with other musicians or CA$80 when he plays alone. Also, *laserenad* does not last one to two hours like before, though, according to Ton Charles, it must be at least five songs long. Even though it is becoming more financially appealing for musicians to play at weddings, they do not get more than a few opportunities per year to play this music. As a result, not many young Seychellois are interested in learning and perpetuating this repertoire. Also, a student in her twenties at the National School of Performing Arts confessed to me that it is not "sexy" to play traditional music, and she was embarrassed to tell her friends that she was learning and practising this repertoire. Beyond music, the traditional wedding ceremony is being forgotten by Seychellois. The country's cultural authorities have deemed it endangered.

To address this issue, the Department of Culture has invested in promoting and managing activities that enable Seychellois of all generations to learn about and experience the Creole traditional wedding as it was during colonial times. As anthropologist David Berliner reminds us, preserving and transmitting culture to future generations is now a value (2010, 36). The emphasis on the transmission of the practice and the values that accompany it is part of a fear of change and loss. It is characteristic of the heritage approach (Charles-Dominique 2013).

The Creole traditional wedding is a part of Seychellois heritage, and in Seychelles, heritage has to be shown and shared. In the context of postcolonial Seychelles, preserving intangible cultural heritage necessarily goes with touristic promotion (see Parent 2016b). This became even more true with the fusion of the Department of Culture and the Ministry of Tourism in 2012. According to many of the cultural workers I interviewed, Seychellois better appreciate their heritage when tourists (or foreigners) show an interest in it. This can be explained by an inferiority complex, understood in the sense of the "cultural cringe", first mentioned by the Australian A.A. Phillips (1950), often noticeable in postcolonial societies.

Tourists getting married in Seychelles is not a new phenomenon, and the number of wedding visitors has been rising steadily in the last ten years. According to the National Bureau of Statistics/Department of Immigration and Civil Status of Seychelles, more than two thousand weddings took place in the archipelago in 2017. However, not all weddings celebrated in the country offer a deep local cultural dimension. Most of the time, as recalled by Seychellois researcher and musician Ralf Amesbury, musicians perform a "*serenade* of Creole and international romantic songs in a ceremony that is held on the beach" (2018, 15). The weddings are sometimes set up by the hotels where couples are staying or are suggested by tour operators or agents, and the ceremonies last about thirty minutes. Musicians get paid directly by travel agencies and do not know how much the clients have paid for their service (ibid.).

State-controlled touristic development initiatives characterize tourism in

Seychelles. Indeed, most of the hotel institutions were nationalized during the 1970s and 1980s before becoming privatized. This privatization (often in the hands of foreign entrepreneurs) was motivated by the economic difficulties the country has experienced. As a result, Seychellois authorities continue to jointly navigate with private companies. Beyond the Ministry of Tourism, an organization based on a public-private partnership, the Seychelles Tourism Board, established in 2005, supervises most aspects of the tourism industry in the country. The economic and political strategy linked to tourism development in Seychelles mainly relies on its rich flora and fauna and the calm and insularity of a Seychelles retreat. In 2010, Alain St Ange, a descendant of *Grand Blancs* from La Digue, became the CEO of the Seychelles Tourism Board and launched the Seychelles Brand. The essence of this Seychelles Brand is Seychellois identity, charm and hospitality and the serenity and stability that the country enjoys. Taking use of the human dimension and the meeting of cultures found within Seychelles was a new approach for the leaders of the industry, some of whom would soon become leaders of the country as well. In March 2012, the president of the country, James. A. Michel, reshuffled the cabinet, attaching culture to the Ministry of Tourism. The new Minister of Tourism and Culture was none other than Alain St Ange. St Ange is a well-known businessman with a strong experience in organizing big cultural events. For example, St Ange initiated the International Carnival of Victoria in 2011, which soon became the biggest cultural event in the country, along with the Creole Festival. Tourists and Seychellois can hear, see and taste Seychelles' cultural heritage at the Creole Festival. Traditionally, programming focused on staged music and dance performances, some workshops and conferences and local cuisine. With the new Ministry of Tourism and Culture and St Ange at its head, a new activity has been introduced into the programming: the Creole traditional wedding.

Since 2012, in collaboration with some local organizations and individuals, the Ministry of Tourism and Culture has coordinated the annual event during the Creole Festival. Although focused on local culture, this initiative supports a broader promotion campaign of Seychelles as a destination for brides and grooms. This includes, for example, the organization of a delegation of nineteen Chinese couples, together with thirty-two Chinese media houses, twelve high dignitaries and a group of potential Chinese investors in June 2012 to promote Seychelles as a honeymoon destination (eTurboNews 2012).

The first Creole traditional wedding was arranged by the Seychelles Creole Festival committee (under the Ministry of Tourism and Culture), in collaboration with the Beau Vallon District Administration and the Seychelles Tourism Board in 2012 and celebrated the union of a Russian couple. The event, called *tifin* (a local word that originally means light traditional snacks, served during tea time or feasts like weddings, anniversary ceremonies and birthdays), was included in the programming of the Creole Festival. In 2014, two traditional weddings took place during the Creole Festival and have been widely publicized in the Seychelles and regional media. The first one took place on Praslin Island and was coordinated in partnership with a local NGO called Women in Action and Solidarity. A Polish couple and a Seychellois couple got married in a ceremony, during which some two thousand inhabitants of the district accompanied them for *laserenad*. On the same day, on Mahé Island, a German couple got married in a *tifin* organized in collaboration with Beau Vallon District. For the occasion, Minister of Tourism and Culture Alain St Ange and Principal Secretary for Culture Benjamine Rose were among those present for the wedding ceremony.

During this type of Creole traditional wedding, couples have the option to celebrate their union in a Catholic church, where the ceremony is celebrated mostly in the Creole language, to add more to the "exotic experience". The bride and groom express their vows, reading them in Creole. Following the religious ceremony, residents of the community are invited to join the newly married couple for *laserenad*, to walk to *lasal vert* in the company of musicians. For the occasion, the dress code is strict, and Seychellois wear their best clothes, sometimes referencing outfits from the past. Then, some guests are invited to join the couple in *lasal vert* for the feast. For the wedding on Praslin, some two hundred residents paid CA$40 to be part of the wedding celebration alongside the guests of the newlyweds and to have access to food, drinks and music until late at night. Grilled fish, octopus curry, fish coconut curry, traditional cake, papaya jam, *kalou* or *toddy* (white alcohol made of fermented palm tree sap), and Marie Brizard liqueur

Figure 3. Musicians during a Creole traditional wedding on Praslin Island, during the 2014 creole festival, with Charles Davidson Lesperans on violin. *Credits*: Romano Laurence, Seychelles News Agency.

are usually available for the enjoyment of the guests. What is now called *tifin* actually consists of a re-enactment of the Creole traditional wedding.

Minister St Ange sees this as a way to save and revitalize a part of the Creole cultural heritage, which tends to be relegated to the past. Local authorities are hoping that Seychellois will better acknowledge local culture when this aspect of Seychelles culture is recognized and appreciated by foreigners. This point of view joins Madina Regneault's thesis on the relationship between culture and tourism in Mayotte. She wrote:

> Cultural tourism can be seen as a vector for identity preservation. Operating as a 'developer' would be a way for the Mahorais to become aware of their cultural wealth (and in particular their musical heritage) and therefore to preserve it. (2011, 107)

The minister has discussed his desire to share Seychellois culture with foreigners in many interviews with journalists. One could also see the phenomenon as a commodification of local culture by the ministry itself. Long considered harmful to local cultures, touristification or commodification of culture may stimulate the survival of certain traditions (Cravatte 2009,

610; Graburn and Leite 2009, 47; Guilbault 2014, 309, and so on). Concretely, selling traditional weddings to tourists is also a way to finance such activities, which would be difficult to do locally, and to give younger Seychellois the opportunity to experience the way of life of previous generations and learn about their history. As a Seychellois who got married in one of these events said in an interview for a local newspaper, "a traditional wedding is more difficult to organize as there should be a parade, songs, speeches and traditional band, all of which we would not have been able to afford" (Meriton-Jean 2014, 3).

In the process of touristification, some parts of the tradition are forgotten, while others remain. For practical reasons, the whole ritual is simplified to the exchange of vows followed by the banquet. The music repertoire is reduced to a few songs that are repeated – musicians therefore no longer need to master a large repertoire. Some specific traditional food and snacks (*tifin*) are preserved, and Seychellois participating are asked to wear traditional, or at least clean clothes, and to behave appropriately in order to create the desired atmosphere. Henry Johnson's words about Balinese music can be adapted to the Creole traditional wedding case:

> Tourism can be seen to influence both change and non-change. Change in the sense that either new structures are devised or old ones are adapted to suit the tourist market or tastes, and non-change in that sometimes traditions are adhered to so that tourist performances become fossilized events that on the one hand represent an idealized [Seychelles], and on the other hand hinder change. (Johnson 2002, 13)

The case of the Creole traditional wedding is an example of how the ministry is taking the lead in preserving a tradition, though in a form that is adapted to a touristic context. We can question the sustainability of such an initiative. Most people participating in these events as musicians or actors are mostly elders or children. Middle-aged people are poorly represented. Soon enough, very few musicians will be able to play *laserenad* because they have not mastered either the repertoire or the instruments. Many questions remain: Preserve for whom and for what? Who decides? Who benefits?

CULTURE, HERITAGE AND TOURISM IN THE SEYCHELLES
OF THE TWENTY-FIRST CENTURY

At the beginning of the twenty-first century, culture, heritage and tourism worked hand in hand in Seychelles. The Cultural Revolution of the early 1980s can be seen as a period of folklorization of local music and culture, and this process created heritage, as understood by Comaroff and Comaroff. They wrote that heritage is culture named and projected into the past, and simultaneously, the past congealed into culture.

> . . . It is identity in tractable, alienable form, identity whose found objects and objectifications may be consumed by others and, therefore, be delivered to the market." (2009, 10)

There is no doubt that Creole traditional weddings are now conceived as a national heritage, alongside cultural practices recognized during the revolution. The problem with this is that once recognized as heritage in Seychelles, a cultural practice becomes the property of the nation, represented by the state (Parent 2016a; 2017). This means that the Department of Culture decides what should or should not be preserved and how. Only a few members of the community – usually people close to or working within the ministry – are involved in this top-down cultural heritage management. Anthropologist Sandra Evers (2010) suggested that the Seychelles Copyright Act underpins many restrictions on freedom of speech criticism by stipulating that folklore's copyright "vests in the Republic" (Copyright Act, Part II, article 7).

Like many other researchers studying music and culture in islands, I am concerned with issues that are directly connected to the postcolonial condition (Rommen and Neely 2014; Guilbault and Rommen 2019). I see in the touristification of Creole traditional weddings a risk that Seychellois feel even more dispossessed of their cultural heritage. I asked, along with Hafstein, "when is protection not a means of dispossession?" (2014, 30). This approach to heritage focuses more on the (tradable) objects – the ceremony, the food, the music – than on the expertise and creativity of individuals. This is in line with Ton Charles's comment about the lack of recognition of musicians, a situation denounced by several individuals during my research.

The Creole wedding is likely to become exclusively associated with tourists, as some music already is. At the same time, Seychellois who participated in these events would probably say that they had a wonderful time. We can even imagine that the experience has strengthened the feeling of belonging to the Seychellois nation and culture, which is probably also the ministry's purpose, whether conscious or not.

The experience of the tourist couples could, to a certain point, fit within the current of cultural tourism. These weddings can be perceived as a local development project in which the experience of the tourist goes beyond the ephemeral, characteristic nature of the leisure trip, aiming instead to leave a meaningful trace and even to have a lasting impact on the local population (Doquet and Le Menestrel 2006, 6). Cultural tourism can thus support values and, in this case, contribute to keeping an intangible cultural heritage alive. Not having interviewed the newlyweds, I am unable to determine the values that guided their choices. Doquet and Le Menestrel warned us, however, of power relations underlying tourist encounters, writing that "the tourist remains the hero of the journey" (2006, 7). Indeed, newspaper articles describing the weddings focused more on the identity of the newlyweds than the Seychellois who contributed to the success of these events.

With the traditional Creole wedding, the ministry not only encourages initiatives but is also a full participant in the rehabilitation and touristification of culture. This kind of activity is considered falling within the culture division. Before the fusion of tourism and culture into one ministry, many artists complained that the arts and culture in Seychelles did not receive enough attention or recognition from the government. When the Ministry of Tourism and Culture was created, musicians and artists felt confident that arts and culture would finally be considered valuable contributions to Seychellois social life and the tourism industry. In the confrontation between the interests of cultural authorities and those of the tourism representatives, needless to say, the latter prevailed. As a result, culture has been used to promote tourism. I remember when the international cooperation director at the Culture Division of the ministry told me she was overloaded organizing the weddings of nineteen Chinese couples coming to Seychelles to get married. Culture is not under the Ministry of

Tourism anymore and has not been since 2016, but it is still a part of the tourism development plan.

As a small archipelago country whose postcolonial history is marked by the omnipresence of tourism, Seychelles represents an exceptional laboratory for studying the relationships between music, culture and tourism. Very few researchers engage in investigations on tourism in relation to culture and music in the South West Indian Ocean islands. It is, however, a promising field of study. As Jocelyne Guilbault observed in the English-speaking Caribbean (2014, 307), research on culture on these islands first served nation-building processes with the need to develop better knowledge and appreciation of the country's cultural wealth. In parallel, all efforts to attract and satisfy tourists have been politically understated in terms of research priorities. The same could be said about Seychelles. The global influence of postcolonial and cultural studies makes itself felt in Indian Ocean islands studies. I am confident that it will soon contribute to the theoretical development of music, island, festival and tourism studies.

Moreover, it is easier to write about Seychelles, tourism and culture in the global COVID-19 pandemic by questioning the viability of a touristic culture and asking, what happens when tourists are no longer present? On this, only time will tell.

REFERENCES

Amesbury, Ralf. 2018. "From Sun, Sea and Sand to Seychelles Sound." Master diss., Université Panthéon Sorbonne and Seychelles University.

Berliner, David. 2010. "Anthropologie et transmission." *Terrains* 55:4–19.

Campling, Liam, Hansel Confiance, and Marie-Therese Purvis. 2011. *Social Policies in Seychelles*. London: Commonwealth Secretariat and United Nations Research Institute for Social Development.

Charles-Dominique, Luc. 2013. "La patrimonialisation des formes musicales et artistiques: anthropologie d'une notion problématique." *Ethnologies* 35 (1): 75–101.

Chaudenson, Robert. 1992. *Des îles, des hommes, des langues*. Paris: L'Harmattan.

Comaroff, John, and Jean Comaroff. 2009. *Ethnicity INC*. Chicago: University of Chicago Press.

Cravatte, Céline. 2009. "L'anthropologie du tourisme et l'authenticité. Catégorie analytique ou catégorie indigène?" *Cahiers d'études africaines* 193–94 (1): 603–20.

Doquet, Anne, and Sara Le Menestrel. 2006. "Introduction." *Autrepart* 4 (40): 3–13.

eTurboNews. 2012. "Chinese Couples Arrive in Seychelles for Tropical Weddings." *eTurboNews*, 15 June 2012. https://www.eturbonews.com/58026/chinese-couples-arrive-seychelles-tropical-weddings/.

Evers, Sandra J.T.M. 2010. "Tales from a Captive Audience: Dissident Narratives and the Official History of the Seychelles." In *A World of Insecurity: Anthropological Perspectives on Human Security*, edited by Ellen Bal, Thomas Hylland Eriksen, and Oscar Salemink, 208–40. London: Pluto Press.

Gay, Jean-Christophe. 2004. "Tourisme, politique et environnement aux Seychelles." *Tiers-Monde* 45 (178): 319–39.

Graburn, Nelson H.H, and Naomi Leite. 2009. "Anthropological Interventions in Tourism Studies." In *Cultural Tourism in a Changing World*, edited by Jamal Tazim and Mike Robinson, 203–14. Clevedon: Channel View.

Guilbault, Jocelyne. 2014. "Afterword." In *Sun, Sean, and Sound. Music and Tourism in the Circum-Caribbean*, edited by Timothy Rommen and Daniel T. Neely, 306–15. New York: Oxford University Press.

———, and Timothy Rommen, eds. 2019. *Sounds of Vacation. Political Economies of Caribbean Tourism*. Durham: Duke University Press.

Hafstein, Vladimir T. 2014. "Protection as Dispossession: Government in the Vernacular." In *Cultural Heritage in Transit. Intangible Rights as Human Rights*, edited by Deborah Kapchan, 25–57. Philadelphia: University of Pennsylvania Press.

Johnson, Henry. 2002 "Balinese Music, Tourism and Globalisation: Invention Traditions Within and Across Cultures." *New Zealand Journal of Asian Studies* 4 (2): 8–32.

Kœchlin, Bernard. 1981. *Musique traditionnelle de l'océan Indien: Seychelles*. Paris: Centre de documentation africaine / Radio-France internationale.

Meriton-Jean, Sharon. 2014. "Saying 'I do' in Seychelles – Beach and Traditional Creole Wedding for Polish Couple." Seychelles News Agency, 27 October 2014. http://www.seychellesnewsagency.com/articles/.

Moka, Cindy. 2016. *Lepok Ze Resi*. Victoria: International Creole Institute and Department of Culture.

Parent, Marie-Christine. 2012. "When Tourism Contributes to the 'Heritagization' of Traditional Music: The Case of the Seychelles." *Conference Proceedings – Soundtracks: Music, Tourism and Travel*. Leeds Metropolitan University.

———. 2015. "Représentations publiques de la diversité culturelle en milieu créole: Le cas des Seychelles (océan Indien)." In *La Diversité des Patrimoines. Du rejet du discours à l'éloge des pratiques*, edited by Daniela Moisa and Jessica Roda, 39–64. Québec: Presses de l'Université du Québec.

———. 2016a. "Being on Both Sides: The Ethnomusicologist Between Official Institutions and Musicians." *COLLeGIUM. Studies across Disciplines in the Humanities and Social Sciences* 21: 62–81.

———. 2016b. "Le festival « *Dimans moutya* » aux Seychelles: (re)construction et « sauvegarde » d'un patrimoine musical au travers de sa mise en tourisme." *MUSICultures* 43 (2): 41–65.

———. 2017. "Le *moutya* à l'épreuve de la modernité seychelloise. Pratiquer un genre musical emblématique dans les Seychelles d'aujourd'hui (océan Indien)." PhD diss., Université de Montréal and Université Côte d'Azur.

———. 2020. "Comprendre le concept de « *moutya otantik* » en tant que patrimoine: Mémoire, représentations et constructions de l'authenticité d'une pratique musicale de tradition orale en contexte postcolonial." *MUSICultures* 47:189–212.

Phillips, Arthur Angel. 1950. "The Cultural Cringe." *Meanjin* IX (4).

Picard, Michel. 1992. *Bali. Tourisme culturel et culture touristique.* Paris: L'Harmattan.

———, and Robert E. Wood. 1997. *Tourism, Ethnicity and the State in Asian and Pacific Societies.* Hawai'i: University of Hawai'i Press.

Regneault, Madina. 2011. "Mise en scène des patrimoines musicaux à La Réunion et à Mayotte." In *Territoires musicaux mis en scène*, edited by Monique Desroches, Marie-Hélène Pichette, Claude Dauphin, and Gordon Smith, 93–111. Montreal: Les Presses de l'Université de Montréal.

Rommen, Timothy. 2014. "Introduction. Music Touristics in the Circum-Caribbean." In *Sun, Sean, and Sound: Music and Tourism in the Circum-Caribbean*, edited by Timothy Rommen and Daniel T. Neely, 1–14. New York: Oxford University Press.

Republic of Seychelles. 1980. *Statistical Bulletin, Fourth Quarter*, no. 3. Victoria: Government Printers.

University of Texas Library. n.d.a. "Indian Ocean Area." Perry-Castañeda Library Map Collection. https://www.lib.utexas.edu/maps/islands_oceans_poles/indianoceanarea.jpg.

———. n.d.b. "Seychelles." Perry-Castañeda Library Map Collection. https://legacy.lib.utexas.edu/maps/islands_oceans_poles/seychelles.jpg.

Part Two

MUSIC, DANCE AND ISLAND IDENTITY

Chapter Five

The Traditional Daur Music and Dance Festival Kumule on the Island Meadow by the Amur River

HOLGER BRIEL

FOR THOUSANDS OF YEARS, THE VAST AMUR BASIN straddling the borderlands between China and Russia has been home to nomadic tribes. While many of them have become settled, often because of support, guidance and requests by the governmental bodies charged with overlooking them, nomadism still plays a significant role in various tribes' folklore, mythologies and rituals. This chapter will introduce the Daur tribe, living in China's Heilongjiang province. Their rituals will be described through the lens of what is arguably their largest and most important festival, *Kumule*.

DAUR HISTORY

Mostly unknown outside of China and Mongolia, the Mongolic-speaking Daur or Dagur people (Khalka Mongolian: Дагуур/Daguur; simplified Chinese: 达斡尔族) are one of the fifty-six ethnic minorities officially recognized by the Chinese government. According to the 2010 census, they comprise about one hundred and forty thousand people. Preceding censuses recorded much lower numbers.

> Dagur are not numerous. Before establishment of the People's Republic of China, the Dagur population was decentralized and population growth was slow. In

1982, a State census indicated a population of 94,014 Dagur, an increase of 42,14 (18 per cent) over the 24 years from the 52,000 reported in the 1958 census, and a further growth of 46,000 (96 per cent) over 29 years from the 48,000 reported in a 1953 census. In 1888 (the 13th year of Guang Xu's reign), based on Heilongjiang, a book by the Commercial Section of the Middle East Railroad Bureau, the Dagur population, including those living in Xinjiang, was 31,000. There obviously has been dramatic population growth, that is, a growth of 50 per cent between 1888 and 1953, especially after the foundation of the PRC. (Stuart, Li and Shelear 1994, 2)

With numbers going up, albeit from a very low base, today the Daurs mainly live in Inner Mongolia, in Qiqihar and along the Amur (Heilongjiang) River near Heihe, Northwestern China, on fertile plains and river islands that were settled during the Palaeolithic era (cf. plates 1, 2 and 3).

The Daurs speak a form of Mongolian, originating from the Altaic language group. Prior to the 1911 revolution they spoke Manchu, but

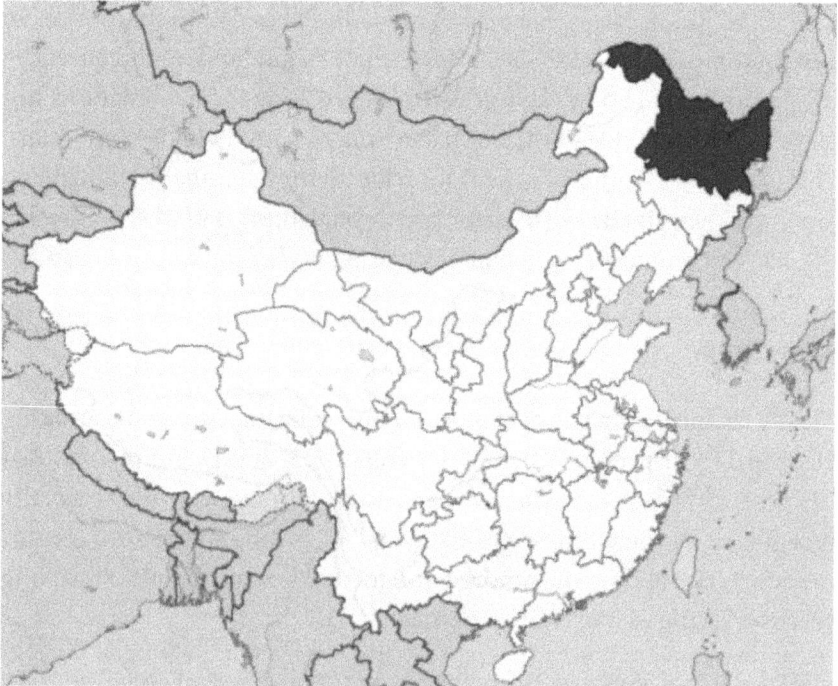

Figure 1. Traditional and contemporary Daur settlements

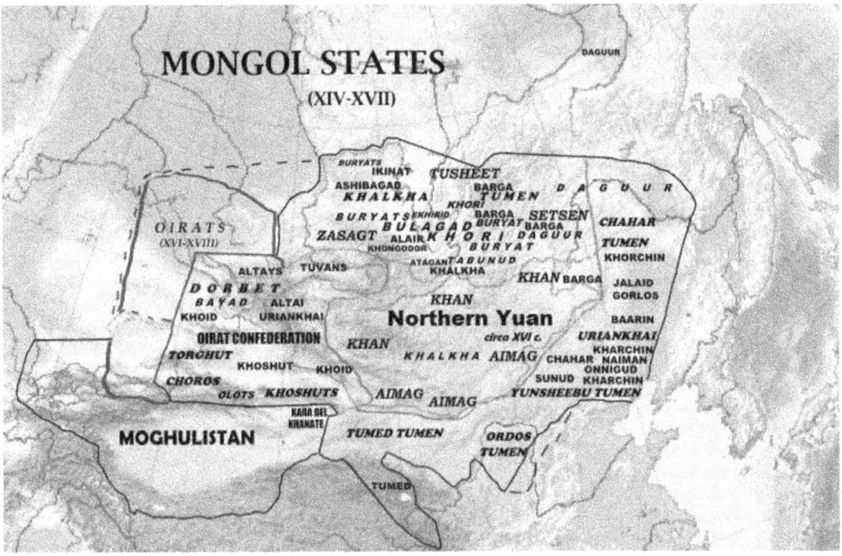

Figure 2. Daur (Daguur) settlements in the 16th century. Credits: Khiruge, CC BY-SA 4.0, File: Mongolia XVI. png, Created: 1 January 2014.

Mandarin replaced it after the revolution. While they have been nomadic for most of their history, like many other tribes, they eventually settled to become a semi-agrarian society. Their name possibly originates here, with Daur meaning "cultivator". Another source traces their name back to the reign of Emperor Gaozu, founder of the Tang dynasty, who ruled from 618 to 626 CE. Remnants of one of his garrisons in Northeastern China were called "*da hu li*", meaning "Those who hunt big foxes" (Cartwright 2017). This latter theory is strengthened by the fact that some of their central folk tales and gods are associated with foxes. For example, *Aoli Barken*, the Fairy Fox Spirit, is one of the most important nature spirits for the Daurs. Stuart, Li and Shelear (1994, 31–32) wrote that "it was worshipped in a miniature temple in each family's courtyard. If there was no temple, it was placed in a storehouse, which was off-limits to women. Offerings were pigs, sheep, chickens, liquor and fruits." The same goes for another spirit, the *Koton* or *Huaran Barken*, which is based on a similar fox spirit and worshipped in family courtyards. The Daurs were not the only tribe to worship it; Manchus and Oroqens did as well.

China-USSR Border: Eastern Sector

Figure 3. The 64 Villages area (University of Texas Library n.d.)

Other gods also clearly speak to the origin of the Daurs. Thus, there is the *Bogol Barken*, the oldest of the Daur gods. According to legend, when the tribes moved from the north banks of the Heilongjiang River, *Bogol Barken* was their only god, but *Bogol Barken* comprised many parts. The water/river theme is very much present in the worship of this *Bogol Barken*, and its chant goes as follows:

His birthplace is on the Heilongjiang River,
And his ancestral place is on the Huangjiang River.
He screams on the Ji River,
Swims in rivers,
Jumps in gullies,
Wanders in deserts.
He has connections in the Mo River,
And has descended in a towering rage (Stuart and Li 1994, 29)

When it comes to Daur poetry, water imagery is prevalent, especially in the long-form pastoral idyll. Here is a short and telling excerpt from a longer poem:

Time flies like rivers,
Spring has returned and winter has gone,
A man lives in the world,
He rarely lives to be 100,
Life is difficult to manage,
And is hard for both you and me,
As we busily work,
Seasons change before you know.
Spring comes,
Snow melts on the ground,
Dried grass has rotted away,
The land comes to life again.
The sun warms the ground,
Breezes caress our faces,
Warm spring breezes blow,
Bringing life to nature.
We go out to listen,
And hear quails converse,
We look into the distance,
And gain pleasure at heart (Stuart, Li and Shelear 1994, 48)

Water imagery here is closely related to the change of seasons and the lifespan of men and women, displaying the close relationship with and dependence of the Daur upon the land, the river waters and the changing seasons. The water theme is not only central to Daur mythology, it can also be found in other tribes in the area. For instance, the Oroqens trace their ancestry back to the survivors of a great flood (Stuart and Li 1994, 2–3)

Today, many Daurs can still speak their language, but there is no written script. Even the poem above is a transliteration from Mandarin. According to one Daur folk tale, their written language was lost when a turtle attacked a returning Buddhist monk from the West, and the scripts were lost to the sea (Stuart, Li and Shelear 1994, 94). In the Heihe region, many do not even speak their own language because of the strong influence of Mandarin, particularly because of the population increase related to the (often forced) influx of Han during the Cultural Revolution. In the documentary film *On the Black Dragon*, which will be discussed below, one Daur interviewed by the river next to his village stated that "it is sad that 50% of people in the area are not local anymore", implying that native communities had been forced into minority status over the last fifty years or so. However, the most recent Han migration was the last of many, dating back to early Qing times, with all of them reducing the numbers of the older tribal settlers.

Most Daur groups remain close to others with the same family name (*hala*). Halas are then further divided into different clans (*mokon*) who would typically live in the same village. Most Daurs believe in Shamanism or, via their Mongol ancestorship, Tibetan Buddhism. Daur historic records, along with those of the Ewenki and Oroqen tribes, reach back to the Khitan tribes who founded the Liao Dynasty (916–1125 CE) when their forebears were nomads roaming the vast steppes of Mongolia and Northeastern China. In the mid-seventeenth century, their lands were conquered by the emperors of the Qing dynasty. At that time, the Qing Dynasty quickly found itself under pressure from Russian explorers in Northeastern China. As early as 1651, Yerofey Khabarov (1603–71) and his men besieged and took important Daur towns such as Yaxa. A defeat of Russian forces near the junction of the Sungari and Amur Rivers in 1658 checked their initial advance, yet there would be further military clashes before the 1680s, when a concerted Qing attack on the Russian fort at Albazin forced a negotiated border in the Treaty of Nerchinsk (1689), which resulted in the Russians abandoning large swathes of the Amur region. While this geopolitical struggle played itself out, it was the locals who bore the brunt of the attacks.

Having originally left the area because of rumours of Russian cruelty, the

Daurs battled the Russians but could not win against Russian guns (Forsyth 1994; Wood 2011). During the reign of Emperor Shun Zhi (1644–62), many of the Daurs moved south and settled on the banks of the Nenjiang River. The struggle with Russia would continue for centuries until 1858, when the forced Treaty of Aigun ceded these lands to Russia for good (in Russian appearing as *Priamurye*, the "Lands along the Amur"). In 1860, areas as far down as Vladivostok were added to the Russian holdings, in effect ending any Chinese influence there. While the Treaty of Aigun allowed Qing subjects to live in sixty-four villages north of the Amur in the Heihe and Aigun regions, there was still unrest. Russian records show that in 1870, 10,646 Qing subjects lived in the area, five thousand four hundred of which were Han Chinese, four thousand five hundred Manchu and one thousand Daurs. In 1894, the overall population of Qing subjects had increased to over sixteen thousand (Timofeyev 2003). A considerable number of Chinese had also settled in the largest city across the river in Blagoveshchensk.

But this was still not the end of political strive in the region. The border wars took an even more traumatic turn for the locals. In 1900, tragedy struck yet again when, during the Boxer Rebellion, Qing forces attempted to blockade the Russian river trade and attacked Blagoveshchensk, the Russian city located directly across from the Chinese town of Heihe. The Russian military governor of the Amur region, Konstantin Nikolaevich Gribskii, ordered all Chinese living on Russian soil to be pushed into the Amur River. This applied to over thirty thousand people. Estimates vary, but up to eight thousand men, women and children were thus brutally murdered (Timofeyev 2003, table 11). The local Han Chinese and minority groups never forgave Russia for this massacre and, in following battles, almost always sided with the enemies of the Russians.

The struggle between the locals, China and Russia continued throughout the Japanese occupation and Russian and Chinese civil wars. Due to ethnic cleansing by the Stalin regime in 1956, many of the indigenous communities, including the Oroqens and Daurs, fled across the border to China, again darkening the Sino-Russian relationship and bringing hardship to local communities. It took until the 1991 Sino-Soviet Border Agreement with China to officially renounce sovereignty of the sixty-four villages, and

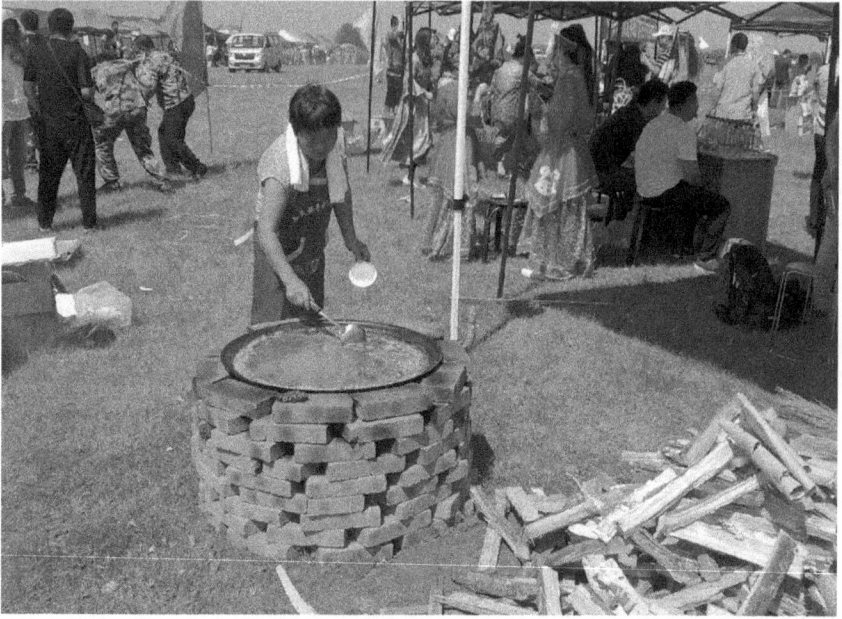

Figure 4. Preparing traditional Daur food (Holger Briel, 2017 CC)

the overall Sino-Russian border conflict was finally settled in 2004 in the Treaty of Vladivostok (cf. Paine 1996; Maxwell 2007).

Not surprisingly, it took until the 2000s for a more collaborative note to be struck in this border region, with cross-river trade and travel slowly opening up (cf. Lin 2017; Zhang 1998). Since 2018, a new bridge spanning the Amur River near Heihe has been built, and Sino-Russian business relations and tourism are finally progressing.

When trying to understand the underlying historic and cultural patterns of this vast area, it is important to point out that, rather than merely following the chronology of Chinese dynasties and Russian Czars, which lends itself to the creation of facile linearist historiographies, a closer analysis of Chinese dealings with neighbouring cultures yields very rich results. The study of Sinicization of the margins of the various Han dynasties demonstrates that the rise of China was not because of an imaginary unity and superiority of people all claiming to be descendants of the Yellow Emperor but involved the interplay of a variety of aspects, such as climate, geography and profitable interactions with native peoples (cf. Crossley 1990). This was something that played itself out in all areas of Han expansion. Thus, regarding the Han expansion towards the South of China, Shin (2006, 2) stated:

> The essential story of China's expansion, according to many a historian, is the emergence and development in the borderlands of a variety of formerly non-existent political, social, and economic relationships. To extend its political reach to the southern border zone, the Chinese state for much of the imperial period is said to have had to embrace and promote the institution of native chieftaincy. The stories of acculturation, similarly, opt to emphasize the profound influences Han and non-Han peoples have had on one another.

Furthermore, Rawski (2015) convincingly argued that throughout its history, China has been largely shaped by its relations with its neighbours in the North and East, Japan, Korea, the Jurchen/Manchu, Russia and the Mongol States, and its development must therefore be viewed within a dynamic regional framework. Daurs, Oroqens and Mongols had been neighbours of the Han for a long time, and it was these relations that influenced the development of all parties involved. The intermingling of cultures would then also produce hybrid cultures in the form of shared linguistic traits, cultural practices and religions. Furthermore, music, folk tales and festivals would all be the result of this common ancestry. The Daur music festivals shall be discussed in more detail in the following section.

DAUR FESTIVALS

One festival celebrated in most of these cultures is the Spring festival, *A'nie*. The Daur *A'nie* is in many ways very similar to that celebrated by the Han communities:

> People rose before dawn on the first day of the first moon. Women began preparing breakfast, and men burnt incense and worshipped heaven and the gods. Tables were prepared in the west part of the courtyard, where incense was burned. A bundle was burnt for heaven, seven sticks were burned for Ursa Major, nine for Guniangshen (Girl God), one for Zaoshen (Kitchen God), and three for each of various other gods.
>
> These offerings beseeched the God of Heaven and other deities to bestow peace and a good harvest. Veneration of deities was followed by toasts and kowtowing to elders in return for *yirele* (blessings). After a breakfast of dumplings, people

dressed in new clothes. Close *mokon* relatives grouped together and, led by the senior elder, began visiting families in order of generations. For three years after the death of elders, a table was placed on the south side of *kangs* on New Year's Eve to venerate them. Visitors paid tribute to the deceased by offering tobacco and kowtowing [to the table]. Various forms of entertainment followed. On the first or second day of the first moon [first lunar month], people rode on horseback or in sleds to make New Year visits to other villages. On the 15th of the first moon (Kaqin), people dressed in new clothing and ate *waaq*. Some ate dumplings. On the night of the 14th, people kowtowed and burned incense to the gods. The 15th was the last festival day. (Stuart, Li and Shelear 1994, 18)

Other traditional Daur festivals include the festival of the second day of the second moon festival, when pig head meat is consumed; the Day of Pure Brightness (*Hanshi*), when graves of ancestors are visited; the fifth day of the fifth moon, when "people rose early and bathed in rivers, or cleaned their faces with dew. A special herb was picked and placed in the ears. This made the body immune from diseases. Dumplings, meat pies, and *hele* (buckwheat noodles) were then eaten" (Stuart, Li and Shelear 1994, 18); the Netherworld Festival on the fifteenth day of the seventh moon; a food celebration on the fifteenth day of the eighth moon, when offerings of moon cakes and watermelons were made to the moon; the Thousand Lanterns Day on the twenty-fifth day of the eighth moon; the celebration of the Kitchen God on the twenty-third of the eighth moon; and *Buntunn*, celebrated on the twenty-third of the twelfth moon. Elders are honoured, firecrackers are set off, and predictions are made for the coming harvest in the new year. Each family also lights a fire in front of their dwelling and keeps it going until the beginning of the new moon.

KUMULE

Apart from these festivals, since the late 1950s, a new festival has been celebrated by the Daurs, and it is this festival which will concern us in the remainder of this chapter. Every June, the Daur communities in China celebrate their biggest communal festival of the year, *Kumule*, which highlights their more recent history via dance and song. Originally, a large segment of the Daur community in Heilongjiang continued to live on the Russian side of the Amur River, but in 1956, many of them were forced to flee to China due to Stalinist ethnic cleansing policies. The *Kumule* Festival restages this traumatic flight across the river. Some of its elements also hearken back to the time when they lived as nomads and travelled the land, some to the time when, in the seventeenth century, they first had to flee from the Russians.

In June 2017, a group of communication and media students from Xi'an Jiaotong Liverpool University and I travelled to Heilongjiang to interview with several minorities living in the area around Heihe, the largest Chinese city on the Amur River and to create a short documentary featuring these communities. We intended to interview members of the Manchu, the Daur, the Oroqen and the Eweki tribes. As it turned out, we were successful except for the Eweki community, who, given our timeframe, lived too far downriver to make a journey to their community viable. Furthermore, we interviewed with administrators and anthropological, political science and arts staff at Heihe University. Individual interviews were set up with minority members in the Daur communities near Aihui and with Oroqen and Manchu individuals in their traditional villages surrounding Heihe. The Daurs also invited us to join in their *Kumule* festival on a grassland island near Heihe in the wide Amur River basin, the border between Russia and China for almost two thousand miles.

Before we made our way to Heihe, we had already had several kick-off meetings at our university to prepare for the trip, work out the logistics and distribute roles. It was decided that all participants would be responsible for taking photographs, interviewing and filming and that the final products, the interviews and a short film summarizing the project would contain images and footage from everybody. This ran the danger of having some uneven material, but it would ensure that everybody was represented in all aspects of the project. The film, entitled On the Black River, can be viewed at https://vimeo.com/375873740. It has English and Chinese subtitles, but the discrete interviews are only available in Chinese at this time.

The *Kumule* festival is the one time of the year when the whole Daur community comes together to interact with each other, share food, worship and remember the hardship of the flight from their old villages across the river in Russia. The dramatic re-enactment of this flight in song and dance is the centrepiece of every *Kumule* Festival, designed to remind the Daurs where they come from and teach their children their cultural history.

Figure 5. Traditional Daur dress on display before a reconstructed Daur hut (Holger Briel, 2017 CC)

We were invited to join in the celebrations and to interview some of the participating actors. The festival was spread out across the meadow, with archery contests, horse riding and jousting at various locations. Traditional Daur huts had also been erected to show off their erstwhile living arrangements. Prior to the musical performance, the Daurs engaged in offering animal heads and liquor to the gods and circled clockwise around a large round structure made up entirely of mid-sized stones. Every Daur would pick up one or several stones to throw onto the structure, thereby petitioning the gods to give health to them, their children and their elders. Garlands of colourful triangular pieces of cloth had been draped around the trees and tents, in a Tibetan fashion, petitioning the gods for good luck and health. Traditional musical instruments were on display and were played, such as grass and oak flutes and the *mokulien* or *mukulian*, a mouth string organ traditionally played by women. People also gathered around storytellers who performed the folk tales of the Daurs, such as "A Farmer's Song", "Song of the Fishermen" and "Song of the Lumbermen", all authored by eminent Daur storyteller and author Qin Tongpu. However, these were written down in Mandarin, and when we visited, they were also told in Mandarin.

While musical instruments were being played, such as the above-

Figure 6. Daur warrior in front of sacrifice and traditional roundhouse made of stone (Holger Briel, 2017 CC)

mentioned *mukulian*, all eyes were on the stage as the *Kumule* performance was about to begin. The music for the performance came from a large PA system and was not played live. The dancers took the stage and re-enacted the fearful and sad days of life in their old village, the famines and the dramatic flight across the river, to crescendo in the joyous arrival in the new world. The performance lasted for about an hour and a half, and the dancers visibly moved the audience. Of particular interest to us was the great care the adult audience took to explain the meaning of the musical and theatrical performance to their children. Many had tears in their eyes. For a people without a written language, it is festivities like this one that allows the passing on of collective memories to the next generation and allows for a feeling of awe for one's own heritage within a cultural world dominated by the other.

For the Daurs, music has always been an expression of their manifest place in the world. One is struck because much of it is already geared towards dancing. This is particularly true for *Zhandal* (work songs), which were typically performed in the open air. A few were performed during the festival as well. Stuart, Li and Shelear (1994, 64) described them as follows:

Figure 7. Kumule Dance performance (Holger Briel, 2017 CC)

Zhandals are sung in forests, the open air, and while driving ox carts. Words were not fixed, but mostly improvised according to the singer's emotions. More often than not, words were not sung, but replaced by sounds like *nayeyao*. The pitch was high, and such songs were melodious and full of trills. This was a special feature of Dagur music ... Lyrics were composed by folk artists and the music and lyrics became folksongs.

Other songs performed were decidedly dialogic and typically sung by women, often with several groups joining in at different times. In many ways, such traditional music plays an important part in safeguarding intangible heritage. This is, of course, true for all minority cultures (cf. Stuart and Li 1994; Davis 2013)

While the reason for the *Kumule* is fairly recent, its dramaturgy and choreography are not. Traditional Daur dances have a very similar kind of choreography, for instance, the *Lurigel* or *Lurigele* dance, which combines dancing and singing:

"Lurigele" gives priority to group dances, which mainly manifest scenes of hunting and production activities. During the dance, there are more movements on the upper body and arms of the dancer, while the basic steps under feet are sidesliping [sic]. At first, a light and slow dance song was sung, the dancer would begin dancing gently to the song, standers-by can join the group at will, then the dancing atmosphere became intense, rhythm became faster, dancers kept shifting and changing positions, and when it reached the climax, dancers give out ... cries such as "Zheheizhe", "Dehuda", etc. and step in forceful tempo together. "Lurigele" stems from the laboring and production life of the Daur people, so there are contents and dancing images of collecting, carrying water, fishing, flying, birds fights etc. in the dance. (Anon, Lurigele 2012).

Another particular feature of this dance is that dancers enact a form of playful communal ethics while dancing. As the dance gets faster, "a dancer places one hand on the waist, and the other hand reaches out toward her partner. The hands moved in turn, suggesting fighting. At this moment, a third party might have joined the 'weaker' dancer and 'confronted' the 'stronger' one" (Stuart, Li

Figure 8. Daur community leader (Holger Briel, 2017 CC)

and Shelear 1994, 66). While set within a scenery of fighting (for survival, for instance, in hunting, from which many of the individual moves of the dance can be traced), it nevertheless becomes clear that a member of the community is always there and ready to help other members in times of need. As such, the dance is a performed ethic intended to teach members of the community what attitudes it takes to retain strong communal bonds.

Kumule fulfils several tasks: it performs the content of the recent history of the Daur, and its performative aspects keep traditional formal elements of such a retelling alive. It allows people to participate in the actualization of historic events and presents a pedagogy for their young.

THE FUTURE

Over the years of its existence, the Daur *Kumule* festival has continued to serve as a reminder that traditional ethnic music deeply and positively affects members of minority communities. It also provides such communities with the opportunity to display to the outside world a coherent and historic account of their being in the world. As became clear during the interviews, the Daurs (and by witness accounts, also the Oroqens) feel a deep gratitude towards the People's Republic of China for, in effect, granting them asylum in the late 1950s and supporting them in resettling thereby building housing for them and providing agricultural machinery and schooling for their children. However, this came at a price. At least, in some ways, they are no longer able to live their traditional lifestyle. For instance, they are prohibited from possessing hunting rifles for most of the year. They must also accept an overwhelming predominance of Han Chinese in their traditional settling areas. While they are once more allowed to travel to Russia for family reunions and trade, when it comes to identity papers for travelling, they must wait like all other Chinese citizens. Or, as an anthropology professor from Heihe University stated during the interviews, "They are like everybody else and do not have special privileges. We are all the same now." This practice is unlike those in other parts of the world, for instance, in Borneo or the Amazon, where indigenous communities are granted certain travel privileges when traversing borders that they neither chose nor perhaps accept. Also, when it comes to higher education, the Daur are still woefully underrepresented. All interviewed representatives of Heihe University denied that they had ever taught members of minority communities in the area.

Kumule allows the Daurs to display their musical and choreographical heritage to the wider world and to reconfirm their own traditions. It is beneficial that they can openly display their culture and music. The festival is already an update of their traditions, as its content combines traditional singing and dancing with more recent content about their flight from Russia. One wonders, though, whether this will be enough to sustain their culture in the future. On this account, the Oroqens have it easier, as they are a larger minority, and scholars have more thoroughly analysed their customs. They also have a recently built cultural heritage museum in their village northwest of Heihe.

Yet they and their other minority neighbours would all benefit from more private, government and international support. It is one thing to play one's traditional music; another to present it more regionally, nationally or, indeed, globally.

What would, therefore, be desirable is an initiative to liberate traditional Daur ethnic music from its folkloristic and, at times, stale niche. Often, it ends up as something only older people from remote regions listen to and perform. Many state-sponsored minority music displays typically follow a pattern such as the one described by Kaiman and Jacobs (2011):

> At the forefront of state-sponsored minority representation are the "song and dance troupes" that appear regularly on television. These shows portray minorities as exotic and unthreatening – with bright clothes and wide smiles and who are fanatical about singing and dancing. Many disparate minority groups often perform on stage together to symbolize ethnic harmony. Songs are often performed in Mandarin.
>
> The lyrics are frequently apolitical paeans to the rugged allure of China's borderlands. In 2009, the Mongolian singer Wulan Tuoya had a major hit with the crisp, karaoke-friendly "I Want to Go to Tibet". The song's music video looks like a public relations campaign for Tibetan tourism, juxtaposing government-financed group dances with video clips of the Beijing-Lhasa express train.

In order to show how limiting such displays are and what kind of disservice they are doing to the respective ethnic groups, it is enough to point out that none of their songs have become part of the national music scene. Yet, nationally and internationally, there are several excellent examples of how to do it better. Generally, over the last thirty years or so, "ethnic" or "world" music has had an incredible impact on global music tastes. While these categories are perhaps problematic, given that all music is ethnic and worldly, its impact cannot be denied. One example of this influence is Daniel Barenboim and Edward Said's *West-Eastern Orchestra* (1999) for classical music, or, more recently, the Israeli-Iranian neo-traditional band *Sistanagila* (Schult 2019). Both use the connecting (and healing) power of music to bring together minorities or communities traditionally at odds with each other, updating traditional music and creating a musical hybrid in and for a hybridized world. In their endeavours, traditional music is culturally and musically recontextualized, thereby decentring its traditional message and deconstructing its place in the pantheon of ethnic music. Musical recontextualization and invigoration have also worked very well for the Sami in northern Scandinavia, with Norwegian Sami singer Mari Boine's fusion oeuvre or the music performed by Iranian-born musician Sina Vodjani (for example, Sacred Buddha, Membran/Pastels, 2006), incorporating electronic chill-out and traditional Tibetan music.

Of late, one can also observe the beginnings of a similar musical hybridity in China with Tibetan music and, perhaps surprisingly, with rappers such as Gong Ba and Baya and their band ANU (which translates from Tibetan to teenagers). Their very successful 2018 single, "Ga Ga", landed them an appearance at the very popular Chinese singing competition *Singer 2019*. Another example is Sichuan singer and actress Tan Weiwei's 2016 song, "Reaction", which was performed during the 2016 Chinese New Year Spring Festival Gala. In this song, Tan used elements of the *Huai Yin Lao Qiang* opera from the end of the Ming dynasty from Shanxi province and combined them into a riveting dance and song combination. One can also point to Hanggai, an internationally well-established Mongolian rock band that combines traditional Mongolian music with rock; to singer-songwriter Mamer from Xinjiang; to Zhang Quan and Shan Ren (the Mountain People, whose singer, Xiao Budian, is from the Buyi minority); bands made up of minority musicians from Yunnan and Guizhou; and Guangdong-based Hakka-dialect rock trio Jiu Lian Zhen Ren. Often, elements of traditional orchestration are used, but lyrics are decidedly modern and express the needs of today. Issues discussed range from city life to the fear of losing one's ethnic identity. All these examples attest to the opportunity for traditional Chinese music to break through its clichéd niche and influence national or even global music streams.

It is heartening to see that such diverse musical artistry is finally finding an ever-larger audience and that musical tastes in China are diversifying beyond Mandopop and Cantopop, truly incorporating ethnic plurality in the creative process. More than a single country, China is a subcontinent, with many of its fringes contributing to its successes. Rawski (2015, 11) wrote: "Faith in the ability of the peoples on the geographic and cultural periphery to adopt Chinese ways was a hallmark of Chinese frontier policy from ancient times onward, reflected in official documents." The converse is, of course, true as well. Hopefully, with the higher visibility of hybrid events like the *Kumule* festival, minorities such as the Daurs will be able to use their traditional arts as a platform for examining their contemporary lives in a multicultural and creative setting. The talent and desire for it are certainly visible.

REFERENCES

Anon. 2012. "'Lurigele' Is a Kind of Representative Folk Dance in Daur." Made in China 17 Dec 2012. https://resources.made-in-china.com/article/culture-life/ynmxQtLoWJIz/Lurigele-Dance-of-Daur-Ethnic-Minority/.

Briel, Holger. 2017. "On the Black Dragon." https://vimeo.com/375873740.

Cartwright, Mark. 2017. "Emperor Gaozu of Tang." *World History Encyclopedia.* https://www.ancient.eu/Emperor_Gaozu_of_Tang/.

Crossley, Pamela Kyle. 1990. "Thinking about Ethnicity in Early Modern China." *Late Imperial China* 11 (1): 1–35.

Davis, Thalea C. "Across the Red Steppe: Exploring Mongolian Music in China and Exporting It from Within." Master's thesis, Western Michigan University.

Forsyth, James. 1994. *A History of the Peoples of Siberia*. Cambridge: Cambridge University Press.

Kaiman, Jonathan, and Andrew Jacobs. 2011. "Ethnic Music Tests Limits in China." *New York Times*, 16 July 2011. https://www.nytimes.com/2011/07/17/world/asia/17music.html.

Lin, Yuexin Rachel. 2021. "White Water, Red Tide: Sino-Russian Conflict on the Amur 1917–20." *Historical Research* 90 (247): 76–100. https://onlinelibrary.wiley.com/doi/full/10.1111/1468-2281.12166.

Maxwell, Neville. "How the Sino-Russian Boundary Conflict Was Finally Settled: From Nerchinsk 1689 to Vladivostok 2005 via Zhenbao Island 1969." In *Eager Eyes Fixed on Eurasia*, edited by Iwashita Akihiro, 47–72. Sapporo: Slavic Research Center, Hokkaido University. http://src-h.slav.hokudai.ac.jp/coe21/publish/no16_2_ses/02_maxwell.pdf.

Paine, S.C.M. 1996. *Imperial Rivals: China, Russia, and Their Disputed Frontier*. Armonk, NY: M.E. Sharpe.

Rawski, Evelyn S. 2015. *Early Modern China and Northeast Asia: Cross-Border Perspectives*. Cambridge: Cambridge University Press.

Schult, Christoph. 2019. "Iranisch-israelische Band Sistanagila Mit Volksliedern gegen die Ohnmacht. *Der Spiegel,* 29 November 2019. https://www.spiegel.de/kultur/musik/sistanagila-iranisch-israelische-band-mit-volksliedern-gegen-die-ohnmacht-a-1298317.html.

Shin, Leo K. 2006. *The Making of the Chinese State: Ethnicity and Expansion on the Ming Borderlands.* Cambridge: Cambridge University Press.

Stuart, Kevin, and Xuewei Li. 1994. "Tales from China's Forest Hunters: Oroqen Folktales." *Sino-Platonic Papers* 61. https://sino-platonic.org/complete/spp061_oroqen_folktales.pdf.

———, Xuewei Li, and Shelear. 1994. "China's Dagur Minority: Society, Shamanism, and Folklore." *Sino-Platonic Papers* 60. *Sino-Platonic Papers* 60. www.sino-platonic.org/complete/spp060_dagur_folklore.pdf.

Timofeyev, Oleg Anatolyevich. 2003. Russian-Chinese Relations in the Amur region, Mid-19th – Early 20th Centuries. Parts 1 and 2 [Тимофеев Олег Анатольевич. Российско-китайские отношения в Приамурье (сер. XIX – нач. XX вв.). Часть 1+2]. Blagoveshchensk: Blagoveščenskogo Gosudarstvennogo Pedagogical University.

University of Texas Library. n.d. "China-USSR Border: Eastern Sector." Perry-Castañeda Library Map Collection. http://www.lib.utexas.edu/maps/middle_east_and_asia/china_ussr_e_88.jpg.

Wood, Alan. 2011. *Russia's Frozen Frontier: A History of Siberia and the Russian Far East 1581–1991.* New York City: A&C Black.

Zhang, Yongjin, and Rouben Azizian, eds. 1998. *Ethnic Challenges beyond Borders: Chinese and Russian Perspectives of the Central Asian Conundrum.* London: Palgrave Macmillan.

Chapter Six

Soca, Utopia and Resistance

Shauna Rigaud

SOCA'S PROPENSITY TO PRIORITIZE MELODY OVER LYRICS HAS positioned it as a music genre that puts pleasure above the political. Its rise as carnival music sets it apart from calypso by offering rhythm and a pace-centred sound instead of the social commentary often found in calypso. This assumption of soca's use value relegates it to "jump and wave" music. Thus, it was not surprising when rising soca artist Nailah Blackman proclaimed to her followers on Twitter, "People might hate me for saying this, but why does soca have to be a fake genre? Why does it always have to be happy, party, clean, like why can't we just talk about some regular shit" (@nailahblackman, 4 September 2019). Blackman's tweet reinforced the idea that soca was only and could only be concerned with happiness and parties. It did not and could not portray "regular shit" because it was framed by the pleasure of carnival. However, Blackman's tweet was met with comments from DJs, other soca artists and fans who rejected her claim. "Regular shit", they insisted, *was* discussed in soca music. Twitter users flooded her comments and mentions, listing soca songs and artists that regularly dealt with the lived realities of Caribbean people, the ugly and the beautiful, the "regular shit" that Blackman claimed was missing in the genre. Her assertion, though, continues a narrative about soca music that removes it from its origins of resistance and, as such, soca struggles to reclaim that space even in the imagination of some of its artists.

Soca music as a genre has grown in popularity since its introduction into the musical culture of Trinidad Carnival in the late 1980s. As an art form now closely associated with Trinidad's Carnival, scholarly discussions of soca can be tied into larger conversations about carnival in the Caribbean and its role in identity formation, performance, and culture. Often, soca is seen in conversation with calypso music and as part of calypso's development. Scholar Lorraine Leu described soca music as a successor to calypso (2000, 49). In Leu's discussion of the development of the genre, she highlighted the relationship between calypso and soca, including the contention between the two as the latter carved out a space for its artists and performances. This kind of opposition, Leu mentioned, connects to conversations about technology's role in music's development. Nabeel Zuberi (2001) noted that musical developments can be seen as "either an older organic and authentic form of musical expression representing a community has been destroyed by the new technologies, or that ethnicity melts away in this synthesized global melange" (132). For some, because soca is seen as the young people's sound and the sound of carnival, does not mean it is necessarily disengaged from the political. Indeed, as scholars like Leu have noted, soca being disengaged from the political is far from the case. Leu (2000) pointed to an opportunity for soca to open new types of participation in the culture in terms of race, class and gender. Leu (2000, 51) noted that female artists are much more prevalent in the soca scene than in the history of calypso, and audiences see cross-ethnic performances as a regular experience, harkening back to soca's origins but also soca's role as part of a continued space of marking Trinidad identities. Jocelyne Guilbault (2004) also explored soca's relationship with identity politics in her article, "On Redefining the Nation through Party Music". Guilbault examined how soca, as a new sound, "redraws the map of carnival space" (2004, 230). Guilbault laid out some critiques of soca as being part of the commodification and globalization of carnival, with some alleging that soca artists have "fallen prey to the 'rules' of the global market: turning original musical compositions (here meaning traditional calypso) into cultural commodities and adopting foreign aesthetics at the expense of local musical values" (232). However, what Guilbault highlighted is that soca artists see the genre as an attempt to understand and display the nation in contemporary terms, extending it beyond the local scene (234).

While most conversations of soca focus on Trinidad Carnival, Susan Harewood (2008) discussed the effects on the musical industry in Barbados of state policies that regulate and, in turn, create specific ideas about citizenship and identity in Barbados. In regulating calypso tents during the island's Crop Over festival, the NCF mandates that only artists from state-sponsored tents could compete; artists had to be residents of the island for at least five years, and lyrics had to be vetted (2008, 214). These regulations for the calypso tents also became the rule for its soca competition, Soca Royale. Trinidad, however, opened up its Soca Monarch, now renamed International Soca Monarch. Artists outside of Trinidad and Tobago were welcomed to perform for the first time in 1996. The International Soca Monarch competition thusly marks itself as a competition of the very best in soca music and winning it means that the artist has reached the high standards of Trinidad soca, the mecca of soca music.

While melodically and lyrically distinct from calypso, it can be argued that soca also highlights the same political, social and cultural issues as calypso in its griot form. Megan Sylvester (2020) made this claim in her research, asserting that "soca music, like calypso music can illustrate important social and political issues such as, prosperity or poverty, economic depression, war, ethnic and racial rivalries and tensions, gender relations and orientation, demographic shifts, and culture wars" (109). Sylvester's focus on narratives of resistance in soca explored narratives pushback against respectability, which is "part of the legacy of the colonial system of values" (113), and then reconstruct and redefine lived experiences. Understanding the cultural work that soca does, Guilbault (2010) revealed how soca transmits certain values and knowledges through pleasure (17). In her study, she focused on the social intimacies that happen on stage and in the audience at live soca shows. She embraces the role that pleasure plays and attempts to re-situate soca as more than just party music.

The following discussion attempts to bring together both Sylvester and Guilbault's scholarly work to engage in a theory of utopian desires. Soca's reputation as a vehicle for pleasure should not discount its ability to illustrate "regular shit" while expressing utopian desires. Soca music was created in response to real-world needs, resting on visions of hope in difficult situations. Below I offer a history of soca music and, through the analysis of the genre, discuss how feelings of utopia are expressed and resistance is displayed.

RESPONDING TO THE SOUL OF A COUNTRY

Soca music is said to have been created in 1973 by Trinidadian calypso artist Lord Shorty, now known as Ras Shorty I after converting to Rastafarianism. According to Ras Shorty I in a 1995 interview, he wanted to create a "new *energy*" (GBTV CultureShare Archives 1995) among listeners of calypso music that reflected and responded to the political climate and the history of the twin island nation. Trinidad's history as a Spanish, French, Dutch and British colony created a revolving door and constant influx of enslaved Africans and colonists to the island from the metropoles. In 1833, when slavery was abolished, Trinidad, now a British colony, met the new demand for non-enslaved workers with indentured labourers from India. This mix of Europeans, Indians and Blacks started Trinidad and Tobago on its journey as the land of "callaloo". The term Callaloo, a crop and a local dish transported from the Atlantic Slave Trade now described the ethnic mixture of cultures and peoples in Trinidad and Tobago. This blend of history, ethnic makeup and economic challenges as a Caribbean country helped to set the stage for the political unrest of the 1970s that was the catalyst for the creation of soca music.

On 21 April 1970, the government of Trinidad and Tobago declared a state of emergency following Black Power protests against wealthy ruling Indians and Europeans. Anti-Black racism, dating back to colonialism, stratified the country by class and colour, with Afro-Trinbagonians at the bottom. By the late 1960s, the bulk of the population in Trinidad was Black, at 38.6 per cent, followed by East Indian, 32.6 per cent (Sudama 1983, 84). Poverty on the island lead to an increase of unemployment among youth, while at the same time it bred an increase in feelings of nationalism and awareness of racial discrimination (Nicholls 1971, 449). Youth at the time felt that neither the People's National Movement government nor the opposition party, the Democratic Labour Party, was addressing their economic needs. Demonstrations led by mostly Afro-Trinidadians directed their anger towards the minority White elite and the more visible East Indian population. However, leaders of the Black Power Movement on the island understood that to win any power over the government, a united Black and Indian population was needed.

In creating soca music, Ras Shorty I was responding directly to this political crisis. He said that "the purpose of soca…was to bring the East Indian and the African of Trinidad together" (GBTV CultureShare Archives 1995). He wanted to create a new sound that incorporated the youth and was distinctly Trinidadian. To do this, he created a new genre that combined musical instruments of classical Indian music with calypso, creating a fusion that he hoped would unite Blacks and Indians (Kitt 2015). Ras Shorty I originally named the new sound "Sokah" – "so" for the soul of Trinidad (not American soul music, as is often thought) and "kah" representing the East Indian influence, as it is the first letter of the Sanskrit alphabet (GBTV CultureShare Archives 1997). Later, a journalist interviewing Ras Shorty I would mistakenly spell the new genre "soca", and it has remained that way.

Ras Shorty I (as Lord Shorty) recorded his first album with the new sound, *The Love Man* in 1974. He received criticism from other Trinidadian musicians who said that his new music was ruining calypso and disgracing Indian music. Responding to those critiques, Lord Shorty's next soca album, *Endless Vibrations* in 1975, removed the traditional Indian instruments, replacing the dholak with the drums, the dhantal with the triangle and the mandolin with the guitar. He also included disco elements while maintaining the structural integrity of his creation (O'Neill 2016). These changes allowed soca to develop quickly as a new genre and were picked up by other Trinidadian artists, allowing it to become the music of the Caribbean and, more specifically, the music of carnival. Since then, it has evolved into several subgenres: groovy, power, ragga and chutney soca (it is chutney soca that most closely mirrors the original sound of the music) and has been exported to the United States, Canada and England as it has grown in popularity and through the migration of Caribbean people.

FINDING UTOPIA IN SOCA

Before understanding how soca music works to represent utopian values, we must first understand the role of utopia in popular culture. Merlin Coverley's (2010) examination of utopian imagery throughout literature gives us one of the first definitions of utopia from Sir Thomas More's book, *Utopia* in 1516, as an "imaginary place with perfect social and political system; ideally perfect place or state of things" (in Coverley 2010, 9). Coverley noted that this new word inspiring More's title combines two Greek terms, *outopia*, meaning no-place, and *eutopia*, meaning good-place (2010, 9), setting us up to understand utopia as a longing for things not yet realized.

Early scholarly work on the use of utopia in entertainment often goes back to Richard Dyer's "Entertainment and Utopia", a chapter in *Only Entertainment* (2002). In his text, Dyer used the 1930s Hollywood musical as the focal point, exploring the use of representational and non-representational signs to understand the political work of entertainment in general and musicals specifically. For Dyer, the musicals' non-representational signs – colour, texture, movement, rhythm, melody, camerawork – were where problems are resolved and foreclosed through the imaginary resolution of contradiction. The musical's show of abundance, energy, community and excitement presented utopian solutions to the real-world social tensions brought on during the Great Depression. Dyer's essay rejected the notion that entertainment should be dismissed as only entertainment, that is, only part of capitalist consumption. Instead, he takes seriously entertainment's role in its imaginary to produce pleasure and relief as a response to real-world needs. For Dyer, entertainment recognizes material problems and addresses them through specific elements that create utopian hope. Entertainment offers the image of something better, the feeling of hope that our day-to-day lives do not provide (20).

Dyer's goal of recovering a type of imagined hope shares a connection with Bakhtin's (1984) carnivalesque and with Trinidad's Carnival and soca music. Trinidad's Carnival relies on its Bakhtinian nature, the rendering of the social order as "upside-down" (Bakhtin 1984), where dark is light, poor is rich, and absence becomes plentiful. The carnival imagines an alternate world, one of excess and abundance, a utopia that contradicts its actual circumstances. As Megan Sylvester noted (2020), Trinidad's Carnival is influenced by the country's economic and political conditions, ultimately displaying the anti-hegemonic symbols of contestation and opposition through its music:

> Soca music simultaneously appeals to current, social behavioural patterns of debauchery, wantonness and excess. Given the significant shift in lyrics to become more explicit, it may seem odd to suggest that Soca music reflects similar

political, social and cultural themes as its musical forefather, Calypso music. Nevertheless, my research suggests that Soca music, like Calypso music can illustrate important social and political issues such as, prosperity or poverty, economic depression, war, ethnic and racial rivalries and tensions, gender relations and orientation, demographic shifts, and culture wars. (109)

For Sylvester, the political and social issues highlighted in soca lyrics represent what she calls narratives of resistance, "the antitheses to established heteronormative and hegemonic societal tropes" (2020, 109). Additionally, it is important to note that resistance is not just the act of pushing back against hegemonic tropes. Resistance also comes as imagining something new – imagining hope, imagining desire, imagining utopia.

Dyer's work functions to ground an understanding of entertainment forms and the ways that entertainment produces feelings of utopia in non-representational signs – that is, through contradictory images that address real world needs. Dyer presents categories of entertainment's utopian sensibility, where he aligns the non-representational signs to specific utopian feelings produced by a historic reading of the time, the 1930s. These feelings are "temporary answers to the inadequacies of the society which is being escaped from through entertainment" (1992, 25). In Dyer's analysis, for example, the social tension of scarcity and poverty within society are answered in the musical with images of abundance, imagining the end of poverty alongside the equal distribution of wealth. Fragmentation, the loss of housing and anti-collective action are answered in the musical with images of community and communal interests. Interestingly, Dyer (1992) notes that not all inadequacies of society are addressed in the musical, observing that issues of gender and race are missed out because of dominant ideologies at the time and in the genre. Dyer's work opens us up to think about how other inadequacies in society might be resolved with other utopian solutions and in other genres.

This is where Dyer, Guilbault and Sylvester's work potentially come together. In thinking about the recovery of soca as a genre rooted in the reflection of real-world needs, we can turn to the framework that Dyer offers in understanding utopian desires in entertainment, the ways that Guilbault allows us to think about pleasure in soca reflecting specific pieces of knowledge and values, and Sylvester's claim that soca lyrics demonstrate anti-hegemonic values. Further, if we use Dyer as a model to understand social inadequacies and their opposing utopian solutions, we might fill in the gaps that Dyer's analysis leaves in terms of race and gender and further understand how soca approaches real-world issues through pleasure. Just as soca's response to the social inadequacy of poverty can be seen in its reflection of abundance – drinking rum, excessive partying – we can suggest that soca music addresses racial tensions and discrimination by answering it through the utopian solution of reaffirmation and self-determination. Tensions around fragmentation – within the Caribbean, lack of jobs and housing – are met with lyrics of community and issues of patriarchy are met with female agency. Now, it is important to note in Dyer's analysis that the non-representational signs he sees in the musical are concerned with the contradictory signs seen in its filming and stage productions. Soca music videos do not become widely available until the early 1990s. Soca, like its big sister calypso, maintained much of its performances for live audiences, as it still does. Therefore, we must approach this analysis by looking at both the representational and non-representational signs found later in soca videos. Using Dyer, Guilbault and Sylvester's work, we can examine soca's contradictory lyrical imagery that produces utopian solutions and further etch these narratives of resistance.

"SAVAGE"

Shortly after Lord Shorty introduced the new soca genre, Trinidadian calypsonian Maestro recorded tracks with his take on the new rhythm. The 1976 song "Savage" retells the experiences of the Caribbean through the Caribbean diaspora. Well before the popular use of videos to display the images of soca songs, Maestro used his lyrics to provide the contradictory imagery responding to the needs of Caribbeans.

> New York City
> Don't have money
> Anywhere you walk, that's the talk in New York
> Alien getting the finest women
> Telling their congressman,
> They going West Indian.

Savage
They say we West Indian
Savage
They say we ain't human (1976)

In this first verse, Maestro is recalling the experiences of West Indians abroad and stereotypes attributed to this growing group of immigrants in the United States. Migration was used as an economic tool by the members of the Caribbean diaspora to address the economic situation in their countries. As scholar Janet Momsen (2002) noted, as early as the 1800s, many Caribbeans left their countries to live and work abroad, sending money home, or leaving with their families to carve out new homes and new opportunities (49). Emigration from the Caribbean would slow down during the Great Depression but then, in the late 1950s, domestic work programmes would call Caribbean people to places like the United States and Canada. The opportunity to move away from their islands for work gave immigrants opportunities for social mobility while they financially supported their families back on the island through the remittances they sent home. Yet as both Black and foreign, many Caribbeans were met with hostility. "Savage", speaking specifically to the experiences of Caribbeans living abroad, discusses the discrimination and bias faced by immigrants in the United States. Using the term savage represents a clear contradiction with the self-image of those immigrants and the image projected onto them by those in their new homes. Later in the song, Maestro pushes back on this idea of the West Indian's inhumanity. He says,

Strong like lion, hard like iron.
They start to protest
How we does zest without rest (1976)

Maestro's use of "lion" is perhaps a call back to Africa, as an Afro-Trinidadian himself. The imagery of the lion represents strength and even stateliness which, while contradictory to the idea of a "savage", is also playing with the term. Similarly, his use of the image of iron is a reminder to the West Indians listening that they are resilient, hard-working and steadfast. Maestro conjuring up images of the savage to define and redefine the humanity of Caribbean immigrants is part of an intentional reimagining of this experience for immigrants, pushing back on stereotypes used to discriminate and oppress.

"FULL EXTREME"

With the colonization of the Caribbean archipelago in the 1600s, there began a creation of economies that created a flow of both human and natural resources between the colonized and colonial state powers. The development of plantation economies in the Caribbean created monocrop economies with small islands that depended economically on the colonial state and the shift of the world market. As Winston Griffith said, "The laissez-faire philosophy of colonial governments resulted in a monocultural economy, the neglect of domestic food production, the absence of economic linkages and of a manufacturing class, the export of the surplus, the creation of a psychological dependent mentality and no significant material improvement in the social conditions of Caribbean peoples" (2010, 507).

The challenges of these small island economies, both as colonial nations and later independent states, were often taken in up the music of the times. Soca would be no different. In 2015, Trinidad would fall into an economic recession that would ignite the lyrics for Ultimate Rejects' 2016 release, "Full Extreme".

Tell dem ah feeling good
Like a new machine
Like morning dew fresh on the scene
And we go party to the full extreme
And light it up
With gasoline
Oh lord the city could burn down
We jammin still we jamming still
The building could fall down
We jammin still we jammin
Just hold them and wuk them
Hold them and wuk them
No we doh business
Go get on like yuh doh business

Free up like yuh doh business
Woiii go get on like yuh doh business
Woiii now we doh business

Recession doh bother we
Promote a fete and you go see
How we go party to the full extreme
And light it up with kerosene
Oh god the treasury could burn down
We jammin still we jammin still
Economy could fall down
We jammin still we jammin
Just hold them and wuk them
Hold them and wuk them
No we doh business (2016)

In 1866, Trinidad's first successful oil well was drilled, allowing Trinidad to diversify its economy in ways its neighbours to the north could not. Yet it was not until the 1950s that oil became a primary resource for the island (Ministry of Energy and Energy Industries n.d.). By the 2000s, Trinidad's oil and gas resources made up about 40 per cent of its GDP and 80 per cent of its exports. However, by 2014 energy prices were steadily declining and by 2015 the Central bank of Trinidad and Tobago had declared the twin island nation in an official recession (*Jamaica Observer* 2015). In the song, the group calls out these economic problems while clarifying that the problems will not stop them from having fun. In fact, they cannot be hindered by the issues of the economy and the country, said that "they feel good, like a new machine and like fresh morning dew". The worries of the economy will not stop them from enjoying their lives. This is an important assertion to make during hard times. The group's lyrics are not only a reminder but also a demand for revellers to not be swayed by the economic hardships that they may go through individually or as a country and to "party to the full extreme". Additionally, we can see some elements of Dyer's non-representational signs at work. In the official music video, the director moves the viewer from scenes of burned-out cars in the middle of an empty Port of Spain road, with the artists jumping and dancing on top of them to cuts of large performances of the songs and at parties with audience members singing and dancing to the music. The contradictions that those two images give us bring us to the framework that Dyer provides. The social tension here is poverty and exhaustion met with scenes of energy and abundance. Additionally, as the video progresses, the four group members appear to grow in size as masqueraders and spectators are added to the scenes of the empty streets, which can connect us to this utopian solution of abundance.

"OLE AND GREY" AND "LUCY"

As noted earlier, the soca genre opened up the performance arena to women in a way that calypso never did, so to have a conversation about utopian solutions for social tensions of gender, we must begin with a conversation about calypso and women. Scholars note it was, in fact, the artistic work of poor, lower-class women in the 1800s that contributed to the art form that would give birth to calypso as we know it (Hughes-Tafen 2006, 55). The tradition of creating and singing songs to transmit stories of their lives and the lives of members of the community came in the form of witty, vulgar and comedic storytelling by Jammettes, the name given to lower-class women and Chantuelles, also lower-class women who sang in the streets of Trinidad and led songs during kalinda rituals.

While the traditions of calypso were founded in the public performances of Black women, as calypso grew in popularity and became paramount to the carnival tradition in Trinidad, women would be removed from public performances. Respectability politics would emerge, embedded in a Black nationalist agenda that looked at Black women as icons of virtue, while simultaneously inscribing onto them ideals of White supremist and colonial gender roles. As Denise Hughes-Tafen (2006) noted, "Underlying the colonial and national agendas was thus the issue of control that attempted to keep women out of public spaces such as calypso performance in favour of confining them to the realm of the private as home makers, faithful Christians and wives. This desire did not fit in with the realities of non-white women living in slave societies" (60).

With men steering the direction of the genre, calypso more often articulated their lives, leaving little space for women to voice their experiences. Women would become "a topic to be spoken about rather than to be actively included" (Billy 2016). By the 1960s, independence, Black Power and feminist movements in the Caribbean would start a shift in calypso music and its performance. Male artists would begin to celebrate the Caribbean woman in song, rejecting European standards and seeking to foster a new sense of pride in the nation's women (Smith 2004, 41). But it would be the female calypsonian and later soca artist who would ultimately edge herself into the scene and speak to her own experiences. In soca music written by women, gendered norms and identities are explicitly rejected. Female artists renounce the ideas that would deny their sexuality and relegate them to the private space. The ideas of womanhood constructed through a Eurocentric, colonial lens are quickly tossed aside for new images of the Caribbean woman in full control of her own body. In Patrice Roberts's 2015 song, "Old and Grey", she professes her love of carnival through her active participation long after some would find it appropriate. Roberts says:

I outta mi mind, looseness in mi waist /Not ah ounce ah shame
Mashing up mi spine, making up mi face/Not ah ounce ah shame
They done know me a'ready/Wen it come to party
I does wine 'n go down, wine 'n go down, wine 'n go down
Full stop/Now everybody/They does talk about me
With mi hand in d air /'N rum in mi head
Now i doin it/'Til ah ole n grey (2015)

Roberts fully embodies this rejection of the ideal of a respectable woman. She asserts she does not have "an ounce of shame" during her participation in the revelry of carnival. She urges others to look on as she dances to the music and ignores disapproving looks because she is engaging in this act of public pleasure.

In the music video, Roberts spends most of her time dancing alone with the backdrop of the Caribbean behind her – wooden houses and lush green fields. The imagery goes back and forth between her, dressed in full masquerade attire and a full green body suit. Through the scenes, an older woman can be seen picking up pieces of Roberts's costume and another dancing to the lyrics by herself, in direct contradiction to Roberts's youthful body. Additionally, the video presents several cuts of older men dancing by themselves or joining in the scene with Roberts and her small but youthful group of dancers. Just as the older women, the older gentlemen represent a clear contradiction to the exhibition of youth as part of the song.

Similarly, Destra Garcia sings about participating in the pleasure of carnival and soca in "Lucy".

> I grew up as a real good girl/Always home, don't go nowhere
> As soon as I was introduced to Carnival/Dey say I loose
> All down on di ground/Wukkin', wukkin' up mi bottom and it
> Draggin', draggin' all ova town/And dey say I Lucy
> Was neva a partiah/My school bazaar I used to go
> But since I was introduced to Bacchanal
> Dey say I loose/When I drop it hawt
> An I winin' on top di speaker box/An I grindin' an I don't want to stop
> And dey call me Lucy/I looser than . . . Lucy
> I sweeter than juicy/ Dis carnival have meh so damn loose, hey
> Get loose, ah weh yuh get loose (2015)

Garcia's alternate personality, "Lucy", manifests after learning about the carnival and participating in its bacchanal. As Lucy reminisces about her indoctrination to carnival, she recalls that "she grew up as a real good girl", reminded listeners that soca and carnival were not suitable behaviour for respectable women. Hughes-Tafen (2006) explained that early public ordinances prohibited the participation of women calypsonians and social pressures restricted their participation (59). In participating in carnival, Lucy embraces the stereotypical images of "loose" women and harkens us back to the "vulgar" woman of the Jammettes and Chantuelles that were part of early carnival celebrations.

Garcia's official music video is a sharp turn from other videos in the genre at the time, as it is a full animation. The video follows Lucy as a young girl watching women dance on her television – her introduction to bacchanal. The video, which also acts as a lyric video, features bright and vibrant colours and animations of women rolling and swinging their hips to the music. The pleasure produced through watching women enjoying the music and dancing with no limitations pulls Lucy into imagining herself as the main character of the show and, later, the dancehall. The kind of dreariness that might be part of a society that is concerned with the respectability of women is completely contradicted by the brilliant colours and exaggerated bodies that the video depicts.

"LEAVE ME ALONE"

Violence against women gives us another place to uncover the work of resistance that soca music performs. Violence against women has long been an issue, as ideas of patriarchy are often reinforced using violence. Kamala Kempadoo (2004) noted that Caribbean men use sex as a primary means to exert control over and to inflict physical harm on women. Further, she explained how musical language assists in this type of violence in the uses of the terms "stabbing", "nailing", and "slamming", all metaphors for sexual acts performed by men that double as dance terms in soca and dancehall music (3).

In 2012, Antigua's biggest soca band, Burning Flames, released the song "Kick in She Back Door". It quickly became a hit across Antigua, winning Antigua's soca road march, and was subsequently picked up by the rest of the Caribbean and soca lovers overseas. The song was a catchy, groovy soca mix that incorporated the storytelling style of so many other soca and calypso tunes before it. But the story that it told seemed to promote domestic violence and rape and received heavy pushback from women's agencies in Antigua. So, in 2016, when the seventy-seven-year-old artist Calypso Rose released the groovy soca track "Leave Me Alone", many saw the song as an anthem for women and a campaign against violence against women.

> Boy doh touch me/Like you goin crazy.
> Let go me hand/Lemme jump up in d band.
> I dont want nobody/To come and stop me.
> Leave me let me free up/myself let me jump up.
> So leave me alone/I aint goin home (2016)

The over-sexualization of Black women during carnival often makes women open targets for unwanted harassment on Carnival Day. Kamile Gentles-Peart (2016) shares in her book, *Romance with Voluptuousness: Caribbean Women and Thick Bodies in the United States*, that the sexualization and globalization of carnival often acts to empower women while at the same time re-enacts male patriarchal stereotypes of women as sexually available (18). This is eerily reflected in the 2016 murder of Tiarah Poyau at New York City's J'ouvert Carnival Mas because she refused to dance with a man. Her murder would send shockwaves through the Caribbean community and would further emphasize the need to respond to this type of violence through soca music. Calypso Rose's "Leave Me Alone" was a direct response to the harassment and violence that women face under systems of patriarchy. The song reaffirmed the women's right to enjoy a carnival free of harassment as a utopia. The music video cuts between scenes of Calypso Rose and a woman who has essentially run away from her boyfriend to enjoy the Carnival Mas. While she is running through the streets of Trinidad on Carnival Day, her boyfriend is desperately looking for her. It is not until the end of the video that he finds her and pulls her away from the revelry. In their conversation alone, she can convince him to enjoy the carnival, and they head back into the parade of the band. Again here, we find the social tension of dreariness – monotony and predictability – contrasted with the excitement and gaiety of the carnival.

CONCLUSION

Soca's infectious soundtrack moves its listeners both literally and figuratively to places of pure pleasure. Its pulsating rhythms instantly cause revellers to sway, gyrate and bounce, and its lyrics asked them to "forget your troubles" and "lose yourself" in the music. Soca has always held this power: to make people feel, to leave their cares behind. It asserts West Indians are the happiest people and the West Indian region is the best place to live despite the area's political, social and economic challenges. Within its music, one can find not only utopian solutions to these real-world issues but also narratives of resistance that should not be dismissed just because they are bound up in pleasure. Revealing these utopian solutions demonstrates how soca continues to be, in fact, real.

Here, we have been able to look at just a few soca songs and we have begun an analysis of some of its music videos to uncover how utopian solutions present themselves through representational and non-representational signs. We have been able to see how resistance, utopia and pleasure can be tied up together. This kind of examination is far from finished, but can be furthered by looking closer at soca music produced during different epochs in the Caribbean's political development. The hope here is to continue this reclamation of soca as a space where both politics and pleasure are welcomed.

REFERENCES

Bakhtin, Mikhail. 1984. *Rabelais and His World*. Bloomington: Indiana University Press.

Billy, Dizzanne. 2016. "The Rise of Calypso Woman." *Words in the Bucket* (blog), 10 October 2016. https://www.wordsinthebucket.com/the-rise-of-calypso-woman.

Calypso Rose. 2016. "Leave Me Alone." Single.

Coverley, Merlin. 2010. *Utopia*. Harpenden: Pocket Essentials.

Dyer, Richard. 1992. *Only Entertainment*. 2nd ed. London: Routledge. https://doi.org/10.4324/9780203993941.

Garcia, Destra. 2015. "Lucy." Single.

Gentles-Peart, Kamille. 2016. *Romance with Voluptuousness: Caribbean Women and Thick Bodies in the United States*. Lincoln, Nebraska: University of Nebraska Press.

Gentle Benjamin. 2010. "GBTV CultureShare ARCHIVES 1995: RAS SHORTY I 'Interview' Seg#1of2." YouTube video, 3 October 2010. https://www.youtube.com/watch?time_continue=122&v=xoYM97IqrNk.

———. 2012. "GBTV CultureShare ARCHIVES 1997: RAS SHORTY I & AVION BLACKMAN." YouTube video, 29 April 2012. https://www.youtube.com/watch?v=gpLUUlX39ZE&t=620s.

Griffith, Winston H. 2010. "Neoliberal Economics and Caribbean Economies." *Journal of Economic Issues* 44 (2): 505–12. https://doi.org/10.2753/JEI0021-3624440223.

Guilbault, Jocelyne. 2004. "On Redefining the Nation Through Party Music." In *Carnival: Culture in Action – The Trinidad Experience*, edited by Milla Riggio, 228–40. New York: Routledge.

———. 2010. "Music, Politics, and Pleasure: Live Soca in Trinidad." *Small Axe: A Caribbean Journal of Criticism* 14 (1): 16–29. https://doi.org/10.1215/07990537-2009-041.

Harewood, Susan. 2008. "Policy and Performance in the Caribbean." *Popular Music* 27 (2): 209–23.

Hughes-Tafen, Denise. 2006. "Women, Theatre and Calypso in the English-Speaking Caribbean." *Feminist Review* 84 (1): 48–66. https://doi.org/10.1057/palgrave.fr.9400300.

Jamaica Observer. 2015. "Trinidad and Tobago 'Officially in Recession.'" *Jamaica Observer*, 5 December 2015. https://www.jamaicaobserver.com/news/Trinidad-and-Tobago--officially-in-recession-.

Kempadoo, Kamala. 2004. *Sexing the Caribbean: Gender, Race and Sexual Labor.* London: Taylor & Francis Group. http://ebookcentral.proquest.com/lib/gmu/detail.action?docID=199612.

Leu, Lorraine. 2000. "'Raise Yuh Hand, Jump up and Get on Bad!': New Developments in Soca Music in Trinidad." *Latin American Music Review / Revista de Música Latinoamericana* 21 (1): 45–58. https://doi.org/10.2307/780413.

Maestro. 1976. "Savage." Single.

Ministry of Energy and Energy Industries. n.d. "Historical Facts on the Petroleum Industry of Trinidad and Tobago." Government of Republic of Trinidad and Tobago. Accessed 30 November 2021. https://www.energy.gov.tt/historical-facts-petroleum/.

Momsen, Janet. 2002. "The Double Paradox." In *Gendered Realities: Essays in Caribbean Feminist Thought*, edited by Patricia Mohammed, 44–55. Kingston, Jamaica: University of the West Indies Press.

O'Neill, Connor Towne. 2016. "Ras Shorty I: The Soul of Calypso." *Red Bull Music Academy*, 1 June 2016. https://daily.redbullmusicacademy.com/2016/06/ras-shorty-i-the-soul-of-calypso.

Roberts, Patrice. 2015. "Old and Grey." Single.

Smith, Hope Munro. 2004. "Performing Gender in the Trinidad Calypso." *Latin American Music Review / Revista de Música Latinoamericana* 25 (1): 32–56.

Sylvester, Meagan A. 2020. "Narratives of Resistance in Trinidad's Calypso and Soca Music." *Cultural and Pedagogical Inquiry* 11 (3): 105–16. https://doi.org/10.18733/cpi29507.

Ultimate Rejects. 2016. "Full Extreme." Single.

Zuberi, Nabeel. 2001. *Sounds English: Transnational Popular Music.* Chicago: University of Illinois Press.

Chapter Seven

Rebel Salute
A Birthday Party the World Attends

MELVILLE COOKE

LOCAL PULL PRECEDES GLOBAL REACH

REBEL SALUTE IS A LARGE-SCALE OUTDOOR JAMAICAN POPULAR music festival staged on the weekend closest to 15 January, the birthday of Rastafarian vocalist Patrick 'Tony Rebel' Barrett, whom the event celebrates. The 2019 staging at its current home on Jamaica's tourism-focused north coast at Grizzly's Plantation Cove in Priory, St Ann, was over two days, 18 and 19 January, while the first Rebel Salute was a one-day event on 14 January at Fayor's Entertainment Centre in the mid-island town of Mandeville, capital of Manchester parish. At the first staging of Rebel Salute, vocalists performed to recorded music played by a sound system and the second highest proportion of patrons by location came from Jamaica's capital, Kingston, sixty miles away (ninety-six kilometres) (Cooke 2018c). Nineteen years later, in 2013, Rebel Salute was relocated to its fourth and current home, four miles (six kilometres) from renowned tourist destination Ocho Rios, and simultaneously expanded to two days. There were so many overseas patrons that, ahead of the 2018 renewal, Jamaica's minister of culture, gender, entertainment and sport, Olivia Grange, publicized a Jamaica Tourist Board's (JTB) finding that the festival had the highest proportion of overseas patrons among any entertainment event in Jamaica (Lyew 2017).

Tony Rebel attributed the finding to a 2013 JTB Rebel Salute audience survey, which found that over 38 per cent of the patrons were visiting the island specifically for the event (Cooke 2018c). In January 2018, he suggested that the proportion of visitors in the audience was much higher than in 2013, pointing to the organizers' own data collection at the entrance and online ticket sales, which showed that patrons had come from the United States, Canada, England, Belgium, Spain, Italy, Trinidad and Tobago, Barbados, St Kitts and Nevis, and St Maarten, among other countries. He said, "I have no doubt right now that we have doubled that, or gone to one and a half times that" (Cooke 2018c). The impact went beyond the festival and its associated physical locations, as fifty-six of the 2013 overseas visitors stayed to go to other places in Jamaica (Campbell 2014). Queen Ifrica, Tony Rebel's partner and a consistent Rebel Salute performer, identified Dubai, Israel and the Czech Republic among the countries from which the festival has attracted visitors (Campbell 2014). In 2015, Justice Minister Mark Golding said the JTB's survey of Rebel Salute 2014 showed 35 per cent of the audience comprised overseas visitors, most of whom were in Jamaica specifically for Rebel Salute and many of whom came from outside North America, especially from Europe (Cooke 2015b).

Tony Rebel has seen his birthday party's patronage expand from strong local support, as at the inaugural staging, people from Manchester comprised the bulk of the audience, followed by people from Kingston, then St Elizabeth (a parish neighbouring Manchester to which Rebel Salute eventually relocated) and then St James, which is on Jamaica's north coast (Cooke 2018c). After a single staging at Fayor's, the event changed venues to Brook's Park, also in Mandeville, then the Port Kaiser Sports Club in St Elizabeth in 2000, which is where Tony Rebel says he saw the overseas visitor presence growing significantly (personal communication, 29 April 2010).

It is serendipitous that Tony Rebel's birthday falls a month after the official beginning of Jamaica's winter tourist season on 15 December. It runs for four months until 15 April. The reason for Rebel Salute's creation and continued existence, its genesis as a birthday celebration, is reiterated by the organizers before and during each staging. This reinforcement is exemplified by Tony Rebel marking his fiftieth birthday on stage with his children at Port Kaiser in 2012. Also contributing to Rebel Salute's pulling power is that it is one of three annual long-running events in the stage show format – large-scale, extended outdoor events where artistes perform to music played by a band – in Jamaica's annual entertainment calendar. The other two are the week-long Reggae Sumfest festival in Montego Bay, St James, also on Jamaica's north coast and held in July, and the one-night GT Taylor Christmas Extravaganza, held on Christmas Day near Black River, St Elizabeth, on Jamaica's south coast. They are the survivors of a once crowded Jamaican stage show scene, which sometimes saw over twenty stage shows being held between 1 December and 1 January (Cooke 2018e). However, in 2018, the Jamaican government started the Reggae Icons Concert as a centrepiece of Reggae Month (February), a free event in Kingston designed to attract a broad spectrum of Jamaicans and encourage visitors to experience Jamaican popular music in its own home (Cooke 2018d). In 2019, it was announced that Reggae Sunsplash would return in 2020, running from 6 to 8 November, and would be staged at Grizzly's Plantation Cove (Johnson 2019). It had been previously staged at those grounds (then named the Richmond Estate) in 2006 (field observation) as a one-off return of the pioneering Jamaican music festival, which was held from 1978 to 1998 (Cooke 2012). The Boxing Day concert, Sting, was cancelled after its 2015 staging, returning in December 2022 at Grizzly's Plantation Cove before moving back to its accustomed Jamworld, Portmore, St Catherine location in 2023.

NO MEAT, DRUGS, ALCOHOL, LOW SPONSORSHIP

Rebel Salute is organized by Organic H.E.A.R.T., a group of companies run by Tony Rebel and his family, who are predominantly Rastafari. Rastafari, the Jamaican spiritual practice focused on the divinity of His Imperial Majesty Haile Selassie of Ethiopia, emerged in the 1930s and became indelibly associated with the country's music product in the early roots reggae period of the late 1960s to early 1970s. Summarized in Cooke (2018a, 327–29), Nettleford (1978, 1998) and Hill (2013) have both noted that this music output helped to reconcile Rastafari with the general Jamaican society after early resistance and friction. The discord peaked in 1963 with the Coral Gardens incident in Montego Bay and the subsequent crackdown by the

Jamaica Constabulary Force, resulting in open state repression, as noted by Augier, Nettleford and Smith (1962), Campbell (2009) and summarized by Cooke (2018a, 327–29). Holt (2002), as cited in Carah (2010), said that the advertising industry thrives on the production of difference, while Kilbourne (2000) pointed out that "advertising often exploits cultural icons of rebellion and anticommercialism" (60). Rastafari fits the commercial bill in both instances, and the attraction to Rastafari is certainly part of Rebel Salute's authenticity and overseas visitor pull. However, other elements that the Jamaican government has identified as attracting tourists to the country are inherent to the festival.

In August 2016, Minister of Tourism Edmund Bartlett said that of the 2.1 billion people who use social media worldwide, the words most associated with Jamaica are food, music and love – in that order. Within that context, he invited ideas for sustainable festivals and programmes that the Jamaican government could market (Cooke 2016b). Love is central to Rastafari, and hence Rebel Salute, which focuses on Jamaican popular music with a predominantly Jamaican line-up, and food is an essential part of the festival, which had booths lining its perimeter at Port Kaiser and now has an extensive, defined food court at Grizzly's Plantation Cove, which patrons are repeatedly encouraged to visit during the festival (field observation). However, true to its Rastafari roots, the festival maintained a mantra of "no meat, no alcohol" (Rebel Salute n.d.), the exception to the former being fish, which sets the foundation for an overwhelmingly vegetarian menu, differentiating the festival in the market. Queen Ifrica, in her dual role as co-organizer and performer, noted the importance of food to the Rebel Salute experience, said, "Rebel Salute is an event for two days, and tourists enjoy the fact that they can come to an event and spend two nights and hear some real authentic Jamaican music and be exposed to some different cuisine" (Campbell 2014).

However, Rebel Salute's official diet, which is rooted in the Rastafari ethos of Tony Rebel, has implications for sponsorship support, which provides a context for JTB's relationship with Rebel Salute. Tony Rebel said:

> One of the problems that we always had, though, is that because it's a non-alcoholic event and no meat event, is like the companies that are willing and have the money to give as sponsorship is mostly people who sell those kind of

things. And so it pose a serious difficulty on us to get sponsorship. So we have to target different people or different organizations and that was one of the things that . . . it helped – it was a hindrance, and it was also a help because a lot of organizations who have sponsored Rebel Salute really would not sponsor us if we were selling alcohol and it is a big selling point to certain types of organizations. So it has helped in one way and mash-up in a next way. (personal communication, 29 April 2010)

At that point in its Port Kaiser years, Rebel Salute had already had stints with two title sponsors, multinational telecommunications company Cable and Wireless and Jamaican fruit juice provider Tru-Juice, and was in the first year of a three-year deal with multinational carbonated beverage-focused company Pepsi. Perceptions of incongruity between Pepsi and Rebel Salute had been acknowledged at the announcement of the partnership at the Hilton Hotel, New Kingston, on 29 December 2009. Pepsi's marketing manager, Denise Dixon, immediately addressed the doubts that were raised, listing "it does not have that ring" and "an unholy alliance" among the negative feedback they had received and declared that "as with anything new, there will be naysayers and detractors" (Cooke 2009b). The end of Pepsi's three-year Rebel Salute title sponsorship coincided with the final staging of Rebel Salute at the Port Kaiser Sports Club in 2012.

Low JTB support was a long-standing issue, and in 2009, Rebel Salute received J$500,000 from the JTB, while the now-defunct Jamaica Jazz and Blues Festival was granted US$500,000 to support a line-up dominated by North American headline performers (Cooke 2009a). Jahyudah Barrett, Tony Rebel's daughter who is integral to organizing Rebel Salute, said that the JTB's misperception of the event may have led to the low funding, as the organizers estimated then that 10 to 15 per cent of the audience comprised overseas visitors (Cooke 2009a).

FROM SOUTH TO NORTH COAST

The visitors from overseas and locals who stayed overnight while attending Rebel Salute, which at that point was still at Port Kaiser in its one-night format, would have had limited hotel choices. Tony Rebel emphasizes the community tourism boom related to the event, where people who live close to the venue can rent out spaces in their homes. (This is before the AirBnB phenomenon.) The available hotels were on the smaller side, with guest houses in Junction approximately five miles (eight kilometres) away being the closest dedicated guest accommodation option. There are larger hotels, such as the seventy-five-room Golf View Hotel and sixty-five-room Mandeville Hotel, both in the town where Rebel Salute was first held, which is approximately twenty-eight miles (forty-five kilometres) from the Port Kaiser Sports Club. However, Mandeville is not a noted Jamaican tourist destination; the nearest to Rebel Salute's Port Kaiser venue is in Treasure Beach, St Elizabeth, twenty-two miles (thirty-five kilometres) away via the South Coast route. Jahyudah Barrett noted that people attending Rebel Salute stayed in Treasure Beach but claimed to know of hotels that hosted Rebel Salute patrons but were not on JTB's website (Cooke 2009a).

Although there are over twenty accommodation options in Treasure Beach, they are quite small. For example, one of the larger properties, the Treasure Beach Hotel, has thirty-six rooms. Much of the accommodation is in cottages and villas. Emphasizing the community tourism orientation around Rebel Salute in its Port Kaiser years, Jahyudah Barrett said, "the whole community benefits. They have their own business they conduct at that time", added that community members reported to a political representative that it is "the only time they get to eat a *big food*" (make a lot of money) (Cooke 2009a). However, Kenya Barrett, another of Tony Rebel's daughters who is heavily involved in organizing Rebel Salute, opined that this was not valued by the JTB, as "they are thinking that a tourist is not going to want that. That is the idea of tourism. That is where people are going: community tourism. People are giving up the five-star hotel and going to a hideaway spot where they can relax" (Cooke 2009a).

In addition to the dearth of dedicated hotel space nearby, at its Port Kaiser venue, Rebel Salute was some distance from Jamaica's international airports, located in its two major urban centres. The Norman Manley International Airport on the south coast in Kingston, Jamaica's capital, is eighty miles (128 kilometres) away from the Port Kaiser Sports Club and the Sangster International Airport in Montego Bay (often referred to as Jamaica's tourism capital) on the north coast is seventy-one miles (114 kilometres) from Port Kaiser across the width of the island via a largely uncomfortable, winding road network. Using the coastal route, which has a better road surface, increases the distance to 130 miles (209 kilometres). Compounding this was a tendency for traffic jams entering and especially leaving the Port Kaiser Sports Club after stagings of Rebel Salute. In response, organizers brought in the police specifically for traffic control. At one staging, prior to the police managing the traffic, I spent two hours moving less than one hundred metres in a parking area while attempting to leave a Rebel Salute staging (Cooke 2018b).

All these visitor drawbacks – distance from international airports, inferior road networks, lack of large-scale dedicated accommodation close to the venue – were resolved by Rebel Salute's move from Port Kaiser on Jamaica's south coast to Grizzly's Plantation Cove on Jamaica's north coast in 2013 (Gilchrist 2012). The festival was simultaneously expanded to two days, and the organizing entity's name was changed from Flames Productions to the Organic H.E.A.R.T. Group of Companies. However, the event's organizers have made it clear that the relocation was not primarily because of those concerns but because of an issue with the venue. They reported that ahead of Rebel Salute 2013, a large hole was discovered below the Port Kaiser Sports Club's Outfield, posing the danger of collapsing and endangering patrons. Although this hole could have been filled, there was no guarantee of a permanent solution to ensure patrons' safety (Brooks 2012). From the outset of the relocation, when a billboard was mounted at Grizzly's Plantation Cove indicating that it would be Rebel Salute's new home, organizers emphasized the event's consistency. Organizing committee member Maxsalia Salmon said, "Our sign says it all. New home, new format, same Rebel Salute" (Cooke 2012). In making a personal physical connection with the new host parish for the festival, Tony Rebel identified a thread running through his childhood that binds all the Rebel Salute venues, noting that he grew up in Mandeville, where he could see parts of St Elizabeth, then grew up and went to school in St Ann (Coke 2012).

Grizzly's Plantation Cove is along the North Coast Highway, which has significantly reduced travel time between Montego Bay and Ocho Rios while increasing travel comfort. The controlled access Highway 2000 (renamed the Edward Seaga Highway in 2018 (*Jamaica Observer* 2018), honouring a former Jamaican prime minister) has had a similar effect on St Catherine parish, its entrance a short distance from Kingston and Ocho Rios. An increase in hotel rooms in St Ann, affording quick, easy access to Grizzly's Plantation Cove, began before Rebel Salute's relocation. The 600-room Grand Bahia Principe in Runaway Bay, St Ann, was opened in January 2007, and the 856-room Riu Ocho Rios was opened subsequently (Cooke 2012). The expansion continued into the following decade, as the 705-room Moon Palace in Ocho Rios opened in 2015. Because Ocho Rios was a famed tourist destination, the JTB already had a strong presence in the town. But JTB's involvement with Rebel Salute served as part of a push towards concentrating on experiences to supplement the traditional sun, sand and sea tourism model that Jamaica's tourism industry had been relying on.

CULTURAL, REGGAE PRESERVATION

Speaking at the New York City launch of Rebel Salute 2018 on behalf of Tourism Minister Edmund Bartlett, senior Tourism Ministry advisor Delano Seivwright, said:

> Rebel Salute continues to draw Jamaicans and tourists alike in one place to celebrate reggae music in one place. Rastafari and reggae music are the backbone of Jamaican culture, the backbone of our tourism product. Tourism is in strong growth mode, and more and more visitors want varied experiences. To ensure that that growth is sustained, we need more events like Rebel Salute. One of our main strategies for achieving sustainable tourism is by promoting the sector as a catalyst for cultural preservation and enrichment. Recent international tourism trends have pointed to a shift from the traditional 'sun, sea and sand' phenomenon towards interactive, experiential tourism, one of tourism's fastest growing sub-sectors, appealing to markets interested in gastronomy, nature, heritage and cultural experiences like Rebel Salute. (Hines 2017)

The Ministry of Tourism's strategy of "cultural preservation and enrichment" dovetails perfectly with Rebel Salute's long-standing tagline, "The Preservation of Reggae" (Gardner 2022). The emphasis on experience is consistent with a trend towards experiential marketing (Schmitt 1999, in Cooke 2018a), which "approach[es] consumers in an expanded range of everyday spaces, which in turn are often organised around the promotion of brands rather than specific products or services" (Moor 2003, 40). Brand

Jamaica, which the JTB promotes in its efforts to attract tourists to Jamaica, is superimposed on the birthday celebration, establishing an association in media as well as a physical presence at pre-festival events and at the festival with a booth space and advertising paraphernalia (field observation). In moving to St Ann, Rebel Salute's organizers were intent on expanding the festival's range of experiences. Ahead of the 2013 staging, Tony Rebel said, "Rebel Salute was always about a lifestyle, and that includes cuisine, Jamaican folklore and is family oriented". Jahyudah Barrett added, "We have all the elements, but the emphasis has always been on music. We never got to highlight the other elements of this lifestyle. For the 2013 staging, we will be doing more of that. You will see the other elements on an equal footing" (Cooke 2012).

The Jamaican government was not always so supportive of the Jamaican popular music festival experience. Stephen Davis, in *Reggae Bloodlines: In Search of the Music and Culture of Jamaica* (1992/1977), quotes a JTB memorandum of 10 October 1975:

> [A] good part of the attraction of reggae music to its metropolitan audience is the anger and protest of the lyrics. We obviously face a contradiction between the message of urban poverty and protest, which reggae conveys, and that of pleasure and relaxation inherent in our holiday product. In short, when we promote reggae music, we are promoting an aspect of Jamaican culture that is bound to draw attention to the harsher circumstances in our lives. All the articles written on the sound so far do this. Our view is that we should leave other agencies and local music interests to carry the ball from here.

That stance reflected a critical requirement of experiential marketing, that it should be "filled with banal pedestrian content; otherwise, it could take on a political life of its own (like other public spaces)" (Carah 2010, 104). However, that approach seems to have been relaxed by the Jamaican government for Rebel Salute, grounded in Rastafari, which has long used Jamaican popular music to express strong opinions about local and international issues. At the 2014 staging, deejay Queen Ifrica reiterated opinions expressed at Jamaica's 2013 Independence Grand Gala, organized by the Jamaican government and held at the National Stadium, Kingston, on 6 August. The microphone was turned off after Queen Ifrica performed the song "Keep It To Yourself" (which contains anti-homosexual content), demanded that Jamaica's anti-sodomy laws remain and appealed to Prime Minister Portia Simpson Miller for marijuana's legalization (Cooke 2018a). Following protest from the Jamaica Forum for Lesbians, All-Sexuals and Gays (J-FLAG), the Ministry of Youth and Culture (which organized the Grand Gala) said in a public statement that it would "be reviewing the system of contractual engagement of artistes for national events to ensure there is no recurrence of an incident in which one artiste was accused of using anti-homosexual lyrics at Tuesday's Grand Gala – the main Independence event" (*Jamaica Observer* 2013).

When Queen Ifrica reaffirmed her stance at Rebel Salute 2014, there were no public statements from the JTB, the government agency which had a strong sponsorship presence at the festival (Cooke 2018a). At the 2019 staging, Ugandan performer Bobi Wine criticized his government extensively, to a strong positive audience response; and Queen Ifrica appealed directly to Jamaican Prime Minister Andrew Holness, who attended the festival and hugged her from the front of the stage after her appeal, that Jamaica not rescind its laws against buggery (field observation).

MARIJUANA EXEMPTION

In assessing Rebel Salute's attractiveness and authenticity, the connection with marijuana and an evolving Jamaican legal framework around it has to be taken into consideration. In my experience, marijuana is consumed heavily at many entertainment, political and sporting events, especially outdoors, in Jamaica. Rebel Salute has been no different but perhaps comes under more scrutiny because of its inherent connection to Rastafari, many of whose adherents consider marijuana a sacrament. Tony Rebel has said that this marijuana connection may have contributed to what he considers the inadequate sponsorship that the festival has experienced (Cooke 2017).

Ahead of its 2016 staging, the festival was granted an exemption under the Dangerous Drugs (Amendment) Act 2015. A Ministry of Justice fact sheet on the amended Act states:

> Persons who are adherents of the Rastafarian faith, or Rastafarian organiza-
> tions, may apply for an event promoted or sponsored by them to be declared an
> exempt event. In order to apply, the event must be primarily for the celebration or

observance of the Rastafarian faith. Where an event is declared exempt, persons who attend the event will not be liable to be arrested, detained or prosecuted for smoking ganja or possession of ganja at the event or transporting ganja to the event as long as they have complied with the amounts and conditions specified in the order declaring it an exempt event. (Cooke 2015a)

In handing over the official document of the exemption, Justice Minister Mark Golding quipped that what has been happening informally could now take place formally, and Tony Rebel acknowledged that the police have generally exercised discretion with marijuana use at Rebel Salute (Cooke 2015a). Even before the exemption, I have seen only one instance of the police attempting to take marijuana from one of the numerous vendors who ply their trade in the Rebel Salute crowd (in the early 2000s at the Port Kaiser Sports Club). Since receiving the exemption, Rebel Salute has hosted the Herb Curb, a space within the festival's grounds but away from the main audience area, for education on and discussion about issues related to marijuana (Cooke 2016a). Rebel Salute is not the first event in Jamaica to have been granted the exemption – the first was Rastafari Rootz Fest 2015 in Negril, Westmoreland (Cooke 2016a) – but having the exemption adds to perceptions of Rebel Salute's authenticity, an essential component of the experience that adds to the tourist experience.

LOCAL APPEAL

Jamaica continues to experience record tourist figures. The Jamaica Information Service reported on its website on 1 January 2018, that there were 4.3 million visitor arrivals in 2017 (Gardner 2018). In January 2019, the Ministry of Tourism reported on its website that there were 202,192 visitors to Jamaica that month, an increase of 9 per cent over the same period in 2018. The JTB broke down the figures by arrivals in Kingston and Montego Bay, with no distinction for Ocho Rios. Still, ahead of the 2019 staging, Rebel Salute listed its hotel accommodation partners as the Pegasus Hotel (Kingston), Hilton Hotel (Montego Bay), Jewel Resorts, Moon Palace, Jamaica Inn, Melia Braco, Club Ambiance and Cardiff Hotel (all in St Ann) on its website. This was in addition to crediting several other properties, all close to its current home, for their support.

Rebel Salute is to Ocho Rios on Jamaica's north coast in the winter tourist season, Carnival is to Kingston on the island's south coast in the Easter Road March period, and Reggae Sumfest is to Montego Bay in the summer, creating the experience that the JTB is relying on to attract visitors. Rebel Salulte's distinguishing features are its origin and continued presentation as a birthday party for its chief organizer, its mantra of no meat or alcohol, and its connection with Rastafari, which facilitates a marijuana exemption. Rebel Salute has, from the outset, maintained a format of (almost) exclusively Jamaican popular music performers, with the inclusion of Ugandan Bobi Wine at the 2019 staging a rare exception (field observation). Other overseas-based performers, such as British band Aswad and New York–based Shinehead in 2013, tend to be either Jamaicans who have migrated, of Jamaican descent, or closely affiliated with Jamaicans through the country's popular music. Thus, a sense of Jamaican identity is maintained throughout the performances. Reggae Sumfest has, since 2016, also taken on an all-Jamaican popular music performer format with significant success, and Carnival has notably attracted a huge following of Caribbean people. Whether or not their composition of visitors coming for the event will match or surpass Rebel Salute's remains to be seen.

However, with the high proportion of visitors to Rebel Salute has come another concern for Tony Rebel: that more Jamaicans should attend his birthday party. He is insistent that, while many people visit Jamaica for Rebel Salute and when he walks the grounds he sees familiar faces from as far back as Brooks Park, there are many Jamaicans who experience his festival only through the media who should be able to experience the event first-hand, even if only once. He declared, "when I walk the venue I see people who have followed Rebel Salute from Manchester to St Elizabeth and now St Ann" (Cooke 2018c). In terms of a decline in that core Jamaican resident audience, alienated by Rebel Salute's changes, Tony Rebel said, "some people want to perpetuate that. For some reason they find all kinds of things to say" (Cooke 2018c). While there are some social media postings, he said "we have not seen that on the ground" (Cooke 2018c).

Two months before COVID-19 hit Jamaica, shuttering the entertainment industry, the festival was staged physically in January 2020. A hybrid event – combining footage from previous stagings with limited live performances

– was streamed on 15 and 16 January 2021 (Friday and Saturday). Along with Jamaican viewers, the overseas viewership continued to indicate Rebel Salute's strong tourist pull, with persons logging ion from Germany, The Netherlands, Uganda, Madagascar, Brazil, Bermuda and Japan, among several other countries (Johnson 2021). There was no staging, physical or virtual, in 2022 (Perry 2022); and after COVID-19 restrictions were removed in March 2022, Rebel Salute returned to Grizzly's Plantation Cove on 20 and 21 January 2023. It was, by the *Gleaner's* report, a successful resumption with a larger audience comprising persons of varying ages still wanting more after two marathon nights (Lyew 2023). The 2024 staging was held on 19 and 20 January. When I attended the second night, I saw the names and company logos of several sponsors shown repeatedly on digital screens inside the Grizzly's Plantation Cove venue. This indication of substantial sponsorship was confirmed by thirty-six sponsors being thanked on the festival's website, with Pepsi named first and the four government entities included. The level of current sponsorship support for Rebel Salute is a possible area for future research.

REFERENCES

Brooks, Sadeke. 2012. "Rebel Salute, a First for New Richmond Estate Venue." *Gleaner*, 30 December 2012. http://jamaica-gleaner.com/gleaner/20121230/ent/ent6.html.

Campbell, Curtis. 2014. "Rebel Salute Continues to Attract International Attention – Global Fans Seek out Reggae's Mecca." *Gleaner*, 28 December 2014. http://jamaica-gleaner.com/article/entertainment/20141228/rebel-salute-continues-attract-international-attention-global-fans.

Carah, Nicholas. 2010. *Pop Brands: Branding, Popular Music and Young People*. New York: Peter Lang.

Cooke, Melville. 2009a. "Rebel Salute gets $500,000 from JTB." *Gleaner*, 13 December 2009. http://old.jamaica-gleaner.com/gleaner/20091213/ent/ent4.html.

———. 2009b. "Pepsi Doubts Addressed at Rebel Salute Launch." *Gleaner*, 31 December 2009. http://mobile.jamaica-gleaner.com/20091231/ent/ent2.php.

———. 2012. "Rebel Salute's Move Means So Much More – Bigger Tourist Town to Re-enter the Music Festival Market with Two-Day Event." *Gleaner*, 16 September 2012. http://jamaica-gleaner.com/gleaner/20120916/ent/ent1.html.

———. 2015a. "Rebel Salute Given Marijuana Exemption." *Gleaner*, 19 December 2015. http://jamaica-gleaner.com/article/lead-stories/20151219/rebel-salute-given-marijuana-exemption.

———.2015b. "Numbers up for Rebel Salute." *Gleaner*, 20 December 2015. http://web5.jamaica-gleaner.com/article/entertainment/20151220/numbers-rebel-salute.

———. 2016a. "Herb Curb Under Control." *Gleaner*, 13 January 2016. http://jamaica-gleaner.com/article/entertainment/20160113/herb-curb-under-control.

———. 2016b. "Food, Music and Love – Bartlett Identifies Three Words Most Associated with Jamaica." *Gleaner*, 15 August 2016. http://jamaica-gleaner.com/article/entertainment/20160815/food-music-and-love-bartlett-identifies-three-words-most-associated.

———. 2017. "Missing Sponsors Irritate Rebel Salute – Marijuana Still an Issue for Some Companies." *Gleaner*, 10 January 2017. http://jamaica-gleaner.com/article/entertainment/20170110/missing-sponsors-irritate-rebel-salute-marijuana-still-issue-some.

———. 2018a. "Sell off or Sell Out?: Experiential Marketing Using the Massive Jamaican Dancehall Market, 2005–2015." MPhil thesis, University of the West Indies, Mona.

———. 2018b. "Sandz Yes – But Don't Forget Jazz and Blues – Target Traffic Control, Not Only Venue Choice." *Gleaner*, 6 January 2018. jamaica-gleaner.com/article/entertainment/20180106/sandz-yes-dont-forget-jazz-and-blues-target-traffic-control-not-only.

———. 2018c. "Rebel Salute Holds Visitor Record – Organisers Believe Figures Now Higher Than 2013 Survey." *Gleaner*, 7 January 2018. http://jamaica-gleaner.com/article/entertainment/20180107/rebel-salute-holds-visitor-record-organisers-believe-figures-now.

———. 2018d. "One Iconic Event – Annual Concert Projected to Pull in Reggae Pilgrims." *Gleaner*, 18 February 2018. http://jamaica-gleaner.com/article/entertainment/20180218/one-iconic-event-annual-concert-projected-pull-reggae-pilgrims.

———. 2018e. Music and More – Rebuilding the Silly Season. *Gleaner*, 21 April 2018. http://jamaica-gleaner.com/article/entertainment/20180421/music-and-more-rebuilding-silly-event-season.

Gardner, Claudia. 2022. "Rebel Salute Returns January 2023." *DancehallMag*, 23 August 2022. https://www.dancehallmag.com/2022/08/23/news/rebel-salute-returns-january-2023.html.

Gilchrist, Carl. 2012. "Rebel Salute Moves to St Ann." *Gleaner*, 5 August 2012. http://jamaica-gleaner.com/gleaner/20120805/ent/ent3.html.

Hines, Horace. 2017. "Government Salutes Festival." *Jamaica Observer*, 6 November

2017. http://www.jamaicaobserver.com/entertainment/government-salutes-festival_116192?profile=1119.

Hope, Donna. 2006. *Inna Di Dancehall: Popular Culture and the Politics of Identity in Jamaica*. Kingston: University of the West Indies Press.

Jamaica Observer. 2013. "Queen Ifrica's Performance Prompts Ministry Review." *Jamaica Observer*, 10 August 2013. https://www.jamaicaobserver.com/news/queen-ifricas-performance-prompts-ministry-review/.

———. 2018. "It's Now the Edward Seaga Highway.". *Jamaica Observer*, 13 June 2018. https://www.jamaicaobserver.com/news/its-now-the-edward-seaga-highway/.

Johnson, Richard. 2019. "Reggae Sunsplash is Back." *Jamaica Observer*, 28 August 2019. http://m.jamaicaobserver.com/entertainment/sunsplash_173430#disqus_thread.

———. 2021. "A Virtual Salute." *Jamaica Observer*, 17 January 2021. https://www.jamaicaobserver.com/entertainment/a-virtual-salute_212414.

Kilbourne, Jean. 2000. *Can't Buy My Love – How Advertising Changes the Way We Think and Feel*. New York: Free Press.

Lyew, Stephanie. 2017. "Rebel Salute to Continue for Another 25 Years – Adam Stewart Pledges to get Festival More Sponsorship." *Gleaner*, 21 December 2017. http://jamaica-gleaner.com/article/entertainment/20171221/updated-rebel-salute-continue-another-25-years-adam-stewart-pledges.

———. 2023. "Great Performances, Surprises as Curtains Close on Exciting Rebel Salute 2023." *Gleaner*, 23 January2023. https://www.pressreader.com/jamaica/jamaica-gleaner/20230123/281994676615455

Moor, Elizabeth. 2003. "Branded Spaces: The Scope of 'New Marketing.'" *Journal of Consumer Culture* 3 (1): 39–60. doi: 10.1177/1469540503003001929.

Perry, Kediesha. 2023. "Rebel Salute on Next Year." *Jamaica Observer*, 22 August 2022. https://www.jamaicaobserver.com/entertainment/rebel-salute-on-next-year/.

Rebel Salute. n.d. "About Us." https://www.rebelsalutejamaica.com/about-us_01_2023/#:~:text=Rebel%20Salute%20has%20maintained%20a,all%20others%2C%20since%20its%20inception.

Chapter Eight

A Celebration of Music, Movement and Memory
The Archival Significance of St Kitts's "Sugar Mas"

STANLEY H. GRIFFIN

ISLAND FESTIVALS IN THE CARIBBEAN, ESPECIALLY CARNIVALS, ARE much more than large crowds enjoying great foods, enticing music, fascinating costumes and vivacious dancing. These annual seasonal events are opportunities for society to recall historic narratives, celebrate communal accomplishments, document current happenings via the signatory and prevailing cultural art forms, and re/present and share new meanings for the festival with its varying characteristic composite elements. Thus, the Caribbean carnival can be considered a storehouse of deliberately selected materials, namely the various cultural expressions, and as spaces to experience the articulation and meanings kernelled in the activities of the festival. The St Kitts and Nevis National Carnival, more popularly known as "Sugar Mas", is held annually in December, with its festivities culminating on New Year's Day with a grand carnival parade through the streets of Basseterre, the capital of the twin-island federation. Sugar Mas bears all the usual features of a Caribbean carnival, with its calypso and soca music, queen and teen talent shows, food fairs and displays. However, there is a strong link between the island's history of sugar production, the customs rising out of the experiences of the enslaved and the Sugar Mas celebration. This chapter is based on historical and ethnographic research methods seeking to analyse the meanings and purposes of a carnival held at the end of the calendar year, a time usually associated with Christmas and New Year celebrations. This study considers Sugar Mas to be a living archive, a celebration of music, movement, and memory jam-packed with expressions of significant historical information, simultaneously documenting and providing access to current details of social value.

Festivals are vital communal activities in small island communities and nations. They are opportunities to celebrate territoriality, commemorate historical events and reinforce cultural identities. For the Caribbean, with its histories of racial stratification and cultural differences, festivals are meeting points for unifying, if only temporarily, its constituents. Islander ways of living and artistic expressions, such as folklore, carnivals, festivals, music and language, differ from other metropolitan mainland nations, which are often the Caribbean's socio-economic colonizers. Thus, festivals are important means of maintaining societal cohesion while challenging the status quo and systemic inequalities and oppressions. Judith Bettelheim, John Nunley and Barbara Bridges, in their examination of Caribbean festival arts, maintained,

> Festivals are no longer regarded as mere rites of reversal, when class struggles and repression can find a public forum, nor as politically neutral expressions. They do provide an arena for negotiations in political power, they simultaneously codify and package vibrant arenas of cultural production. As cultural products, they have superseded traditional social relations as a basis of shared values and sensitivities. Cultural productions have become the generative basis of shared myths, lifestyles, and even worldviews. (n.d., 242)

Festivals in the Caribbean are gatherings with multi-layered meanings and purposes.

Island festivals showcase the cultures that are emerging out of the experiences and histories of the people and are crucial to appreciating the various forms of Caribbean nationalism that have emerged from circumstantial and inherited divisions. Cultural philosopher Rex Nettleford (1995) aptly described this phenomenon of the Caribbean nation: "Despite the diversity of Caribbean life and the surface fragmentation evident in multiple small sovereignties (all with standard bureaucratic rigidities), there are 'submarine' unities manifested in shared cultural identities and sense of community on which functional economic co-operation, if not immediate political integration, can be built" (10). These acts of solidarity are performed in festivals, which are essential elements in the constant evolution of national identities and island economies.

An island festival is, therefore, not an end in itself. Islanders and visitors coming to the island for the festivities see festivals as "a respite from normal routine" imbued with "an ideological sense" (Guerrero 2013, 175). Paulina Guerrero, in her study of Puerto Rican street festivals, posited, "Festivals serve two functions. First is the symbolic inversion of everyday life or the flipping upside down of reality. The second is the mirroring of everyday life during the festival, and this is sometimes a performance of exaggeration or enhancement of everyday events" (175). It is this ability to re-enact, embellish and document ordinary lived experiences that give each island festival its unique content and purposes. Thus, island festivals are windows to the soul of island communities wherein their concerns and commemorations are laid bare and made tangible.

Finally, festivals are vital access points to creating, commemorating and reinforcing traditions that include the cultural expressions that best reflect the socio-cultural interests of its constituents. Memory institutions in the Caribbean, such as galleries, libraries, archives and museums, are debilitated by the dynamics and politics of colonialism and the economics of globalization. Far too often, the holdings marginalize most of its communities with its global northern focus and representation of the small, racialized elite. These works are often written about the island through an imperialist lens while diminishing the inclusion of regional content. Anthropologist Karen Fog Olwig, in her ground-breaking study of the Eastern Caribbean and, in particular, the island of Nevis, observed the use of festivals as means of revitalizing eroding cultural knowledge and re-emphasizing cultural meanings and identities: "The reification of a culture of the past, which these cultural celebrations represent, is not a unique phenomenon. It can be seen to be part of a more general interest in cultural identity, ethnicity and roots which have emerged as people look for local identities in a world which is increasingly experienced as a global ecumene" (1993, 154). For these reasons, Sugar Mas in St Kitts is a key island festival that examines the interconnections of festival, identity, cultural heritage, history, and socio-economic politics on the Caribbean island.

THE GENESIS OF CARIBBEAN COLONIALISM

The island of Saint Christopher, popularly known as St Kitts, has been a site of rich and complex cultural history. St Kitts is a tropical island in the Leeward Islands of the Caribbean Sea of 176 square kilometres (sixty-eight square miles). It is known for its rich volcanic soil and lush mountain ranges at its centre, where the highest peak of the country, Mount Liamuiga, 1,156 metres (3,793 feet), can be found. There are also many rivers descending from the mountains, which provide fresh water to the local population (The World Factbook 2019). Historically referred to as the "Mother Colony of the (British) West Indies", St Kitts was the launching pad of British colonialism in the Caribbean and the site of much of the imperialist activity that marked the European expansion in the region (Simmonds 1987, 277).

When Christopher Columbus encountered the islands Nevis and St Kitts, respectively, in November 1493, he found thriving communities of indigenous Amerindian peoples, namely the Tainos and Kalinagos (Dyde 2005; Beckles 2008). The rock carvings found around the island are evidence of their presence there. By the time British and French settlers landed in St Kitts (in 1624 and 1625, respectively), the Kalinagos had been, according to Hilary Beckles (2008), "inhabiting the islands long enough to perceive them as part of their natural, ancestral, survival environment" (78). Thus, the Kalinagos mounted a fierce and protracted resistance. The British and French united their efforts against the Kalinagos, who by then had established a "poison arrow curtain" that separated the islands captured by the Spanish and those still in Kalinago possession (79). The Anglo-Franco colonizers, rather than try to overthrow the already settled Spanish in the nearby Greater Antillean islands (Jamaica, Cuba, Hispaniola and Puerto Rico), fought the Kalinagos "partly because of the perception that Kalinagos were the weaker, but also because of the belief that Kalinagos were the 'common enemy' of all Europeans and that solidarity could be achieved for collective military operations against them" (79). Once the Kalinagos were defeated, St Kitts became the primary station for British and French expansion into the Caribbean.

After much military conflict between the French and British – who occupied various parts of the island – the French surrendered the island to the British in 1713. This made way for the British to fully develop, initially, a tobacco smallholding economy using white (mostly Irish) indentured workers and, later, a sugar plantation economy based on imported enslaved labourers from Africa. However, the battles between the French and British had already shaped the island's landscape with bases and forts, chief among which was the expansive Brimestone Hill fortress that is listed on the UNESCO World Heritage Site (UNESCO World Heritage List n.d.). This European sparring dynamic also influenced the island's culture. Place names illustrate the tension. The name of Basseterre, the nation's capital, is, like several other place names, derived from French, though its pronunciation is based on English. The island's culture is also fashioned by the lived presence of the white indentured and African enslaved, as found in the island's creole language, St Kitts Creole, which includes traces of French as well as other African and English languages (Lewis 2009).

THE CENTRALITY OF SUGAR

By the turn of the eighteenth century, St Kitts was the richest colony in the British Caribbean per capita because of the trade in sugar. Sugar cane cultivation was central to life in the colony, which included the extensive slave laws, racism, classism and conservative Christianity that crafted the norms and values of present-day Kittitian society. Karl Watson (2003) referred to a statement made in 1676 by an enslaved person in Barbados that describes the reality of plantation life in St Kitts: "The Devil was in the Englishman, that he makes everything work, he makes the Negro work, the Horse work, the Ass work, the Wood work, the Water work and the Winde work" (64). The landscape was transformed into sugar plantations or military fortifications. The natural resources, as described by the enslaved, either worked on or for the plantations. This is in addition to the forced control of the imported human resources. Yet, there were acts of resistance by the enslaved masses. These ranged from overt rebellions, such as the 1690 uprising (Craton 1982; Historic St Kitts n.d.), to instances of marronage (Zacek 2007), to daily acts of defiance. More importantly, the resistance to the system of slavery took on cultural forms, for example, in the retention of rhythms, design of costumes, storytelling and singing calypsos, and the ingredients and preparation of foods, which would inform the island's signature cultural activity called "Christmas Sport". For, as Karen Fog Olwig (1995) maintained, "many aspects of slave culture were not directly oppositional in nature, but rather worked within the institutional frameworks established and recognized by the colonial society" (55). Christmas Sport would be used later to localize and affirm Kittitian identities in the post-independence period.

The enslaved population in St Kitts was emancipated in 1838, as in other parts of the British West Indies, even though that declaration of freedom changed very little on the ground. The drudgery of plantation life continued unabated right until the 1930s, and the labour rebellions triggered similar reactions around the Caribbean. Trade unions emerged out of these riots, and trade unionism became central to renegotiating the economic, political and social structures of Kittitian society, including its cultural expressions. Even with all these political changes occurring, Christmas Sport remained a constant feature of plantation and Kittitian life. Masqueraders, with their fife and drums, would celebrate the Christmas break and dance their way around villages and permitted spaces in Basseterre. Christmas Sport, or masquerade, is also a feature of the Kittitian and Nevisian diaspora as its performance forms part of their "cultural equipage" in Bermuda, the Dominican Republic, the Virgin Islands and other parts of the world (Nettleford 2003, 2).

SUGAR AS POST-INDEPENDENT IDENTITY

St Kitts and Nevis gained its independence from the United Kingdom in 1983 to become the smallest sovereign state in the Western Hemisphere with a population of approximately 53,094 (The World Factbook 2019). Sir Kennedy Simmonds, former Prime Minister of St Kitts and Nevis (1983–95), aptly described the daunting effect plantation society has had on St Kitts. He posited, "the plantation . . . was a total economic institution, which blurred any distinction between economic organization and society on one hand, and chattel slavery, on the other, which deprives workers of any personal rights, including the right to own or cultivate land" (Simmonds 1987, 278). Even with independence, the institutions that built Kittitian society were not intended to support a free, democratic community of citizens. Plantation society contradicted this imagined community, as famously described by Benedict Anderson (1991): "regardless of the actual inequality and exploitation that may prevail in each, the nation is always conceived as a deep, horizontal comradeship" (7). Sir Kennedy Simmonds (1987) accurately described the challenges of a post-emancipation society attempting to decolonize itself while affirming its identities fully:

> The task of undoing the effects of three centuries of colonialism is, of course, not easy. The task defies a unidimensional approach to accomplishing such a human feat. In a very real sense, the ingrained political values and deep-seated economic structure of the past cannot be substantially altered by policies that, at best, are seemingly designed to nibble at the edges of well-established social, political and economic institutions. These institutions, throughout the colonial period, have developed a life of their own and have determined the limits of change and development during the long post-independence era. (285)

The difficulties of surmounting colonial impositions would also be found in the genesis of St Kitts's Carnival. The various racist, classist and religious divisions came to bear on and are contested by the Carnival.

With the announcement in 2005 (Historic St Kitts n.d.b) that the island would close its sugar cane plantations and factory for good to replace this industry with tourism, there was much discussion about the major issues that were rooted in plantation society (Richards 2005). Concerns included the ownership and use of lands and the potential of tourism to fully employ the large labour force once attached to the sugar industry, as well as, more importantly, the cultural identities that were previously grounded in the dynamics of the various sugarcane plantations. In their study, "Developing Sugar Heritage Tourism in St Kitts", Rachel Dodds and Lee Jolliffe (2012) observed the clear links between the island's historic reality and tourism efforts:

> The attractions in St Kitts . . . have a strong connection to both the colonial and post-colonial history of the island, which included sugar monoculture, for

example, the St Kitts Scenic Railway and the plantation inns. Sugar heritage that permeates all aspects of the history of the island is thus woven into the interpretive story of the attractions, as some remains of the industry are still quite evident in the physical landscape and architectural remains, as well as in the intangible culture of local folklore and cuisine (for example, the local sugar cakes). (125)

Some may argue that this effort at industrializing Kittitian plantation heritage may be difficult given the awareness of the horrors and inequities of sugar plantation life. However, Dodds and Joliffe posited that the weak economic infrastructure occasioned by the sugar industry could form the basis for a unique and robust heritage tourism product. They maintained,

> [The island's] sugar heritage as a resource has potential for contributing to sustainable growth and development of the tourism industry in St Kitts. Small-scale sugar attraction development by local entrepreneurs supported by government and with the involvement of community-based organizations and volunteers will be the most suitable way forward. This would ensure that the people of St Kitts directly benefit from the commodification of their heritage, while preserving this heritage for future generations. (126)

The Sugar Mas Carnival demonstrates the possibility of grounding a nation's identities, uniting the society in ways only possible in a carnival while offering a truly unique festival – at a time of year when other markets are not focused on their tourism products. Within and through this celebration of music, movement and memory, St Kitts reaffirms its narratives, documents its present realities and reinforces its economic prowess.

CELEBRATING CHRISTMAS SPORT

> You didn't have to see them to know they were coming! Troupes of masqueraders wearing trinkets and Christmas bells could be heard from afar, backed by the melodious sounds of a string or steel band and the driving beat of the big drum. Here and there, they would stop and have displays. Biblical stories, like David and Goliath, were classics. Slugging matches would break out, and the Sergeant would arrive to pacify and handcuff the belligerents. Clowns and Mummies and Bulls entertained the throngs crowding the streets. (De Baecque 1994, 28)

Jerome De Baecque captures the rhythm, movements and vivaciousness of the various participating characters in his description of a scene of masqueraders performing Christmas Sport. The festivities of Christmas Sport took place traditionally in the two weeks leading up to Christmas Day and Boxing Day (25 and 26 December, respectively). Sugar factories were customarily closed during this time and plantation work ceased, allowing labourers their time to "leh go!" (entailing dance in the streets, sing calypsos and told stories, in addition to preparing special foods that are linked to the festivities of Christmas).

A key feature of the Christmas Sport is the Masquerade. Masquerade is the most colourful of all the other creolized expressions of Christmas Sport (Brathwaite 1974). The art form consists of costumes, drums and movements, which will be value-added features when fused with the imported Trinidad-model carnival. The colourful costume is a central component to the music, movement and memory of performing Christmas Sport. It "consists of several pieces of garments that include a multi-coloured shirt and pants, apron or mantle and cape made of materials of kaleidoscopic beauty and decorated with ribbons, mirrors, handkerchiefs or tassels and small bells. This costume is completed with a decorated wire-meshed mask, a multi-coloured headdress of peacock feathers and a colourful dance wand or thunder axe" (Byron 2004, 32). This traditional dress has been dated back some three hundred years to the days of slavery. With most of the enslaved from the Yoruba-speaking Oyo Empire of West Africa, the design of the costume is replete with Yoruba religious significance. The religion of the Yoruba peoples is founded on ancestor worship. Through spirit possession, the ancestors descend and commune with worshipers. According to Byron, "the costume, therefore, has its origins in the cultural and religious beliefs of the slaves" (32), and this is illustrated in the use of peacock feathers as headdresses.

MEMORY IN DRESS AND MOVEMENT

Halstead Byron showed that the wearing of feathers in Yoruba culture is considered a strong medium for attracting and communicating with the ancestors. Thus, since peacocks were abundant on the island, the giant plumes shed by males in October and November were gathered for use in headdresses during the Christmas season. Several other arguments have been proposed to explain why peacock feathers are gathered and used in this way. One suggestion refers to the mating behaviour of peacocks in which the male peacock dances for the hen before mating. Since the peacocks dance for their mate, the claim is that "peacock feathers are not only beautiful to look at, [but] they are meant [for use in the] dance" (Gaugert 1988, 2). An old Bermudan masquerader offers another plausible explanation that hints at the feelings of self-empowerment that come from participating: "The peacock is a proud bird, so we wear its feathers" (Gaugert 1988, 2). One may, therefore, say that the proud male peacock's feathers on the head of an enslaved and demoralized dancer were a silent yet powerful – and creative – means of resistance against the racist social and cultural oligarchy of the plantation society.

The thread of Yoruba tradition is interwoven in other aspects of the costumes used in Christmas Sport. The mirrors that are sown into the kaleidoscopic cape capture the viewer's image and link that individual to the spirit world. Hence, mirrors are considered "windows to the spirit world" (Gaugert 1988, 1). Likewise, the handkerchiefs and scarves stood for the pieces of cloth that were attached to the dress of Yoruba worshippers at funeral rites. The cowrie shells worn on the priestly vestments of Shango priests are represented by small bells worn on the cape and the legging of the pants. The wire-meshed mask, dyed pink, was used "to mimic the actions of the master and his spouse during the end-of-crop and Christmas celebrations on the plantations during slavery" (Byron 2004, 33). The predominant use of the colour red is also linked to Yoruba mythology. Red is believed to be the favourite colour of the god of thunder, Shango. Thus the costume becomes a visual witness to the Shango beliefs. The thunder axe in the hand of the masquerader signifies the power of Shango. Moreover, the entire masquerade performance of music, dance and dress are all ways to attract and worship this Yoruba deity, Shango.

Christmas Sport was seen as entertainment staged by the labouring poor performers for the pleasure of the ruling elite. Masqueraders will perform songs with movements that jeered at the masters, making light of any notable occurrence of the previous months outside the homes and halls of the plantocrats. Fog Olwig (1993) argued that within this planter-permitted activity were opportunities for "acceptable resistance", and she referred to these acts as "performative culture" (55). Under this label, she listed the singing of work songs in the field, songs that were "rather critical of the slave system" (55). Other performative cultural acts took place "within a framework of traditions closely tied to the patriarchal society of early modern England and therefore of a more inclusive kind" (55) – especially in the Christmas celebrations. Christmas Sport, Fog Olwig rightly stressed,

> represented a challenge to the whole plantation society, because they presented a formally accepted structure through which the enslaved could display their own culture of music and dance, which otherwise had to be performed more or less under cover in the slave villages on the different estates. By boldly displaying this important aspect of their culture within the framework of English folk traditions right in the homes of the planters, the enslaved thus challenged the planters on a cultural terrain which implicated the planters themselvesby making their culture public through traditions of the old English rural society. (57–58)

Resistance, as illustrated by Christmas Sport, was a multi-layered and complex means of pushing back against the hegemonic pressures the enslaved faced on the plantations.

The street also became the site of cultural and political contestation against the establishment. Storytelling, including a form called "Neaga Business", and composing songs were key features of the Christmas Sport. However, these stories and songs not only entertained but also caused violent reprisals that led to increased censorship of performance. In fact, even after emancipation, where masqueraders were now free to parade the street, the players were forced to begin their celebrations in front of the local police station for the performance to be vetted. Nevertheless, this attempt at "imposing a form of censorship on anything the players said or did concerning the rulers that could be considered defamatory, obscene, or even seditious" (Mills and Jones-Hendrickson 1984, 15) did not escape the ingenuity and creativity of the actors who "succeeded admirably in exposing in a disguised form the gross injustices, social hypocrisy and moral deficiencies of the pretentiously superordinate and 'cultured' upper class" (17).

The masquerade also served a pivotal political role on the plantation. During the turbulent labour rebellion years of the late 1930s and 1940s, almost all the territories of the British West Indies were facing strikes from the black working classes. Facing the longest strike in the colony's history, following deadlocked negotiations between the labour union of sugar workers and the plantocracy, Christmas Sport became a negotiation tool. Llewelyn Bradshaw, a trade unionist-politician who later became the first premier of the state of St Kitts and Nevis, cautioned those who participated in Christmas Sports to refrain from such entertaining activities. He believed "they should not entertain bukra [the white elites] any longer because they were the same villains who were intractably refusing to agree to decent wages and working conditions for the labourers" (quoted in Mills and Jones-Hendrickson 1984, 18). Christmas Sport was also a key political weapon in the efforts to protest for improved wages and conditions.

MEMORY IN MUSIC

The masqueraders step out on the street to the rhythms of a three-piece folk band commonly called the Big Drum. The Big Drum comprises the kettle drum, on which a variety of enticing rhythms are tapped out, the bass drum, which holds a constant beat, and the bamboo fife, which thrills the listener with various high-pitched melodies. This band and its instrumentation could be traced to two distant ethnic entities in the Old World. Gaugert (1988) maintained, "this group of instruments played together as an ensemble can be traced to Europe in the late Middle Ages. Fife and Drum bands were popular with British regiments. The enslaved Africans no doubt substituted their 'Big Drum' for the bass drum" (3). Byron (2004) further asserted, "although the drum originated in Africa, the particular make of the Big Drum can be traced to Europe. The kettledrum resembles the snare drum used in military and acoustic drum kits while the bass drum is similar to that of the marching bands" (34). The Big Drum was creolized by using cattle skin to get the required boom and timbre. The Big Drum clearly beats the combination of several cultures into one electrifying pulsation. Like the Big Drum, however, the fife was also creolized. Byron contended that the fife also found its way from Africa: "The fife is a traditional seven-hole wind instrument made locally from the female bamboo plant" (34). As it is now difficult to find female bamboo, PVC and aluminium, other materials have been substituted to fill this musical role. Nonetheless, while the music played for the masquerade dances (to be discussed below) is traditional, the fifer is allowed to play contemporary calypso melodies, from medium to up-tempo, for the Fine Dance.

The masquerades perform six different dances: the Quadrille, Fine, Jig, Wild Mas, Waltz and Boillola. It is indeed noteworthy that the first three dances have French names. Gaugert (1988) attributed this to the French influence and presence on St Kitts, especially during the tenure of Governor Lonvilliers de Poincy. Within this timeframe, French dance instructors toured the world, instructing their Creole citizens on the finer points of French dance routines. The Quadrille dance originated in seventeenth-century France and is the first dance in the masquerade's routine. Dancing at a fairly slow pace, an even number of dancers "pair off, shake hands, bow and then go through a series of structured, well-coordinated movements. Dancers are expected to perform the same movements in unison" (Byron 2004, 33). While the Quadrille had not been introduced into England prior to 1815, Gaugert asserted that "it may very well have been danced in English Great Houses on St Kitts and Nevis before that time" (1988, 3). He, therefore, argued that this instruction trickled down to the dances of the enslaved. As the masquerade drill progresses, greater skill is required from the dancers as movements grow more complex and require greater agility. Each dance move has been traced back and linked to particular African cultures and historic periods, thus making the movements documentary records of particular times and spaces.

The masquerade performance was a source of community pride, especially among working classes on both St Kitts and Nevis. Frank Mills and J.B. Hendrickson noted, "for several years, the people of St Kitts awaited the Masquerades of Nevis, particularly those of Gingerland, Nevis" (Mills and Jones-Hendrickson 1984, 12). While one could not ascertain whether there are any differences or uniqueness in the performances of the various community masquerades, it is quite clear that these dancers are the pride and joy of their neighbourhoods. Christmas Sport was seen as an activity of the labouring poor and unfit for the involvement of the elite sectors of Kittitian society. Christmas Sport contrasted with Eurocentric Christmas activities, which included carolling, religious worship, family time and private social gatherings. In contrast, the masquerade was seen as loud, noisy, disgraceful and vulgar by the Black and Brown middle classes and upper-class Whites of society. Not surprisingly, Christmas Sport was suppressed by the police, even with the support of trade union leadership. Christmas Sport was not seen as a unifying national activity but as a customary activity that formed part of the local Yuletide season. Accordingly, one may presume there were no public opportunities or spaces for the elites of Kittitian society to engage in carnivalesque festivities such as those celebrated in other Caribbean islands, like Trinidad.

INTRODUCING AND LEGISLATING A NATIONAL CARNIVAL

Trinidad Carnival is a pre-Lenten carnival that starts a few weeks after the Christmas holidays with a season of events from calypso singing competitions, themed parties, beauty pageants and teen shows, steel pan orchestra tournaments to food fairs and children's parties. The season culminates in two days of street dancing, partying and costumed bands of revellers parading in the streets from morning till midnight. Dubbed "The Greatest Show on Earth", Trinidad Carnival is a model for national carnivalesque festivals and has inspired carnivals developed in other Caribbean islands (which did not have such customs) and in the cities with a Caribbean diaspora (Business Wire 2012). The idea of a carnival in St Kitts was inspired by and based on the Trinidadian version. According to records at the National Archives:

> In June 1957, Basil Henderson, Major L.N Alphonso, Tony Lawrence, Leroy Coury, Alexis Knight, E Vanterpool and Al Barker formed a temporary committee entrusted with the planning of St Kitts' first Carnival. It was felt that a Carnival along the lines of the Trinidad one would help the economy and give visitors something to look forward to. By the end of that year, St Kitts had its first queen show, Calypso Show and street parade full of colourful troupes. The first one was a resounding success, and soon, plans were underway to make it an annual event. (Historic St Kitts n.d.a)

One may also argue that the carnival model found favour with the elites who desired the opportunity to revel in ways that were distinguished from Christmas Sport:

> Basil Henderson, Secretary of the Steel Pan Organization, returned from Trinidad with the idea of introducing a carnival based on the Trinidadian model. This type of street performance was fast becoming a trend in the Eastern Caribbean. The idea was embraced by the upper classes of society because they saw in it a possibility of an economic recovery by attracting visitors to St Kitts. However, with the introduction of Carnival, the traditional Christmas sports were pushed into background and the public interest was directed towards the Queen Shows, Calypso, and street jamming. (Historic St Kitts n.d.c)

Consequently, there were two separate festivities, though both were arguably carnivals, taking place at the same time and in contradiction to each other, with obviously different participants and audiences. Undoubtedly, the early St Kitts Carnival faced much opposition, especially from the Church – which had difficulty accepting this flagrant form of revelry at a time of year it believed was meant for religious reverence – and from political rivals. As one might imagine, politics in such a small society affects every sphere of life, including its carnivals. Emerging from the politics of the day were several carnivalesque activities, Christmas Festivities, which focused on the traditional Christmas Sport, and from another political corner came "Soul Carnival", which followed the Trinidadian style of carnival. There was no romanticized unifying festival in Kittitian society, as the seriously divided society could not agree on how to come together even for play. It must be noted, therefore, that while Christmas Sport was a community-oriented and community-driven cultural activity, Carnival was an organized event with private investment and divided interests rather than the national unifying event it is today.

In 1971, the government of the day organized a national celebration in which Christmas Sport became a main feature, with bands of revellers participating in the Carnival Parade. An Act of Parliament, the National Carnival Committee Act of 1971, was passed to cement this unified national event further. This piece of legislation outlined how the carnival would be organized, resourced and held accountable for its output and products.

Schedule II of the Act dictated the activities to be held as part of the carnival. This did not quell the politics and challenges facing carnival, as inequities in prizes and performances still blight the event. There are still major questions concerning the authenticity of Christmas Sport performances and the level of attention and investment traditional folk performers and events receive. However, by legislating a carnival, politicians could craft a national space for including all the varying races and classes, including tourists, as part of the national island festival.

St Kitts Carnival evolved again with the attainment of independence in 1983. The carnival reinforced narratives of national unity and cultural identities, seeking to celebrate this next stage in the social and political life of the state. This is a common characteristic of national island festivals in the Caribbean. Carnivals in the Caribbean have been used as a political tool to promote notions of political stability and social unity. Keith Nurse (1998) observed this in his writings on carnivals in the Caribbean:

> The carnivals of Latin America and the Caribbean have evolved to be dynamic and politically engaging . . . Carnivals are a reflection of the configuration of social forces and the conflict that arises from them, as well as the submerged aspirations and tensions of the respective societies . . . Throughout the Caribbean, the carnivals in the post-independence period have been expressions of island identity, regional harmony and black identity. (86–87)

In the 1990s, serious efforts were made to revive and include Christmas Sport in the Carnival. This inclusion of the folk culture helped to nationalize the carnival, linking the masquerade, with its colourful costumes, vivacious rhythms and movements, to nationalism. Masquerade bands were registered, allowing for fairness in the distribution of resources, and local folk culture was introduced into the school curricula. Consequently, when the historical link between the sugar industry and the island's economy was severed in 2005, the idea of a Sugar Mas, the popular nickname for the carnival, took on greater significance. A particular popular Kittitian soca hit, "People's Suga", with its catchphrase, "De people just can't get enough of the Sweetness", seemingly reverberated and reinforced the continuity of the island's identity rooted in the sugar cane in an age of much economic and social uncertainty (South Florida Caribbean News 2006).

The St Kitts Carnival has certainly grown from being a one-week Trin-idadian-style festival with steel pan recitals, formalized calypso competi-tions, carnival queen pageants and parades and street dances. Today, Sugar Mas is now a carnival with a season of its own, starting in November and culminating on New Year's Day (1 January). Besides the many privately organized fetes and grand parties with live performances, there is a wide variety of folk-oriented, youth-focused and community-organized events. Of note are folk shows and exhibitions, food fairs that include the large migrant communities (from the Dominican Republic, Jamaica and Guyana) resident on the island, and Christmas Sport masquerade competitions. The season also encompasses Christmas-focused events, thus including this socio-religious festivity in the kaleidoscopic carnival season.

THE ARCHIVAL SIGNIFICANCE OF SUGAR MAS

Archives are traditionally defined as places where materials or records of enduring value are held, preserved and made accessible for use. It is customary to perceive archival materials as paper-based items bearing priceless details. However, any format – from the kinetic to the textile to the digital – with informational and transactional information can have archival significance. Richard Pearce-Moses suggested that a record ought not to be defined by the format in which the valuable details are inscribed, but by how the item is used and fits into the creator's activity. He posited:

> records are defined in terms of their function rather than their characteristics, the definition is stretched to include many materials not normally understood to be a record; an artifact may function as a record, even though it falls outside the vernacular understanding of the definition. For example, an artefact may serve as a record if it is preserved to bolster human memory or to demon-strate accountability. [Thus,] a record has fixed content, structure, and context. (Pearce-Moses 2005)

Based on this redefinition, the various elements of Sugar Mas can be con-strued as records of Kittitian society.

> All the particular components of Sugar Mas meet the criteria of a record; that is, they have fixed content, context and structure. The cultural elements have

established subject details, with expected performative formations and per-spectives. Additionally, these record items have meanings that are integral to understanding the nation's culture, history and identities. Michael G. Smith (2004) theorized that culture is an important weapon in the movement towards independence and self-realization, especially in societies that are still reeling from the effects of colonialism. He added that "as colonial peoples move to freedom, the connections between their culture and nationalism are important but various. Questions of cultural unity and distinctiveness typically emerge within contexts of nationalist action seeking autonomy . . . cultural distinctiveness has great values for nationalist movements. For a people emerging from tutelage, cultural distinctiveness may be used to justify demands for independence" (364–65).

Undoubtedly, Sugar Mas, as a festival, is a multi-layered, complex island cultural festival that is based on the memory of historical experiences and postcolonial re/constructions of Kittitians. As part of the annual perfor-mances of their cultural expressions and identities, Kittitians have imbued Sugar Mas with representations that are consistent in form and structure yet linked to other articulated forms of their historical narratives, such as the colonial-built environment and architecture, language and culi-nary expressions. Through Sugar Mas, folksongs and rhythms pass down traditional knowledge, while new imaginations and ideologies are voiced through the lyrics of winning calypsos and soca songs.

Accordingly, Sugar Mas becomes an archival repository in which per-sonalities, events and even politics are memorialized and, in the art forms, become records of the Kittitian society. The costumes, foods, calypso songs, performances and even dance movements all capture, store, preserve and re/tell the various stories, beliefs and experiences of the island society. Thus, keen researchers can revisit past times and feelings by interpreting the activities and movements of Sugar Mas. The archival value of oral traditions, kinetic movements and artefactual objects has been observed, especially in other postcolonial societies around the world. As Hamilton et al. stated, "the oral record is not the only alternative to public documentary archives. Literature, landscape, dance, art and a host of other forms offer archival possibilities capable of releasing different information about the past, shaped by different record-keeping processes" (2002, 10). Sugar Mas encompasses all these varieties and should be appreciated as a window into the past and a microscope for looking at Kittitian society.

This is vital for a nation that has a somewhat weak traditional archival infrastructure. The National Archives is a small department of the island's government, with a qualified archivist and an assistant as custodians of the documentary heritage. Victoria Borg-O'Flaherty, St Kitts' National Archivist, wrote, "over the three and a half centuries of colonization [the island] acquired a valuable archive which has only rarely been explored, leading many locals to believe that it did not even exist. The archival collection owes its origins to the administrative and legal activities of the colonial period" (2018, 385). Consequently, the records reflect details that were of importance to the white planter class, with the enslaved being documented as subjugated assets of the white oligarchy. Borg-O'Flaherty rightly asserted, "since power and the ability to create archives rested with the island's elite, the records naturally reflect the events they felt were important" (2009, 220). For this reason, the national archives are perceived as the documented memory of the whites, irrelevant and useless to present-day Kittitian society. Jeannette Bastian aptly described this dichotomy of postcolonial societies trying to come to terms with their colonial past: "How do the descendants of the enslaved, the descendants of that transported mass of silenced humanity, find the voices of their past, not the past as documented by the former planters, merchants, and colonial officials, but the past as experienced by their ancestors who created no official records themselves, but enter the record, as transactions perhaps, as property" (Bastian 2005, 28).

A major challenge for the National Archives of St Kitts is promoting the relevance of its holdings to a nation that is documenting itself in other ways. Borg-O'Flaherty (2009) was correct when she said, "the concept of the maintenance and the archiving of records was not easily absorbed especially in a culture where the oral transmission of information predominated. [Therefore,] by recognizing that the archive was an inherent part of the machinery of colonialism, one becomes conscious of its limitations in contributing to the history of the colonized in a post-colonial community. Yet, it is still a source of information about them" (225, 220). The recurring performances in Sugar Mas turn into complementary records to the written plantation registers and deeds in the Archives, showcasing the perspectives of the formerly enslaved.

SUGAR MAS: A 'LIVING ARCHIVE'

Sugar Mas, as a space that allows for articulating and expressing the multiple practices and activities unique and significant to St Kitts, constitutes what is called a Living Archive. Jeannette Bastian posited that a living archive is created and maintained in activities that are consistent in the format of the performances, which carry deep meanings for both participants and spectators.

> Events such as performances, parades, celebrations, and commemorations, while generally recognised as expressions of cultural values may require a considerable stretch of archival boundaries in order to be thought of as archival evidence or even as records themselves . . . Each of these societal events generally do not occur in isolation, but rather form components of a complex matrix, a web of multilayered interconnected formats – visual, oral and textual – that together comprise a self-contained archive of cultural expression. (Bastian 2009, 114–5)

Bastian, in her study of the US Virgin Islands, another relatively close Caribbean island, observed the same disconnect between society and its (colonial) archives. Carnivals and other festivals are more than community events; more importantly, they are opportunities to remember and commemorate past struggles and triumphs. Bastian maintained,

> For post-colonial communities such as the Virgin Islands, archives seem to pose special problems that revolve around the contradictions inherent in the voicelessness of the majority segment of society. With no input in the record-creating process, how can these communities reclaim their history? How can the voices of those who were silent be recovered? How can communities that were the victim of records use these records to build reliable and positive constructs of their past? (2005, 28)

The carnival, with its celebration of music, movement and memory, becomes this vibrant, experiential, positive counter-narrative to the written colonial text.

A key characteristic and theme of the Living Archive festival is its overt connection to memory and simultaneous capability to capture and document present happenings in a society in perceptible ways. Sugar Mas links expressions and meanings of the island's past to present-day celebrations. It concomitantly gives constituents and participants creative opportunities to produce culture, construct memory and document details that are dynamic and up-to-date. Each Sugar Mas celebration has the expected features, which are dancing masquerade bands, costumed revellers, scheduled events, and various competitions and exhibitions. Yet, each year's celebration uniquely articulates different informational content and memory experiences. The music, costumes, songs and activities mirror the concerns, gossip, issues and triumphs of that particular year. The details and perspectives kernelled in the various articulations of the year's festivities will not be accessible in other documentary formats, resources and sources.

The festival is both a creative space and a preserving praxis – a dichotomy not easily unified in the traditional archival context. The traditional archives, with their Eurocentric infrastructural emphasis on fixed formats and static representations, will never be able to fully represent the living and fluid meanings and content that is expressed in artworks, costumes, food, lyrics and rhythms. Thus, no form of research, whether cultural, economic, heritage, historical, political or social, on Kittitian society would be complete without an examination of its festivals. For it is in the Sugar Mas, like the customary institutional archive in other societies, that Kittitians annually deposit the narratives, perspectives and rhythms they collectively acclaim as having enduring memory value for their society. For this reason, it is not uncommon for particular songs to trigger discussions and remembrances on personalities or politics in neighbourly gatherings, especially over drinks. These recollections can be precisely attributed to a specific year, place or person. They can be further triangulated by traditional record forms, such as newspaper reports or government documentation or even social media posts. Hence, Sugar Mas is a dynamic repository that receives and releases memory in dynamic ways and that informs and preserves Kittitian cultural heritage.

SUGAR MAS IN THE POST COVID-19 ERA

Like all aspects of life around the world, Sugar Mas was affected by global lockdowns, travel restrictions and public health protocols in the wake of the COVID-19 pandemic. While it was customary for some major events in the festival season to be broadcast and streamed live online, the pandemic presented new opportunities to maintain interest and extend the reach of participation using virtual modalities. This proved successful as both local and international audiences tuned in in record numbers. For example, for one event in the 2020 "Sugar Mas 49", the following statistics were recorded: "As gathered, from the 'ICONS' live streaming, there has been a recorded twenty-three thousand views on the SKNcarnival Facebook page with over thirteen thousand comments plus five hundred shares along with five thousand four hundred views on SKNcarnival YouTube channel. Viewers and listeners of Sugar Mas events and activities continue to tune into the traditional means of doing so via ZIZ radio and television" (Labour Spokesman 2020). The Minister of Culture, with responsibility for Carnival, Jonel Powell, lauded the successes of the virtual experience, noting that after the pandemic, it would become an additional fixed feature of the festival.

> It's not the regular Sugar Mas that we're accustomed to, but COVID might try to keep us down, but it can't stop us, and we've just pivoted and adapted, and we've uncovered the new norm, and I think everyone can agree that even for next year Sugar Mas 50 when we expect to have bodies in here, we will have to continue this virtual experience because for all of those who can't make it home for carnival, this is making their Christmas and carnival for them, especially this year with COVID and they really not being able to come. (Labour Spokesman 2020)

Undoubtedly, the festivities will reflect the experiences of surviving the pandemic, particularly in the calypsos sung and memories created. As with every societal progression, the festival will continue to evolve and adapt in order to best serve and preserve its cultural knowledge and heritage, as is the expectation of every archive. The internet will become more than an access point, but an additional space for full creative engagement, memory-making and participation in the festival. Additionally, as the island's digital infrastructure and creative and cultural economy develops, Sugar Mas will redound even greater benefits to the nation's international standing and financial stability. More importantly, its role as the nation's memory bank will deepen as it captures and preserves the nation's cultural, and socio-political information.

CONCLUSION

Sugar Mas is, therefore, a vibrant annual exhibition that occurs at a time that is based on the life cycle of plantation work. With its inclusion of the unique expressions of Christmas Sport, Sugar Mas re/presents the past triumphs over colonial conquest, settlement, enslavement and cultural subjugation. It is also a resource for the reinvigoration of the island's economy and interests in its heritage, especially with the closure of the sugar industry in 2005. Sugar Mas, therefore, serves as a living archival repository for reading and accessing Kittitian memory. It allows for documenting the creative imagination of current societal personalities and narratives. It embraces local popular culture for the purveyance of the island's history and heritage. Sugar Mas serves as a point of access or reference for researching the social, economic, political and cultural issues and nuances of Kittitian society. Standing in all its meaning and value to St Kitts, Sugar Mas will continue to grow in popularity and significance "because de people just can't get enough of de 'sweetness'" (South Florida Caribbean News 2006).

REFERENCES

Anderson, Benedict. 1991. *Imagined Communities: Reflections on the Origin and Spread of Nationalism*. London: Verso.

Bastian, Jeannette A. 2005. "Whispers in the Archives: Finding the Voices of the Colonized in the Records of the Colonizer." In *Political Pressure and the Archival Record*, edited by Margaret Proctor, Michael Cook and Caroline Williams, 25–44. Chicago: Society of American Archivists.

———. 2009. "'Play Mas': Carnival in the Archives and the Archives in Carnival: Records and Community Identity in the US Virgin Islands." *Archival Science* 9 (1): 113–25. https://doi.org/10.1007/s10502-009-9101-6.

Beckles, Hilary McD. 2008. "Kalinago (Carib) Resistance to European Colonisation of the Caribbean." *Caribbean Quarterly* 54 (4): 77–94. https://doi.org/10.1080/00086495.2008.11829737

Bettelheim, Judith, John Nunley, and Barbara Bridges. n.d. "Caribbean Festival Arts: An Introduction." In *Caribbean Civilization: A Provisional Interdisciplinary Reader for the Course FOUN 1101 (FD11A) Caribbean Civilization*, edited by A.

Johnson, 237–43. Kingston: Faculty of Humanities and Education, Cave Hill Campus, University of the West Indies.

Borg-O'Flaherty, Victoria. 2009. "Overcoming Anonymity: Kittitians and their archives." In *Community Archives: The Shaping of Memory*, edited by Jeannette A. Bastian and Ben Alexander, 221–34. London: Facet.

———. 2018. "Which Court is the Ball in Now?: A Case Study of Archival Outreach in St Kitts." In *Decolonizing the Caribbean Record: An Archives Reader*, edited by Jeannette A. Bastian, John A. Aarons, and Stanley H. Griffin, 385–96. Sacramento, CA: Litwin Books.

Brathwaite, Kamau. 1974. *Contradictory Omens: Cultural Diversity and Integration in the Caribbean*. Kingston, Jamaica: Savacou Publishers.

Business Wire. 2012. "The Greatest Show on Earth: Caribbean Carnival in Trinidad & Tobago." *Business Wire*, 17 February 2012. https://www.businesswire.com/news/home/20120217005738/en/The-Greatest-Show-on-Earth-Caribbean-Carnival-in-Trinidad-Tobago#:~:text=Known%20as%20"The%20Greatest%20 Show,completely%20immersed%20in%20the%20festivities.

Byron, Halstead. 2004. "King of Nevisian Folklore." *Culturama @ 30*. Charlestown: Nevis Culturama Secretariat.

Craton, Michael. 1982. *Testing the Chains: Resistance to Slavery in the British West Indies*. London: Cornell University Press.

De Baecque, Jerome. 1994. *Nevis: Queen of the Caribbean*. Paris: BTP Images.

Dodds, Rachel, and Lee Jolliffe. 2012. "Developing Sugar Heritage Tourism in St Kitts." In *Sugar Heritage and Tourism in Transition*, edited by Lee Jolliffe, 110–27. Bristol: Channel View Publications.

Dyde, Brian. 2005. *Out of the Crowded Vagueness: A History of the Islands of St Kitts, Nevis and Anguilla*. Oxford: MacMillan Education.

Fog Olwig, Karen. 1993. *Global Culture, Island Identity: Continuity and Change in the Afro-Caribbean Community of Nevis*. London: Routledge.

Gaugert Richard. 1988. "Mas in St Kitts and Nevis." Unpublished.

Guerrero, Paulina. 2013. "A Story told through Plena: Claiming Identity and Cultural Autonomy in the Street Festivals of San Juan, Puerto Rico." *Island Studies Journal* 8 (1): 165–78.

Hamilton, Carolyn, Verne Harris, Jane Taylor, Michèle Pickover, Graeme Reid, and Razia Saleh, eds. 2002. *Refiguring the Archive*. Norwell: Kluwer Academic Publishers.

Historic St Kitts. n.d.a. "Carnival-New Year's Day." Accessed 1 December 2019. https://www.historicstkitts.kn/events/carnival

———. n.d.b. "The Sugar Factory." Accessed 1 December 2019. https://www.historicstkitts.kn/places/the-sugar-factory.

———. n.d.c. "The Survival of the Christmas Sport." Accessed 1 December 2019. https://www.historicstkitts.kn/items-of-interest/the-survival-of-the-christmas-sport

———. n.d.d. "Timeline: A History of St Kitts." Accessed 1 December 2019. https://www.historicstkitts.kn/timeline-history-of-st-kitts.

Labour Spokesman. 2020. "Virtual Sugar Mas Experience to Continue after COVID Pandemic." *Labour Spokesman*, 24 December 2020. http://thelabourspokesman.com/virtual-sugar-mas-experience-to-continue-after-covid-pandemic/.

Lewis, M. Paul. 2009. "Saint Kitts Creole." In *Ethnologue: Languages of the World*, 16th ed., edited by M. Paul Lewis. Dallas, TX: SIL International.

Mills, Frank L., and Simon B. Jones-Hendrickson. 1984. *Christmas Sports in St Kitts-Nevis: Our Neglected Cultural Tradition*. US Virgin Islands: Frank L. Mills.

Nettleford, Rex. 2003. *Caribbean Cultural Identity*. Kingston, Jamaica: Ian Randle Publishers.

———. 1995. *Inward Stretch, Outward Reach: A Voice from the Caribbean*. New York: Caribbean Diaspora.

Nurse, Keith. 1998. "Globalisation and Trinidad Carnival: Diaspora, Hybridity and Identity in Global Culture." In *Identity, Ethnicity and Culture in the Caribbean*, edited by Ralph Premdas, 86–87. St Augustine, Trinidad: University of the West Indies School of Continuing Studies.

Pearce-Moses, Richard. 2005. *A Glossary of Archives and Records Terminology*. Chicago, IL: Society of American Archivists.

Richards, Peter. 2005. "TRADE: Collapse of St Kitts Sugar Sector Leaves Bitter Aftertaste." *Inter Press Service News Agency*, 1 April 2005. http://www.ipsnews.net/2005/04/trade-collapse-of-st-kitts-sugar-sector-leaves-bitter-aftertaste/.

Simmonds, Keith C. 1987. "Political and Economic Factors Influencing the St Kitts-Nevis Polity: An Historical Perspective." *Phylon* 48 (4): 277–86. doi:10.2307/274485.

Smith, Michael G. 2004. "West Indian Culture." In *The Birth of Caribbean Civilization: A Century of Ideas about Culture, and Identity, Nation and Society*, edited by O. Nigel Bolland, 362–72. Kingston, Jamaica: Ian Randle Publishers.

South Florida Caribbean News. 2006. "Nu-Vybes Wins 5th Road March Title and Beat Out Caribbean's Top Bands for VIP Band Award." *South Florida Caribbean News*, 23 January 2006. https://sflcn.com/nu-vybes-wins-5th-road-march-title-and-beat-out-caribbeans-top-bands-for-vip-band-award/.

UNESCO World Heritage List. n.d. "Brimstone Hill Fortress National Park." Accessed 1 December 2019. https://whc.unesco.org/en/list/910.

Watson, Karl S. 2003. *Barbados First: The Years of Change 1920 to 1970*. Bridgetown, Barbados: Author.

World Factbook 2019. 2019. "St Kitts and Nevis." Central Intelligence Agency. https://www.cia.gov/library/publications/the-world-factbook/geos/sc.html.

Zacek, Natalie. 2007. "Reading the Rebels: Currents of Slave Resistance in the Eighteenth-Century British West Indies." *History in Focus*, no. 12. Accessed 1 December 2019. https://archives.history.ac.uk/history-in-focus/Slavery/articles/zacek.html.

Chapter Nine

The Sound of Citizenship
Performance, Politics and Transgression

SONJAH STANLEY NIAAH

'Sound di big ting dem'
(Busy Signal, 2005)

ARGUABLY, KINGSTON IS THE LOUDEST CITY IN THE Anglophone Caribbean and Jamaica, whose national instrument is the sound system, is the noisiest country on the planet. This chapter seeks to analyse decades of observations regarding the historical problems around noise, entertainment and work in Jamaica, where the entertainment sector has been under siege, and its promoters, proprietors and patrons have existed in an antagonistic relationship with the state and enforcers of the law who are charged with protecting lives. Indeed, the use of force by the Jamaica Constabulary Force to regulate entertainment outweighs any other sector or profit-making enterprise, except where private security measures are arranged. Viewed as a case historically, the entertainment sector reveals a thriving culture of enforcement by security forces, which has resulted in high degrees of in/security. Focused on the analysis of culture, in particular, popular culture, Caribbean culture and cultural studies, a significant portion of my work on Jamaican popular culture, documented in the book *Dancehall: From Slave Ship to Ghetto* (2010), has engaged in historically grounded, geographically sensitive, and culturally comparative work. I extend that work here to examine the politics of noise and in/security around Jamaican music.

Located at the intersection of cultural history, cultural geography and cultural studies more broadly, this chapter continued the exploration of Black Atlantic performance, geography and history by placing entertainment practice in a wider comparative and analytical field along a historical trajectory where Africa as a source and sensibility takes shape in a 'new world' of social and political challenges and opportunities. As I thought about my contribution to this collection of essays, I began more and more to ruminate on the hallmarks of Black life across the African diaspora that have been systematically suppressed or prostituted. I have tried to document some of this in papers I have presented over the past few years, namely, "Africa on Stage" and "Of Memory, Prisons, Crime and Profit", where I highlighted dimensions of Black life such as religion, recreation and celebration, especially around music, which have been criminalized and ultimately suppressed. Following the arguments logically, there is a framework within which Africans in the diaspora can argue for reparatory justice based on systematic measures used for cultural erasure.

As I thought more about this chapter, artistes such as Busy Signal, with his notable sound effect – "sound di big ting" (2005) – entered my mind. He was referring simultaneously to the amplified sound of the sound system and to another sound that many fear and around which Jamaica has gained notoriety: the sound of the gun. Within dancehall, and for the artiste, it is a musical rendering of the gun, a tool of destruction that has caused much insecurity. But it is also the weight of sound, the sound system, and the certain way that Jamaica has been heard as the noisiest little place on the planet because of its music. Arguably, Black life and, in particular, entertainment have been suppressed through various forms of oppression in Jamaica to the same degree that Jamaican music has grown correspondingly loud through the sound system to signal agency and resistance. In many ways, the gun and the sound system have occupied a Janus-faced existence, but in this chapter, I want to highlight the similarity in their habitus and operation. What roles have the sound system played for different stakeholders and the public? Can it be compared to the barking of guns? And who have been its real victims? What has been the impact of "sounding the big ting" in true dancehall fashion, or the big sound system?

With the sound system as Jamaica's national instrument, I wish to hone in on the role of the sound system, sound practice, politics and mechanisms of transgression. I also use sound deliberately in contradistinction from the pejorative 'noise' in order to engage in reparatory thinking, to reclaim sound and to make redress to the extent that we have engaged in and enabled pejorative thinking about sound. This chapter is, therefore, activist in its orientation, and I begin by locating Jamaica and the sound system in the cosmopolitan Caribbean at the heart of modernity and globalization in the West. For, as Wardle (2000, 1–2) concluded:

> People from the Caribbean – subject to slavery, the plantation economy, and labour migration – have one of the longest exposures to a global political and economic order of any social grouping. For centuries, Jamaicans have lived at a crossroads of transnational economic, social and cultural dynamics. A central argument here is that they are still living out the aesthetic and moral consequences and contradictions of the Enlightenment and modernity . . . Jamaicans understand themselves as global citizens—as individuals who have the potential for making social and cultural connections with many parts of the world. This sense of self can be identified across multiple contexts—oral performance, music, kinship and friendship, economics and politics. It is also shaped by and reacts against, manifest exclusionary practices in the countries that Jamaicans travel to and work in.

With the foregoing as context, I do three things in this chapter. I say something about the work of entertainment by select citizenry historically, its location in a colonial past, and within contemporary Jamaica and the Caribbean more broadly. I contextualize Jamaica's entertainment practice in a wider geographical, African diaspora sense, to establish the ground for a new vision of entertainment. Additionally, I use Jamaica as a case for putting the creative work around music first in activating creative industries for Caribbean development through analysis of sound as a form of labour, a certain form of practice for select citizenry. This chapter seeks to extend works by scholars such as Orlando Patterson (1974), Tricia Rose (1994), Julian Henriques (2011), Jacques Attali (1985), Walter Rodney (1969), Barbara Browning (1995), Carolyn Cooper, Louis Chude-Sokei, Frantz Fanon (1963) and others in centring the form of practice embodied in the work and politics of the sound system. In particular, I extend notions of "noises in the blood" (Cooper), itself a dub off "echoes in the bone" (Earl

Lovelace), as well as "echo chamber" (Louis Chude-Sokei), or sonic rebel communities in this chapter.

RE/DEFINING NOISE, REINSTATING SOUND

This chapter insists cultural studies grounded in the Caribbean must consider sound as a reference for the power dynamics characteristic of the post-/colonial Caribbean in which people of African descent reside and are consistently engaged in struggles to express, to identify, in space and place. Douglas Kahn, in Noise Water Meat, suggested that "we know they are noises in the first place because they exist where they shouldn't or they don't make sense where they should" (1999, 21). Among others, Marcel Cobussen (2017) highlighted that noise, often defined based on volume, is not the only factor to be considered when trying to understand it. He suggests that other factors, such as context and environment, are crucial. Cobussen advanced a similar view to Kahn's out-of-place-ness, that:

> Sounds are thus not noisy in themselves but can become noise if they occur in a place where they are not supposed to be. Noisiness then becomes a label attached to them. If noise is indeed sound out of place, it implies that any sound occurring in its appropriate place is, by definition, not noise. "Out of place" then refers to disorder, instability, contravention of the expected, undermining the dominant organization, disharmony, etc.

Cognitive dissonance was originally defined as a musical term denoting a clash of sounds or an unpleasant combination of notes, or simply noise. This terminology is being applied to the sounds being made by the descendants of Africans in the Caribbean, which are seen as noise and juxtaposed to the more Eurocentric construct of aesthetically pleasing, acceptable sound. Notably, in the postcolonial world of sound, the acceptance of an audible expression defined as sound or noise depends on the environment but also on who is making the sound and who has the power to define the sound. This results in the issues around sound being subjective or, moral, or even aesthetic.

Against this background, noise in the Caribbean has been constructed to denote those sounds which are created in, or come from, spaces that are deemed immoral within a Eurocentric Christian ideology. This kind of subjective discrimination is often applied to the majority African enslaved (the masses), their descendants and their African-influenced spiritual and performance practices, cultures and memories. From slavery to an era of freedom, tensions over popular cultural expressions prevailed. Pickering and Rice (2017) noted:

> This implies that labels such as "quiet" and "loud" can be mapped onto more overtly moral ones such as "harmonious" and "disharmonious" or "good" and "bad." And the general opinion is that . . . to be quiet is to be good, to agree to cherished classifications, to uphold the sonic and social order and to follow accepted ways of being. To be noisy is to be bad, to disregard convention, and to confuse or ignore classifications and have different and unacceptable ways of being. Noise, far more than just 'sound out of place,' indicates an entire moral system.

The task of re/defining the term noise and understanding its politics, even its pejorative application, can further be traced in the writings of Attali (1985) and Rose (1994), among others. Taken in contradistinction to music, noise can be seen as a representation of chaos, destruction and disharmony in both nature and the violence of society. Attali (1985) offered four cultural stages in which to understand the structure, production and dissemination, moving from ritualized contexts to that of commodity and recorded artefact for reproduction by the start of the twentieth century. Rose (1994) positions Black musics, such as hip hop and rap, as social movements in their political uses against the system – racial, sexual, cultural and aesthetic. While this chapter does not seek to account for the history of use or definition in relation to noise and sound, the adoption of terms such as noise without understanding their intellectual genealogy or history of usage is part of the awareness this work offers. It is cognisant that the question of musical value cannot be subsumed in terms such as noise and that one person's rhythmic purity may be another's disharmony or even another's standard of excellence. The essentially subjective term noise counterposes my argument; the term sound inserts rudimentary physical characteristics that are more objectively isolated and engaged.

SOUND AND THE POLITICS OF CITIZENSHIP: A CARIBBEAN
CULTURAL STUDIES PERSPECTIVE

The politics of Caribbean citizenship, and indeed Jamaican citizenship, are bound up in experiences and discourses around the post-/colonial enterprise. The politics around Jamaican citizenship invoke questions such as Who is the citizen? How do they live in the everyday and have their being? What securities do they enjoy? What are the spaces and habitus of their creativity? What are the symbols, fantasies and products of their imaginings? Who has rights to the nation and its privileges? The citizenry at the heart of this chapter are those involved in the creation and consumption of Jamaican popular music, in particular, amplified music inside the dancehall and around the sound system. Such a citizenry has been produced through particular forms of 'smadditizin' (after Charles Mills 1997, 55) vis-à-vis sound, and the politics of citizenship must be seen through an interdisciplinary lens based on the degrees of disenfranchisement and exclusion. The instruments of the colony and later of the nation, their creators and enforcers (the system) in the colonial era and the postcolonial present have never been favourable in their intentions toward the way the masses have lived and had their being. Arguably, this amounts to somewhat of a departure from the vision of nation-builders. If this statement is too naïve, then it is at least a departure from what can be interpreted from their writings. Leighton Jackson (2014) explained the following:

> The people are in reality the centre of the institutional universe which comprises the State. The objective of laws which are the mechanism to officially order relationships within the state is to bring its institutions in alignment with this truth. Norman Washington Manley echoed this sentiment when he declared that the mission of his generation in creating a new "self-governed" state is "to win political power for the black masses of my country." There is no win if this state does not reflect the people's insight and values, which are in turn reflected in their language and *culture*. (emphasis added, 4)

The extent of the struggle to re-engineer self and society, for even nation builders as they departed from a colonial era, can be explained by the creole term "smadditizin'". A development from the word "somebody", "smadditizin'" is an active Jamaicanism explained the process of becoming somebody. Added to this are the factors of class and hierarchy that dominate the process of becoming somebody, especially for those who are at the bottom of the class and race ladders or not on the ladders at all. Charles Mills (1997, 55) asserted that smadditizin' should be understood as a "struggle for, the insistence on, personhood . . . in a world where, primarily because of race, it is denied", thus smadditizin' is essentially a political, cultural, moral, epistemological and ontological (metaphysical) struggle that is not yet complete, as the structures against which it struggles are "in many ways intact". For those who have been creators and consumers of amplified Jamaican reggae and dancehall sounds, it is correct to assert that the creative process has been their proverbial 'road to Zion', their means of becoming, and of struggle, where reprieve from the making and remaking of the everyday self and identity collides with a world that privileges the colour and class of the colonial and metropolitan ideal, compounded by the competition inherent in the urbanscape.

The complexity of the urbanscape notwithstanding, Orlando Patterson, through research he conducted in five inner-city Kingston communities, reported to the Office of the Prime Minister in 1974 that "every community should have its own sound system". His recommendation was based on the collective bond he observed and the economic and social gains for the communities where music was consumed using sound systems. As sugar and bauxite lost their appeal and financial sustainability, there was something else emerging, such as bars and street corners with sound systems, which became the enterprise of choice for many who found alternative pathways in musical expression. Patterson recommended to the prime minister that each community should have its sound system, a recommendation the government ignored but which the people took up on their terms. The Jamaican case is hardly unique and reflects an ethos across the postcolonial African diaspora. Evidence suggests that in various sectors of life and through time, not least of which is the sector of entertainment, little or no space was made available through a system that included legislative suppression.

"SOUNDING" AND "GROUNDING" THE REASONING

A historically grounded analysis of sound in the African diaspora and the wider Caribbean reveals a high degree of creativity as much as attempts at suppression. Wrapped in the creativity is that underexplored dimension of transgression, of action through sound, sounding, like grounding, which insists on an orientation to action, activism, pushing at the limits of expression, and selfhood, the absolute necessity of expression, and celebration. While grounding is a form of practice intended to raise consciousness through reasoning, honed in discourse, sounding, as in through the sound system, is intended to be heard, amplified audibility, countering disenfranchisement and erasure. The sound system became the voice that was not to be silenced by the system, the same "Babylon system" that Peter Tosh referred to as the "shit-stem". The only good system, after all, is a sound system. DJs were "sounding" off on the system through improvised and carefully orchestrated lyrical virtuoso, both live and recorded. "Sounding the big ting" became a pastime favoured by the Jamaican masses, which gathered weekly to celebrate various dimensions of life.

It is the sound system, like the body as instrument, as a kingdom of memory, a landscape of power, which ultimately gains attention in this chapter. I extend Julian Henriques's thinking about the African body, the African diasporic, and its acts of memory across time and on stage. Henriques pointed to the inextricable link between the body, earth, and sound, at once democratizing access to memory and movement and corporeal power. Whether it was in the work songs, the blues, the studio or dance floors around the sound system, *the body* in these spaces aimed to find and maintain a primal connection (see Henriques 2008, 231). This is the body which historically sought refuge from the days of being forced to dance on the slave ships or disparaged for too much gyration of the hip girdle.. Examining the history provides important insights into how this history can function to serve popular culture scholarship in the re/presentation of the legacies of slavery.

The culture of celebration, indeed, the will to celebrate, the culture of entertainment born in a mostly African experience with cross-fertilization from European and other experiences, has been characterized by an ethos of containment, force and eradication. Barbara Browning's (1995) comments on Brazil clearly show that African-derived performance practices such as samba are referred to as infectious rhythms, placing them in terms of diseases, such as the AIDS pandemic, in need of elimination. Evidence of such elimination is found across the spectrum of African aesthetics, whether as dance, drumming or spirituality, which were banned and regulated in deadly ways. Notably, the politics of noise within the African diaspora from jazz and the blues to calypso, passinho, grime and dancehall have been documented by writers such as Rose (1994), Martis (2016) and Scruggs (2014, 2018), among others. As various states over time have sought to cement the words negro and noise/Black and boisterous together in pathological ways, various populations have remained steadfast in their imperative to live, celebrate and affirm their being. There is an imperative to celebrate even as states have been militant in their attempts to stem the prevailing tide. Martis (2016) documented the following: "I've watched as black people have been silenced, arrested, and even killed for the noise they make. Black people aren't more or less loud than anyone else, and yet the noise we make is feared, scrutinized, and made public. Understanding why there's such a sensitivity – and fear – of black noise is a complex and intricate question that doesn't supply a simple answer."

Closer to home, "the debate in Kingston", according to Scruggs (2014), "is similar to those that have … erupted in New York and New Orleans over the rights of street musicians and dancers to perform in public space". However, during the 1960s, the same kind of animosity existed between those entertainers and the broader populations and, in particular, the state. This shows that killing music in the city has been a long-term goal, continuing today inside more contemporary musical populations such as the Grime generation. An African Diasporic perspective therefore reveals common genetic ties around noise, sound and suppression.

HISTORICIZING ENTERTAINMENT AND CRIMES OF THE STATE

While the likes of Bournemouth Club, Silver Slipper, Myrtle Bank Hotel and other prestigious clubs in Kingston around the 1960s were not seen as a threat, but popular spaces hosting several performers from across the world, there were other ways in which entertainment was being regulated in disadvantageous ways. There had been the enactment and enforcement of law by apparatuses of the state that operated in opposition to the people. A close examination of the history of entertainment revealed that no space was made and temporary "shrubs" were used for the slave dances in the early and mid-nineteenth century. They were sometimes constructed with bamboo and they were demolished after the event.

Waddell reported (1970, 17–18, 147 and 161–62) that slaves in Jamaica had three holidays at Christmas, which lasted one week among the town slaves. His report of the character of slave entertainment, and the physical and philosophical spaces it occupied, was revealing. There was "unbounded revelry" in the "shrub made for the occasion", with crowds dancing "Johnny Canoe", singing and drumming, and set girls. There were "rude and demoralizing 'balls and suppers'" as well as "the soiree", of which the first one, in the schoolhouse, an official space, was introduced "to promote the great cause of temperance and of social improvement". Waddell recounted "revelling and rioting" in the negro yards by "ill-disposed, disorderly people … pervert[ing] their freedom" with singing, drumming and dancing in "the booth" constructed in a certain yard, which the powers of the plantation society were not able to prevent. One resident of the yard was later arrested and jailed for staging the ball and threatened the life of a constable, and Waddell and other "quiet good people rejoiced" that this person would no longer be able to "disturb all their neighbours" with revelry into the morning.

In the same era and across time, sanctions have not been proportionately applied to Eurocentric gatherings and activities of the established Church, until recently, long after Noise Abatement Acts concerning "night noises", which sought only to regulate the entertainment economies in cities such as Kingston, were passed. The table below shows several pieces of legislation that were passed in the anglophone Caribbean, following from the inherited frameworks for noise abatement.

The noise legislation from the 1600s to the 1900s seemed to be largely preoccupied with regulating African sound and expression, specifically the drum and obeah. Because they were defenceless against physical and verbal abuse, gatherings were the most effective weaponry possessed by the enslaved. Although drumming, as a central part of these gatherings, dis-

Table 1. Caribbean Laws Implicating Noise

Name of Legislation	Year	Location
Customs of the Islands Prohibition on Drums and Horns	1688 *amended in 1717	Jamaica
Acts Passed in the Island of Barbados – law against drums and horns	1699	Barbados
Antigua Act	1702	Antigua
Law banning communication by horns and drums	1711 *amended in 1722	St. Kitts
An Act to Remedy the Evils Arising from Irregular Assemblies of Slaves	1760	Jamaica
Act for the Encouragement, Protection and Better Government of Slaves	1788	Dominica
An Act for the Punishment of Such Slaves as Shall be Found Practicing Obeah	1806	Barbados
Act for the Punishment of Obeah	1819	Montserrat
Grenada Consolidated Slave Act	1825	Grenada
Summary Convictions Ordinance	1868 *the anti-Obeah clauses were removed from the law in 2000	Trinidad
Ban of Calinda Bands	1883	Trinidad
The Obeah Law	1898 *still in effect today	Jamaica
The Leeward Islands Obeah Act	1904 *remains basis of the law in several of these countries	Anguilla, Antigua, Barbuda, Montserrat, St. Kitts, Nevis, British Virgin Islands
The Medical Law	1908 *while not explicitly aimed at Obeah practitioners, they were punished under this act for unlawfully practicing medicine	Jamaica
Shakerism Prohibition Ordinance	1912	St. Vincent
Shouters Prohibition Ordinance	1917 *repealed in 1951	Trinidad and Tobago
Noise Abatement Act	1997	Jamaica

turbed the peace of the colonizers, it was not the main intention. Although it was a rebellious act, and was not allowed, drumming was more for communal healing purposes. In a Fanonion sense, the "crystallizing of souls" (1963) that have been dismantled from the day's whipping and abuse is covertly at work/play. It is the putting back together of self, or the putting together of a new self, that is the power of the communal gathering. However, ironically, the drum symbolizes a foreign sound from a foreign land from foreigners, causing it to be defined as noise and unconnected to citizenship.

What the Noise Abatement Act inadvertently suggests is that some people make a sound while others make noise. In order to make a distinction, the state security apparatus has been employed to ensure that no noise crime is committed, or that any noise crime committed must be punished. Since the state in any society is there to prevent violence and maintain the peace, then noise is being perceived not just as disturbing the peace, but as violent and needing to be punished. Since noise disturbs the peace, the peace in this sense has to be the law-abiding non-violent citizenry. This can only mean that the noise makers are not a part of the citizenship and are being othered as lawbreakers, as bad, immoral and violent people.

Correspondingly, the state sees dance gatherings as a den for criminals. Evidence of the state conflicting with the masses can be highlighted in police raids on dancehall events. Venues could be perceived as being under siege. Dance venues throughout the 1960s and 1970s up to the present have been raided with such frequency that locking down the dance became a feature of dancehall life, and film crews could request re-enactment or pay to stage a lock down. Several dancehall artistes have made mention of these lockdowns in their music. In a 1994 paramilitary operation of the Jamaica Constabulary Force anti-crime division, eighty people were detained and one arrested for murder and shooting at the House of Leo Venue (Miller 1994). This raid was thought to have been staged for a British film crew. These ideas were immortalized by Buju Banton, who recorded "Operation Ardent", which details the DJ's experience of a raid in the early 1990s. Opening with blaring sirens, Buju asked: "What's di motive? Why dem keep meddling around the poor people dem business? . . . What more? What oonu want di massive fi do? Every dance wey wi keep oonu mek dem get curfew" (Buju Banton 1993).

The DJ was asking: what does the state want the poor, who have no adequate space in which to live, recreate and re-create self, to do when every attempt at entertainment, especially through the dance, is curfewed? From the 1960s to present day, many more raids than those receiving media coverage have occurred, all causing varying degrees of damage to the community and to people themselves, sometimes to the artists themselves, such as DJ U-Roy. For U-Roy and his team, who had a reputation of being "rude boys" or "bad men", raids, beatings, locking down the sound and arrests were common around them. U-Roy himself was once beaten by the police and subsequently imprisoned and his turntable confiscated because he was creating night noise.

If the reason for raiding street dances is that criminals frequent them, it assumes that criminals are only found downtown and in inner cities, while clubs and parties uptown are filled with law-abiding citizens. For night noise associated with entertainment, police raids take on a severe nature especially when compared to Christian evangelical crusades, church services, and Nine Nights or Dead Yaads. This haphazard enforcement of the law is ultimately discriminatory and serves to violate the efforts of creators of entertainment products.

Additionally, since geographical space helps to determine the definition of noise, it becomes critical to note that successive governments in Jamaica, just as in the colonial period, have not created an enabling environment for the production and consumption of entertainment. As such, much of the sound from dancehalls and night noises exists on the margins, in lanes, on gully sides, parking lots, open lots, etc., that are converted to accommodate dance activity. However, the contradiction is that the Jamaican state seems to protect carnival processions that are more expansive on the streets of Jamaica and disrupt traffic and pedestrians alike. This demonstrates the hypocrisy around noise, as carnival takes control of daylight hours even on business days, for parades involving middle- and upper-class traditions imported with roots from a Catholic European Christian philosophy. Instead of sanctions, there are tangible ways in which the state supports carnival as an active policy to expand its potential as a tourism product. Furthermore, when naked brown bodies are exposed and parading the streets of Kingston in carnival, that is the mostly Brown flesh can afford the skimpy costumes at premium cost. They are fully accepted. However, when black bodies from the inner cities are on display or exposed, the argument becomes discriminatory, condemnatory, shameful and judgemental.

Here, shame is embedded in using terms such as loud or vulgar. The loud and vulgar bodies, and the sounds they gyrate to, are also transferable to and describe the fashion worn by some dancehall patrons: bright, colourful clothing, wigs, nails and accessories are also classed as vulgar, especially fashion that is too revealing. In this sense, the appearance of the person is making too much noise, disrupting the moral silence that black bodies should be subjected to as a kind of under-class or second-class citizen. Additionally, political rallies used for campaigning activities exist outside the scope of the Noise abatement legislation. Political motorcades often take the shape of a merger between a carnival and a dancehall event by virtue of the taking over of the streets to obstruct regular traffic and business activities and the plethora of dancehall and reggae songs that litter their soundtracks.

Because Jamaica is so class stratified, citizenship is tied up with the politics inherited from enslavement, resulting in persons from the middle- and upper-classes, who are largely the business class of owners with means to generate wealth, influencing policies and laws that work in their favour. As such, access to the privileges of citizenship is denoted by their values and morals. It is therefore clear who the real citizens are and how their roles and privileges are reinforced or diminished.

VENUES POLITICIZED

Exploring the concept of entertainment geographies, an analysis of spaces like venues shows that they have retained their character, use and significance for many decades. They could be nomadic, occupying marginal domain, but the wellspring of venues never dries: these spaces are constantly being created or refashioned. Even though they may be outside of Jamaicans' sensibilities and aesthetics of quality in the Nettlefordian sense, they are central to the articulation of a sense of community and cultural identity among the lower class and those abroad, some in spaces of exile.

The police have been an extremely problematic symbol of the tensions between dance patrons and promoters and the state. Even today, the police continue to be accused of provocation, profiling and exerting excessive force. Police were said to profile people into the stereotypical notion of what a "rude boy" or "bad man" looked like in the 1960s. Typical markers used to identify them were khaki clothing and Clarks brand shoes. Police officers were also incensed by the playing of certain tunes. Of these, U Roy explained that Max Romeo's 'Run Babylon' (1975) referencing the way police were menacing and gravalicious was sure to be a dance stopper (U Roy 2002). The police would immediately appear to end the dance by ordering the selector to turn off the sound system. In my early research U Roy recalled:

> Police look for wanted man in the dance. I used to think Bablyon don't want man enjoy themselves back then ... 'Sound system waan turn down' was the constant warning at midnight. If they [had to] come back it's trouble. Sometimes police mash up the dance. Sometimes the Black Maria van was there with the police, and after they line up everybody and search them, they would load the Black Maria. Some of this was just harassment. (interview with the author, Kingston, 24 April 2002)

Foundation DJ King Stitt, in an interview, expounded on police harassment by saying that, for the police, the vocation of being a DJ was tantamount to a criminal offence, such as smoking marijuana. The fact that these activities were often found in the same space – DJs would often be users of marijuana and some of them were Rastafari in their cultural and religious convictions – made it harder to separate the police from dance activity.. Raids have also been tainted by the suggestion that police officers demanded money from dance promoters in exchange for allowing the event to continue. A classic example of this going wrong was the incident at the La Roose venue in St Catherine on 27 January 2003. People at the dance allegedly resisted police bribery, and a shooting incident ensued, leaving at least five injured.

The state, including but not limited to the police, is not the only entity to blame. According to U-Roy, politics did not play such an important role in the raids on dances. Intervention by the police was common and their authority was particularly invoked when "society people" (middle- and upper-class) complained about the noise when sound systems played in venues above Cross Roads. In a report on Television Jamaica's Prime Time News (11 August 2003), it was acknowledged that "uptown" venues – Constant Spring Golf Club, Priscilla's, Weekenz and Villa Ronai, used at the commercial end of dancehall for stage shows – were disturbing nearby residents but were not always subject to stipulations.

Instead, authorities reminded them of stipulations under the Noise Abatement Act (1997) that required them to seek permits ten days prior to the event and to end events by 2:00 a.m. while promising its enforcement.

The accusations of party raiding and locking down have increased since the passing and subsequent re-enforcement of the Noise Abatement Act (1997) and the Places of Amusement (1999) regulations. The Noise Abatement Act regulates both public and private spaces and events and controls noise around several public activities, from political and public meetings to dance events. It states that no person in a private or public setting shall sing, play or sound noise-making or musical instruments or use any loudspeaker, microphone or other means of amplifying sound to a level "reasonably capable" of annoying individuals, particularly residents, visitors and the infirm, beyond a range of one hundred metres from the origin of the sound. The regulations further stipulate that loudspeakers should not be operated at levels capable of annoyance beyond 11:00 p.m. in the case of public meetings, or midnight for political meetings held during political campaigns, or between the hours of 2:00 a.m. and 6:00 a.m. on Saturday or Sunday, and between midnight and 6:00 a.m. on Sunday, Monday, Tuesday, Wednesday or Thursday. Where commission of an offence is proven, sanctions apply as fines not exceeding J$20,000 or imprisonment up to six months. The Act requires that persons intending to stage events capable of disturbing nearby residents seek permission from the police a minimum of ten days prior to the event (The Noise Abatement Act 1997).

As a policing apparatus, the Noise Abatement Act is closely associated with the Places of Amusement Regulations under the Parish Councils Act (1999). Scrutiny of the Kingston and St Andrew Corporation (Places of Amusement) Regulations (1999) further outlines the nature and context of regulating events. The term "places of amusement" is defined as any public place freely accessed by patrons paying a fee or not, including a cinema, club, dance hall, open air dance venue, festival, discotheque, roller disco, skating rink or amusement arcade. Operators of such places are granted licenses upon paying fees ranging from J$2,000 to J$10,000. While the definition of amusement activities is not limited to the staging of dance events, it is safe to say that a large number of these permits were issued for dancehall events.

Since 2018, there has been an increase in calls to revise the Noise Abatement Act because it serves the needs of the state but not always the needs of the citizen, night economy entrepreneur, music promoter or community. Due to combined efforts by the Ministries of Culture, Gender, Entertainment and Sport; National Security; Local Government; and Tourism, it was announced in 2019 that party hours would be extended until 4:00 am, allowing two additional hours for entertainers and patrons in Jamaica over the limited Christmas and New Year holiday periods. While this extension brought criticism from residents and parliamentarians representing citizens, it highlighted that a critical mass was now convinced of the need to relax historically problematic legislative platforms that had not been assessed in light of Jamaica's status as an entertainment capital in the Caribbean. Minister of National Security Dr Horace Chang asserted that the government "must create the balance between the continued growth of our music and entertainment industries, and maintaining public order, safety and well-being of the general public" (Peru 2020).

"NEW WORLD" SOUND LANDSCAPES: THE "UNBOUNDED" RED BULL CULTURE CLASH

Ironically, as Jamaica faltered in structuring its night economy and finalizing frameworks to grow its creative economy, entities far and wide were busy exploiting Jamaica's musical capital. In this section, I analyse the fragile context of luminosity using Jamaican dancehall's relationship and, in particular, the sound system's relationship with the transnational corporation Red Bull. Not only is Jamaica's place on the music video production scene secure, but Jamaican aesthetic practices have populated the commercial performance and video production landscapes around sound clashes staged for global appeal. The sound system clash, a popular dancehall performance mode, became prominent after the 1960s. It has led to increased engagement with indigenous Jamaican music, but it has also resulted in both symbolic and very real violence. By the 1980s and 1990s, sound systems such as Stone Love, Kilimanjaro and Bass Odyssey, among many others, ruled the Jamaican nightscape, and sound system clashes became popular beyond Jamaica to occupy outernational terrains. Violent clashes put a damper on the sound system scene in Jamaica, but they gained popularity abroad in the 1990s when the World Clash events organized by Irish and Chin began in New York. Even though there have been attempts to revive the practice through the Jamaica Sound System Festival, clashes remain a rare aspect of Jamaica's dancehall scene. However, as the sound system clashes at home subsided, they increased on a global scale, especially in metropolitan centres such as New York, Atlanta, London, Lisbon and further afield in Johannesburg.

Most importantly, for those who do not live in such cities, the spotlight has been cast on sound system clashes within the global videoscape inside primary visual repositories such as YouTube, where Jamaican dancehall aesthetics are paraded in such events as the Red Bull Culture Clash. Red Bull has been explicit about its transnational commercialization of the dancehall performance mode usually staged in indoor venues (a departure from the typical Jamaican scene where events are usually outdoors). Originating in 2010, the Red Bull Culture Clash series is hailed as the world's biggest musical battle and has featured artistes, DJs, MCs, rappers and sound systems such as Metalheadz, Skream & Benga, Channel One, Major Lazer, Federation Sound, Wiz Khalifa, Stone Love Movement, Disturbing London, David Rodigan, Unruly (featuring Popcaan), African Storm, Durban Massacre and Tinie Tempah, among many others. The modus operandi is similar to the typical Jamaican sound clash where four sounds (sometimes referred to as crews) compete in four or five clash rounds and success in each round is determined by crowd response. The events have seen up to twenty-five thousand people in attendance, making them some of the most successful one-night events staged around sound system culture globally.

Following the first Red Bull Culture Clash in 2010, the England Riots of 2011 spotlighted Jamaica as accusations circulated about the role Jamaicans and, more specifically, the Jamaican language, played in the successful spread of the riots. Beyond these years, I argue that the consumption of Jamaica as

Figure 1. Flyers of Bass Odyssey's Sound System Festival (Courtesy of Bass Odyssey)

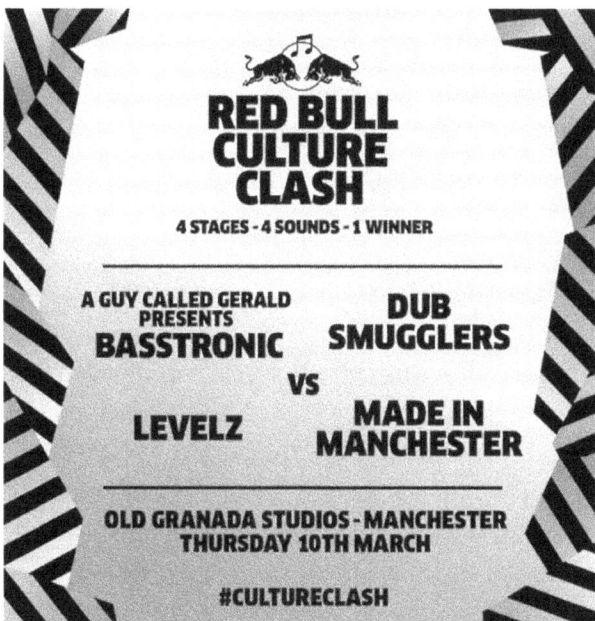

Figure 2. Flyers for Red Bull Culture Clash Events – Manchester and Johannesburg (Courtesy of Red Bull Culture Clash)

Figure 3. Popcaan Dropping Drake's Track "One Dance" at the 2014 Culture Clash (A Nation of Billions 2016))

a product and personality reached a high point in 2013, a saturation point in a sort of boundaryless hegemonic dissolution, and Louise "Miss Lou" Bennett's poem *Colonization in Reverse* captures this idea well. The sound system and the dancehall culture it produced has become productive for many beyond Jamaica's shores.

As Red Bull Culture Clashes sought to cement Jamaican aesthetic practices in specific sites, by 2013 we saw a critical increase in the consumption of Jamaica as a brand, made visible through a different sort of video light in a global landscape. Highlights of 2013 as a year of critical consumption contained the following representations of Jamaica occupying various forms of visual media and their spotlight: the Volkswagon commercial at the Super Bowl Sunday, featured a white man speaking Jamaican and cajoling his co-workers to be happy (TheSuperBowlTV 2013); Beyoncé performed her hit song featuring Grammy-winning act Sean Paul to millions at the same Super Bowl; the BET Awards featured dancehall performances by Beenie Man and Elephant Man, among others; a Saturn ad (Gilpin 2013), which featured the highest symbolic representation of hegemonic dissolution when the burning of the Jamaican flag prompted the ire of Jamaicans at home and abroad so much so that the ad was pulled in short order; Jamaican songster Tessanne Chin won the Voice competition; the 'No Woman No Drive' song (BBC 2013; Wardi 2013), remixing Bob Marley's "No Woman Nuh Cry" and bringing attention to advocacy for Saudi women to be allowed to drive, circulated around the globe; and Major Lazer's release of dancehall music featuring acts such as Sean Paul, Busy Signal, Chronixx and Protojé contributed to him becoming one of the top paid DJs globally. By way of context, therefore, the preceding outline regarding the explicit consumption of Jamaican popular culture highlights the cool factor that Jamaica embodies. My use of the word cool traces back to Farris Thompson's (1973) articulations and subsequent analyses on "an aesthetic of the cool" to engage with the translation of a self-conscious confidence seen in attitude, determination, pleasure in the self, bodily carriage, dress and performance that manifests not only from a certain mental state but also in a performance aesthetic linked to ancestral histories. Moreover, the clash, mobilizing the seriousness of competition and pleasure of play around music, is one of the cool aspects of Jamaican performance that has gained new visibility through the clash. What is arguable, however, is that this visibility is muted by virtue of Red Bull's marketing in an arena

Figure 4. Admiral and Jah Seed Playing on African Storm Sound System, Johannesburg Admiral (*Left*) and Jah Seed (*Centre*). (Courtesy of Red Bull Culture Clash)

of unbounded global media consumption that can easily occlude sites of origin and make way for interpretations of cultural appropriation.

Some demographic information about the consumers of the sound clash content transmitted through Red Bull's site, among others, can be gleaned from online comments. They are youth music lovers, Red Bull Academy/ Culture Clash fans and music aficionados of all ages. Specifically, the online video teasers for the culture clash engaged viewers in the international spread of sound clashes with videos featuring the competitors advertising the event without any reference to Jamaica. The politics of noise, or silence in this case, is also about the virtual absence of Jamaica in the centrality of its own proliferation of dubs and sound systems. However, there was no doubt that Jamaica's musical innovations received global visibility in spite of Red Bull's crafty marketing strategies at the intersection between authentic dancehall culture and the corporate power brokering. In pushing its brand, Red Bull used Jamaica as a backdrop with only cursory mention of Jamaica as site of origin and producer of the cool. Jamaican sound system clashes have transcended national borders to occupy transnational soundscapes, with Red Bull sound clashes at the contemporary centre providing another dimension for analysis of dancehall culture in the context of boundary-lessness beyond the visions of dancehall creators and perpetuators who do not own the means of production in a visual economy.

THE VALUE OF SOUND AS WORK AND BUILDING SOUND CAPITAL

Speculations are that there is an average of over one thousand four hundred live events per day in Jamaica. The total number of licenses issued for places of amusements in the year 2015 was 26,687, according to the Planning Institute of Jamaica's Economic and Social Survey for that year (PIOJ 2016). This figure is a 9.6 per cent increase from the figures shown in 2014 and a 28 per cent increase from 2012 (PIOJ 2015, 2013). These figures are much higher than in 2008, which was reported at 15,700. The numbers reported do not reflect the many illegal or informal dances held without permits.

The formal industry is growing despite the Jamaica Constabulary Force's zero-tolerance approach to enforcement of the Noise Abatement Act. There are notable fluctuations in the number of permit requests between 2012 and 2018, though by 2015, the numbers have levelled. The parishes with the highest number of licenses issued were Kingston and St Andrew and Clarendon, with 9,413 and 3,575 requests in 2015, respectively.

Data from the Ministry of Culture, Gender, Entertainment and Sport and the Jamaica Constabulary Force Operations Branch, shown in table 2, confirm the numbers of permit and extension requests reported above, which indicates the health of the entertainment sector.

The Kingston and St Andrew Municipal Corporation reported revenues of J$28 million from entertainment permits alone in 2017 and 2018 showed a 13 per cent increase in revenue at J$33 million. The Kingston and St Andrew Municipal Corporation is the highest grossing municipality in relation to entertainment events, according to Economic and Social Survey of Jamaica data (PIOJ). While there have been crackdowns under the Noise Abatement Act, the ministry with responsibility for entertainment makes it possible to request a time extension for events to go on beyond midnight during the week and 2:00 a.m. on the weekend. This corresponds with permission from the Jamaica Constabulary Force. Table 2 shows the number of extensions approved for the period 2013–18.

A significant portion of the country's population lives in Kingston and it has a healthy culture of amusement. It, therefore, presents an urgent case for the examination of policies that are sensitive to the history and form of

Table 2: Entertainment permits and extensions issued in Jamaica (2012–2018)

	Year	Permits	Ent Capex	# Of Extensions	Total Value $Ja
	2012	18,956			
	2013	24,790	207,237,300	300	17,124,708,890.00
	2014	18,917	380,755,808	518	13,904,937,490.22
	2015	19,297	365,597,448	348	20,272,798,718.55
	2016	19,146	169,314,000	87	37,260,756,827.59
	2017	19,158	448,643,020	264	32,557,208,246.82
	2018	19,765	423,120,000	342	24,453,119,298.25
Total Average event figure over (7 years)		20,004	1,994,667,576		145,573,529,471.43

entertainment practices. Suggestions regarding zoning entertainment and providing proper venues for staging events should be explored seriously in order to shift the popular stance of policing. In October 2017, Fort Rocky in Port Royal was announced as the first entertainment zone in Jamaica, a space that would be used exclusively for entertainment. However, it is still up to policymakers to look seriously at the problem of raids and police clashes and choose instead to cultivate healthy entertainment practices, especially around dancehall. Entertainment promoters continue to complain about the double-edged sword that characterizes the production and consumption of dancehall and its relationship with the state and its apparatuses. Due to the zero-tolerance approach, promoters feel dance events have been increasingly policed as a method of minimizing criminality. However, at the same time that the authorities are increasing surveillance (such as through Zones of Special Operations, introduced in 2018), there is an increase in the number of events being held, the revenue they earn and the means by which they serve as a release valve for the many who are frustrated by daily "sufferation".

This discussion is significant because it has implications for the development of Kingston as an entertainment and creative industries capital. Kingston's history of music creation was instrumental in being named a UNESCO Creative City of Music. This was an important achievement not only in solidifying the history and achievements of Kingston as an entertainment scene, but an important guide toward continued development as a creative city and music capital of the world. It allows Kingston to work alongside and network with other Creative Cities of Music and provides guidelines on what needs to be done in order to maintain the designation. It is also excellent for marketing the city and strengthening the city's entertainment life.

THE SOUND ECONOMY: TOWARD A CULTURE OF REGULATED SOUND

In seeking to solidify security for the citizenry at the heart of Jamaica's entertainment and celebratory practices so they may fulfil the mandate of contributing to the development of Jamaica as a small island state, it is crucial that entertainment is seen as fulfilling both economic and citizen wellbeing imperatives. Work must continue, seeking not merely the relaxation of stipulations in the Noise Abatement Act but, ultimately, the replacement of said act by a more appropriate Sound Regulation Act that uses sound meters to measure sound both within and outside designated entertainment zones. While the social gains from music and entertainment have been under-researched and underacknowledged, it is critical that we grapple with the postcolonial problem of inheriting philosophical, moral and economic models that could not make visible or quantify the value of creativity to the articulation of the self, the maintenance of cohesive citizenry and to the national budget. This leaves a huge disconnect between what we do to create income and the creativity we engage in for pleasure after work. In conclusion, what I place on the table is the fact that there is a disconnect between what we do for play and what we do for work and income, and therefore what is seen as viable for development. While we have come a long way, there is still much further to go in solidifying security and wellbeing for citizens as they navigate the daily imperatives to celebrate.

REFERENCES

A Nation of Billions. 2016. "They Fed Em to the Lions at Culture Clash." Image. https://nationbillions.com/feed-em-to-the-lions-at-redbull-culture-clash-pop-caan.

Attali, Jacques. 1985. *Noise: The Political Economy of Music*. Translated by Brian Massumi. Minnesota: University of Minnesota Press.

Browning, Barbara. 1995. *Samba: Resistance in Motion*. Bloomington: Indiana University Press.

Buju Banton. 1993. "Operation Ardent." *Voice of Jamaica*. Universal Music LLC.

Busy Signal. 2005. "Step Out" [Single], *Step Out* [Album], Greensleeves

———. 2005b. "Full Clip" [Single] featuring Mavado, *Step Out* [Album] Greensleeves.

Chude-Sokei, Louis. 1997. "Postnationalist Geographies: Rasta, Ragga, and Reinventing Africa." In *Reggae, Rasta, Revolution: Jamaican Music from Ska to Dub*, edited by Chris Potash, 215–27. New York and London: Schirmer Books & Prentice Hall International.

Cobussen, M.A. "Noise, Sounding Art, and Urban Ecology." Paper presented at 46th International Congress and Exposition on Noise Control Engineering (Internoise 2017): Taming Noise and Moving Quietly. Hong Kong, China, August 2017.

Cooper, Carolyn. 1993. *Noise in the Blood: Orality, Gender and the 'Vulgar' Body of Jamaican Popular Culture,* Warwick University Caribbean Studies Series. London: Macmillan Press.

Fanon, Frantz. 1963. "'On National Culture." *The Wretched of the Earth.* London. Grove Weidenfeld.

Gilpin, Jodi-Ann. 2013. "Germany, Saturn to Withdraw flag-burning ad." *Jamaica Gleaner* https://jamaica-gleaner.com/gleaner/20130227/lead/lead9.html. Accessed July 15, 2013.

Lovelace, Earl. 1986. *The Dragon Can't Dance.* New York: Persea Books.

Miller, Anthony. 1994. *Entertainment Report.* Kingston, Jamaica Broadcasting Corporation.

Henriques, Julian. 2008. "Sonic Diaspora, Vibrations, and Rhythm: Thinking through the Sounding of the Jamaican Dancehall Session." *African and Black Diaspora: An International Journal* 1 (2): 215–36.

———. 2011. *Sonic Bodies: Reggae Sound Systems, Performance Techniques and Ways of Knowing.* New York: Continuum.

Jackson, Leighton. 2014. "Language, Culture and the Law: A Theoretical Framework for Paradigmatic Change in Institutional Governance in the Commonwealth Caribbean." Paper presented at the Inaugural Law Faculty Symposium, 25 April 2015.

Kahn, Douglas. 1999. *Noise Water Meat: A History of Sound in the Arts.* Cambridge, MA: MIT Press.

Martis, Eternity. 2016. "The Politics of Being Black and Loud." *Fader,* 28 June 2016. http://www.thefader.com/2016/06/28/the-politics-of-being-black-and-loud.

Mills, Charles. 1997. "Smadditizin'." *Caribbean Quarterly* 43 (2): 54–68.

Ministry of Justice, Jamaica. 1997. *The Noise Abatement Act.* https://moj.gov.jm/laws/noise-abatement-act.

v 1999. *Kingston and St Andrew Corporation Act*: Places of Amusement Regulations. Part X, 193, item (g). Jamaica.

Patterson, Orlando. 1974. *The Condition of the Low-Income Population in the Kingston Metropolitian Area.* Kingston, Jamaica: Office of the Prime Minister.

Peru, Yasmine. 2020. "Extended Party Hours Big Boost to Business – No Word Yet on Consideration for Further Extension of Noise Abatement Act." *Jamaica Gleaner,* 29 January 2020. http://jamaica-gleaner.com/article/entertainment/20200129/extended-party-hours-big-boost-business-no-word-yet-consideration.

Pickering, Hugh, and Tom Rice. 2017. "Noise as 'Sound out of Place': Investigating the Links between Mary Douglas' Work on Dirt and Sound Studies Research." *Journal of Sonic Studies* 14.

Planning Institute of Jamaica (PIOJ). 2013. *The Economic and Social Survey Jamaica 2012*. Kingston: Planning Institute of Jamaica.

———. 2015. *The Economic and Social Survey Jamaica 2014*. Kingston: Planning Institute of Jamaica.

———. 2016. *The Economic and Social Survey Jamaica 2015*. Kingston: Planning Institute of Jamaica.Rodney, Walter. 1969. *The Groundings with My Brothers*. London: Bogle-L'Ouverture Publications.

Romeo, Max. 1975. "Run Babylon." [Single] Attack Label.

Rose, Tricia. 1994. *Black Noise: Rap Music and Black Culture in Contemporary America*. Connecticut: Wesleyan University Press.

Scruggs, Gregory. 2014. "A War on Jamaican Dancehall is Threatening Kingston's Street Life." *Next City*, 18 December 2014. https://nextcity.org/daily/entry/a-war-on-jamaican-dancehall-is-threatening-kingstons-street-life.

———. 2018. "Can a City Famous for its Sound Quiet Down? A Crackdown on Public Music Events is Forcing Kingston, Jamaica, to Rethink how the World-Famous Music City Regulates Noise." *Next City*, 8 January 2018. https://nextcity.org/features/view/can-a-city-famous-for-its-sound-quiet-down.

Stanley Niaah, Sonjah. 2010. *Dancehall: From Slave Ship to Ghetto*. Ottawa: University of Ottawa Press.

Television Jamaica. 2003. "Prime Time News Report." 11 August.

TheSuperBowlTV. 2013. "Get Happy Volkswagen Super Bowl 2013 Commercial." YouTube video, 29 January 2013. https://www.youtube.com/watch?v=09JT-tVxztv4.

Thompson, Robert Farris. 1973. "An Aesthetic of the Cool." *African Arts* 7 (1): 41–91. doi:10.2307/3334749.

Waddell, Hope Masterton. 1970. *Twenty-Nine Years in the West Indies and Central Africa: A Review of Missionary Work and Adventure, 1829–1858*. London: Cambridge University Press.

Wardi, Alaa. 2013. "No Woman, No Drive" [Single], *Loudr*.

Wardle, Huon. 2000. *An Ethnography of Cosmopolitanism in Kingston, Jamaica*. Caribbean Studies 7. New York: E. Mellen Press.

Contributors

HOLGER BRIEL is a distinguished academic in media and communication studies, holding a PhD in cultural theory from the University of Massachusetts, Amherst. He has taught at prestigious institutions worldwide, including New York University, Shanghai Jiaotong University and Aristotle University Thessaloniki. An active journalist and prolific author, he is also the editor-in-chief of the *IAFOR Journal of Cultural Studies* and serves on numerous editorial boards.

MELVILLE COOKE teaches in the Bachelor of Arts, communication arts and technology (BACAT) programme at University of Technology, Jamaica (UTech, Jamaica) and is a PhD candidate in cultural studies at the University of the West Indies (UWI), Mona.

CAROLIN FUNCK obtained her PhD from the Albert-Ludwigs University, Freiburg. She is professor for human geography at Hiroshima University (Japan), Graduate School of Humanities and Social Sciences. Her research focuses on the development of tourism in Japan and sustainable island tourism.

STANLEY H. GRIFFIN holds a BA (Hons.) in history, and a PhD in cultural studies (with High Commendation), from the Cave Hill Campus, University of the West Indies, Barbados, and an MSc in archives and records management (Int'l), University of Dundee, Scotland. Stanley is senior lecturer in archival and information studies and coordinates the graduate programme in archives and records management in the Department of Library and Information Studies, UWI Mona Campus. Since 1 August 2021, Stanley serves as deputy dean for undergraduate matters in the Faculty of Humanities and Education. Stanley thinks and writes (mostly) about Caribbean archives and records, culture, history and heritage.

YACHEN HE is a doctoral student at Hiroshima University's Graduate School of Humanities and Social Sciences. Her research centres on tourism gentrification's effects on local cultures and economies. She also enjoys using maps to trace evolving landscapes.

EMMA LANG is the executive director of the Heritage Trust of Nova Scotia. She holds an MA in museum studies from George Washington University in Washington DC and an MA in folklore from Memorial University of Newfoundland and Labrador.

A.D. McCORMICK is a writer, artist, educator and director of Art Island Center on Naoshima in Japan. He is currently working on a book about Japan's "art islands".

EVANGELIA PAPOUTSAKI, PhD Cardiff, is the SICRI co-convenor (Small Island Cultures Research Initiative). She is the executive editor of ePress at Unitec Auckland, New Zealand; previously associate professor and program lead at the University of Central Asia; former international research fellow at the Center for Pacific Islands Research at Kagoshima University and former UNESCO PNG chair for Freedom of Expression. Her research interests focus on island studies and communication for social change in Oceania and the Asia Pacific regions. She has extensive involvement in editorial roles (*Island Studies Journal and SHIMA, Okinawa Journal of Island Studies, Contemporary PNG Studies Journal* and *Pacific Journalism Review*) and has published three edited volumes on Pacific islands communication and media landscape.

MARIE-CHRISTINE PARENT holds a PhD in ethnomusicology from Université de Montréal and Université Côte d'Azur. Her research deals with intangible heritage, memory and touristic staging issues related to the moutya, a musical genre and practice from the Seychelles islands. She received a Vanier Canada Graduate Scholarship for her PhD research. She is also the French review editor of the Canadian peer-reviewed journal *MUSICultures*.

MENG QU, PhD, is an associate professor and vice-director at Hokkaido University and co-convener at Small Island Cultures Research Initiative (SICRI). His research focuses on creative tourism and rural revitalization in East Asia, demonstrated through involvement in community-engaged art festivals.

SHAUNA RIGAUD is an adjunct faculty at George Mason University and a scholar of the Caribbean, highlighting the experiences and stories that give a more nuanced understand of the region, its history and postcolonial condition. Her research interests include a focus on the Caribbean Diaspora, Performance and Performativity, Black feminism and Caribbean feminism. Her PhD thesis is focused on "Harvesting Home: Economy, Identity and Gender in Barbados's Crop Over Festival." She is also the co-founder of Mayhem246, a concierge company that specializes in providing entertainment experiences during Barbados's Crop Over Festival.

SONJAH STANLEY NIAAH is a Jamaican scholar and cultural activist known for her expertise in dancehall and Black Atlantic performance geographies. She earned her PhD in cultural studies from the University of the West Indies, Mona, becoming its first cultural studies PhD graduate. Stanley Niaah directs the Institute of Caribbean Studies and the Reggae Studies Unit. An advocate for cultural respect and education, she has authored books on Dancehall and contributes to documentaries like Samuel L. Jackson's *Enslaved* and *Move* on Netflix.

JOHN STANSFIELD is a serial social entrepreneur and passionate island dweller. He founded a graduate programme in NGO and community organization leadership and management and has held leadership roles in the polytechnic sector. John holds post graduate qualifications in intercultural practice and has taught extensively across the Pacific Islands. John lives on Waiheke Island on his cooperative organic farm with his partner and a menagerie of rare breed poultry.

Index

f denotes figure; *n* denotes note; *t* denotes table

www.ingramcontent.com/pod-product-compliance
Lightning Source LLC
Chambersburg PA
CBHW030836300326
41935CB00036B/173